THE MISSIONAL CHURCH
AND DENOMINATIONS

MISSIONAL CHURCH SERIES

The missional church conversation continues to grow in importance in providing for many a fresh way into rethinking what it means to be church in our rapidly changing context. This Missional Church Series by the Wm. B. Eerdmans Publishing Co. is designed to contribute original research to this critical conversation. This series will make available contributive monographs as well as edited volumes produced from specially designed consultations.

The Missional Church and Denominations

*Helping Congregations Develop
a Missional Identity*

Edited by

Craig Van Gelder

WILLIAM B. EERDMANS PUBLISHING COMPANY
GRAND RAPIDS, MICHIGAN / CAMBRIDGE, U.K.

Published 2008 by
Wm. B. Eerdmans Publishing Co.
2140 Oak Industrial Drive N.E., Grand Rapids, Michigan 49505 /
P.O. Box 163, Cambridge CB3 9PU U.K.

Printed in the United States of America

13 12 11 10 09 08   7 6 5 4 3 2 1

Library of Congress Cataloging-in-Publication Data

The missional church and denominations: helping congregations develop
    a missional identity / edited by Craig Van Gelder.
        p.   cm.   — (Missional church series)
    Includes bibliographical references.
    ISBN 978-0-8028-6358-4 (pbk.: alk. paper)
    1. Mission of the church.   2. Church.   3. Missions — Theory.
    4. Christian sects.   I. Van Gelder, Craig.

BV601.8.M594   2008
266 — dc22
                                                2008031137

www.eerdmans.com

Contents

Preface

This volume is the second in the Missional Church Series now being published by Wm. B. Eerdmans Publishing Company. It utilizes the missional church conversation as a lens for engaging an important dimension of U.S. church life — denominations and denominationalism. Denominations have been studied from a wide variety of perspectives — historical, sociological, and theological, but have yet to be engaged substantively in light of a missional church understanding. That is the purpose of this book.

The missional church conversation came on the scene in 1998 with the publication of the book entitled *Missional Church: A Vision for the Sending of the Church in North America*. This conversation has now spread into many venues and is language that is being picked up by numerous denominations and faith traditions. It is clear, however, that the use of the word "missional" often means different things to different groups. The most common problem is the tendency to assume that it is just another way of framing the historical understanding of missions in the life of the church — what the church *does*. But the use of the word "missional" within the missional church conversation has in view something much more basic. It is about the very nature or essence of what it means to *be* church.

This current book is intended to help bring further clarity to the word "missional" and to contribute to this ever-widening missional church conversation by engaging the issue of denominations. It is the result of a the 2nd annual Missional Church Consultation hosted by Luther

Seminary in Saint Paul, Minnesota, in November 2006. The theme of that consultation was "The Missional Church and Denominations: Engaging the Challenge of the Denominational Church." The essays contained in this volume are those presented for discussion at that consultation.

Luther Seminary has been engaged in thinking about the missional church for over a decade, but especially since the adoption of its strategic plan in 2000, entitled "Serving the Promise of Our Mission." This plan envisioned the development of a strategic initiative in the field of Congregational Mission and Leadership. Concentrations in this new field are now available in all degree programs, including Master of Arts, Master of Divinity, Doctor of Ministry, and Doctor of Philosophy. Part of the vision of this strategic initiative is to create an ongoing center for research on the missional church that is framed biblically and theologically while being informed by insights from the social sciences. The annual Missional Church Consultation is designed to bring scholars together on a yearly basis to contribute to this growing body of research.

The Wm. B. Eerdmans Publishing Company has graciously agreed to serve as the publisher for the Missional Church Series that Luther Seminary is taking the lead in developing. This series will include both edited volumes that result from the annual consultations as well as selected monographs. It is our prayer that the church of Jesus Christ will be more deeply informed, as well as built up and strengthened, as a result of the contributions made by this series.

CRAIG VAN GELDER
Editor, Missional Church Series

Contributors

Rev. Daniel Anderson holds a Ph.D. (ABD) from Luther Seminary in Congregational Mission and Leadership. He is an ordained minister in the Evangelical Lutheran Church in America (ELCA) and has served in calls both as a pastor and as a worship leader.

Rev. Marion Wyvetta Bullock holds a D.Min from Lutheran School of Theology in Chicago. She is an ordained minister in the Evangelical Lutheran Church in America (ELCA) and has served in calls as a pastor and as an executive staff person for several churchwide agencies at the denomination's headquarters. She is presently serving as the Executive for Leadership Development in the ELCA's Office of the Presiding Bishop.

Rev./Dr. David Forney holds a Ph.D. from the University of Texas. He is an ordained minister in the Presbyterian Church (U.S.A.) and has served in calls as a pastor and theological educator, in the latter capacity most recently at Columbia Theological Seminary. He is presently serving as senior pastor of the First Presbyterian Church in Clarksville, TN.

Rev. Wesley Granberg-Michaelson holds an M.Div. from Western Theological Seminary in Holland, MI. He is an ordained minister in the Reformed Church in America (RCA) and has served calls as a pastor and as the director of the sub-unit on Church and Society of the World Council of Churches. He has since 1995 been serving as the General Secretary of the Reformed Church in America.

Todd Hobart holds a Ph.D. (ABD) from Luther Seminary in Congregational Mission and Leadership. He is associated with the free-church movement and has served in calls with several congregations as a youth minister.

Rev./Dr. Alan Roxburgh holds a D.Min from Northern Baptist Seminary in Chicago. He is an ordained minister in the Canadian Baptist Church and has served calls as a pastor in several congregations. He is presently serving as Vice-President for Allelon and engages in speaking, consulting, generating resources, and conducting research on the missional church.

Rev. Kyle Small holds a Ph.D. (ABD) from Luther Seminary in Congregational Mission and Leadership. He is an ordained minister in the Evangelical Covenant Church (ECC) and has served a call as a pastor since graduating from seminary, and is currently serving as the Missional Schools Project Assistant for Allelon.

Rev./Dr. Craig Van Gelder holds a Ph.D. degree in Mission from Southwestern Baptist Theological Seminary, and a Ph.D. in Administration in Urban Affairs from the University of Texas in Arlington. He is an ordained minister in the Christian Reformed Church and has served in calls as an interim minister, a judicatory staff member, and theological educator. In the latter role, he taught ten years at Calvin Theological Seminary as Professor of Domestic Missiology and since 1998 has taught at Luther Seminary as Professor of Congregational Mission.

Rev. Dwight Zscheile holds a Ph.D. in Congregational Mission and Leadership from Luther Seminary. He is an ordained deacon in the Episcopal Church U.S.A. and has served in calls in several churches, including his present service as Deacon at Saint Matthew's Episcopal Church in Saint Paul, MN. He began teaching at Luther Seminary in 2008 as Professor of Congregational Mission.

Engaging the Missional Church Conversation

What would it look like for a congregation to have a missional identity? This is the question that underlies all the essays in this volume. It is a question that is still very much in process of being answered within what is now known as the "missional church conversation." We believe that we can only answer this question in our context of the United States today by engaging in a thorough critique and analysis of denominations and the denominational local congregation. We also believe that we can only answer this question by drawing deeply on biblical and theological foundations that are informed by Trinitarian foundations. These are the two perspectives that we bring into conversation throughout this volume.

A Changing Context and Changing Church

These are exciting yet challenging days for the church of Jesus Christ as it continues to face massive shifts taking place throughout the world. One of the more interesting shifts, to those of us living in the West, is the growing recognition by churches in the United States that they are now in their own

---

Some of the background information on the "missional church conversation" in this introduction also appeared in the first volume in this series, *The Missional Church in Context: Helping Congregations Develop Contextual Ministry* (Eerdmans, 2007). This will be helpful to the reader who is new to or unfamiliar with the missional church conversation.

mission location. This awareness is generating fresh opportunities for new ministry, but it is also introducing disruption into long-standing practices. Business as usual by congregations in the United States is no longer possible. As a result, many historical denominations are now in serious decline. Alongside this development, significant new movements are coming into existence: the rapid expansion of megachurches, the significant increase in the number of immigrant congregations, the dramatic expansion of the number of congregations along generational lines, and the rapidly growing emergent church movement.

In the midst of such shifts, it is profoundly important to keep returning to the foundations of what it means to be the church of Jesus Christ in the world. This involves the issue of ecclesiology (*ecclesia* = "church"; *-ology* = "the study of"). In the midst of our changing world, we are in constant need of continuing to engage in the *study of the church*, to explore its nature, to understand its creation and continuing formation, and to carefully examine its purpose and ministry.

A discussion has emerged over the past several decades that has been very helpful in focusing our attention on this ongoing study of the church. This discussion is known as the "missional church conversation." It has a number of generative sources, but the most influential by far have been the contributions made by missiologist Lesslie Newbigin as his writings gained wider circulation in the late 1970s and early 1980s.

The Influence of Lesslie Newbigin

In returning home to England from the foreign mission field in the 1970s, Newbigin took up the challenge of trying to envision what a fresh encounter of the gospel with late-modern Western culture might look like. He focused on this issue perhaps most sharply in his book *Foolishness to the Greeks,* where he posed this question: "What would be involved in a missionary encounter between the gospel and this whole way of perceiving, thinking, and living that we call 'modern Western culture'?"[1]

A movement that tried to address this issue emerged in England in the 1980s and came to be known as the Gospel and Our Culture (GOC) conversation. While the GOC discussion first surfaced in England, it soon

---

1. Lesslie Newbigin, *Foolishness to the Greeks* (Grand Rapids: Eerdmans, 1986), 1.

spread to the United States, where it was taken up by a new generation of missiologists who were focusing their attention on addressing the North American context as its own unique mission location.

Newbigin's missiology was largely shaped by the mission theology that was born within the International Missionary Council (IMC) conferences of the 1950s through the 1970s. This was a Trinitarian understanding of mission, or what is commonly referred to as the *missio Dei,* the mission of God. Influenced by the biblical theology movement of the 1930s-1940s, this Trinitarian foundation for mission theology began to take shape at the Willingen Conference of the IMC in 1952 and was later formulated as the *missio Dei* by Karl Hartenstein.[2] Johannes Blauw then gave it fuller expression in his 1962 book *The Missionary Nature of the Church.*[3] Lesslie Newbigin articulated his own expression of this mission theology in *The Open Secret* (1978).[4] Central to his understanding of mission is the work of the triune God in calling and sending the church through the Spirit into the world to participate fully in God's mission within all of creation. This theological formulation understands the church to be the creation of the Spirit: it exists in the world as a "sign" that the redemptive reign of God's kingdom is present; it serves as a "foretaste" of the eschatological future of the redemptive reign that has already begun; and it serves as an "instrument" under the leadership of the Spirit to bring that redemptive reign to bear on every dimension of life.[5]

The British GOC Programme

The British version of the GOC movement that developed during the 1980s came to be known as a "programme," and it was shaped largely by the writings of Newbigin during that period: *The Other Side of 1984* (1983), *Foolishness to the Greeks* (1986), and *The Gospel in a Pluralist Society* (1989).[6]

---

2. H. H. Rosin, *'Missio Dei': An Examination of the Origin, Contents and Function of the Term in Protestant Missiological Discussion* (Leiden, Germany: Interuniversity Institute for Missiological and Ecumenical Research Department of Missiology, 1972).

3. Johannes Blauw, *The Missionary Nature of the Church: A Survey of the Biblical Theology of Mission* (Grand Rapids: Eerdmans, 1962).

4. Lesslie Newbigin, *The Open Secret* (Grand Rapids: Eerdmans, 1978).

5. *Open Secret,* 124.

6. Lesslie Newbigin, *The Other Side of 1984* (Geneva: World Council of Churches,

Newbigin's intellectual leadership of the programme was joined by the administrative and organizational contributions of Dr. Dan Beeby and Bishop Hugh Montefiore. An occasional newsletter began publication in 1989, but the programme culminated in many ways with the National Consultation at Swanwick in 1992. A volume of essays edited by Montefiore, which was entitled *The Gospel and Contemporary Culture,* served as the agenda for discussion at that consultation.[7]

The British GOC programme floundered somewhat during the early 1990s, primarily because of its failure both to secure sufficient funding and to find an institutional home within the church. An effort to merge the GOC programme with the C. S. Lewis Center was made in 1994, but this proved to be short-lived; it was disbanded in 1996.[8] The death of Lesslie Newbigin in 1998 brought an additional sense of closure to his substantive as well as symbolic leadership of the movement in England.

The GOC Network in the U.S.

As the British programme began to gain public recognition, a U.S. version of the Gospel and Our Culture conversation also began to emerge. Several consultations sponsored in the mid-1980s by the Overseas Study Mission Center stimulated interest in the question Newbigin had posed in the Warfield Lectures at Princeton in 1984 (later published as *Foolishness to the Greeks*). A network began to take shape from these early events in the mid-1980s; by the early 1990s, under the leadership of George Hunsberger, the Gospel and Our Culture Network was publishing a quarterly newsletter and also convening a yearly consultation. By the mid-1990s, the movement in the United States had begun to find its own voice beyond the influence of Newbigin, and the Wm. B. Eerdmans Publishing Company began to publish a series of books under the moniker The Gospel and Our Culture Series. To date the following volumes have been published in this series:

1983); Lesslie Newbigin, *Foolishness to the Greeks* (Grand Rapids: Eerdmans, 1986); and Lesslie Newbigin, *The Gospel in a Pluralist Society* (Grand Rapids: Eerdmans, 1989).

7. Hugh Montefiore, ed., *The Gospel and Contemporary Culture* (Herndon, VA: Cassell Academic, 1992).

8. A brief history of the British GOC Programme is available online at: www .deepsight.org/articles/engchis.htm.

George Hunsberger and Craig Van Gelder, eds., *The Church Between Gospel and Culture: The Emerging Mission in North America* (1996).

Darrel L. Guder, ed., *Missional Church: A Vision for the Sending of the Church in North America* (1998).

George R. Hunsberger, *Bearing the Witness of the Spirit: Lesslie Newbigin's Theology of Cultural Plurality* (1998).

Craig Van Gelder, ed., *Confident Witness — Changing World: Rediscovering the Gospel in North America* (1999).

Darrel L. Guder, *The Continuing Conversion of the Church* (2000).

James V. Brownson, ed., *StormFront: The Good News of God* (2003).

Lois Y. Barrett, ed., *Treasure in Clay Jars: Patterns in Missional Faithfulness* (2004).

This literature has focused on understanding North America as its own unique mission location and the church as being *missional* by nature, and it continues to stimulate a very important conversation. There are a number of other books from several different publishers that have also contributed to this conversation, which include the following:

Craig Van Gelder, *The Essence of the Church: A Community Created by the Spirit* (Grand Rapids: Baker Books, 2000).

Richard H. Bliese and Craig Van Gelder, eds., *The Evangelizing Church: A Lutheran Contribution* (Minneapolis: Augsburg Fortress, 2005).

Alan J. Roxburgh and Fred Romanuk, *The Missional Leader: Equipping Your Church to Reach a Changing World* (San Francisco: Jossey-Bass, 2006).

Patrick Keifert, *We Are Here Now: A New Missional Era* (Eagle, ID: Allelon Publishing, 2006).

Craig Van Gelder, *The Ministry of the Missional Church: A Community Led by the Spirit* (Grand Rapids: Baker Books, 2007).

Craig Van Gelder, ed., *The Missional Church in Context: Helping Congregations Develop Contextual Ministry* (Grand Rapids: Eerdmans, 2007).

Richard W. Rouse and Craig Van Gelder, *A Field Guide to the Missional Congregation: A Journey of Transformation* (Minneapolis: Augsburg Fortress, 2008).

The strategic importance of the missional church conversation is taking on an increasing significance in North America, as literature on the subject continues to expand. More and more denominational and congregational leaders are becoming aware of the need to explore more deeply the church's nature and identity. This awareness is coming largely from the increased recognition that the multiple late-modern strategies and programs that have been generated to make the church more effective have significant limitations in addressing systemic issues. This awareness and the need to continue to extend the missional church conversation are the primary impulses that have given birth to this book, which is the second in a new series being published by the Wm. B. Eerdmans Publishing Company, the Missional Church Series.

The Missional Church Series

The purpose of this book is to help extend the missional church conversation by attempting to engage the subject of denominations and denominationalism. Substantive developments in theology, especially the renewal of Trinitarian studies, continue to offer new insights into this conversation. Additional efforts to bring the missional church conversation into direct discussion with particular denominations are now gaining traction, and each 'of the denominations has its own unique history, traditions, ecclesiology, and polity.

This book is the result of the second annual Missional Church Consultation, hosted by Luther Seminary in St. Paul, Minnesota, in November 2006, with the theme "The Missional Church and Denominations: Engaging the Challenge of the Denominational Church." The essays from that consultation are the materials included in this volume and are organized into three sections (see table of contents).

How to Read and Use This Book

As I have noted above, the primary purpose of this book is to extend the conversation about the missional church through an engagement with denominations and denominationalism. The reader will find that the authors draw deeply on the missional literature that has been generated to date; but in the midst of drawing on this previous literature, these authors also contribute some fresh new insights into thinking further about the missional church in relation to denominations.

The first section of four essays contributes to the development of a constructive argument for the missional church by bringing it into conversation with the larger framework of denominations and denominationalism. In the first essay I have set up this discussion by unpacking the DNA that is embedded in the formation of denominations in the United States. I note the inherent organizational self-understanding around a purposive intent that is at the core of understanding denominations, and I offer a perspective on what it might look like for a missional ecclesiology to be incorporated into this DNA. In the second essay, David Forney uses the biblical book of Hebrews to explore what a missional polity might look like within denominational church life. He invites denominations to consider *going outside the gate* as a way of recovering a missional identity.

In the third essay, Alan Roxburgh places the rise of the twentieth-century corporate denomination into context by noting its formation within the development of corporations in the broader culture. He notes the challenges now facing denominations in the midst of the discontinuous change and liminal space that denominations now find themselves occupying. And he offers some suggestions for how denominations might navigate this new terrain. In the fourth essay, Wyvetta Bullock develops a perspective on what a missional ecclesiology and polity for denominations might look like, using the Evangelical Lutheran Church in America as a case study to flesh out her framework.

The second section of four essays provides the reader with specific examples of what a missional understanding of ecclesiology and polity looks like when it is brought into conversation with the particular history, traditions, and theology of specific denominations. Each of these essays draws deeply on Trinitarian understandings for rethinking, reframing, and reclaiming the historical ecclesiologies and polities of these denominations from a missional perspective. In the first essay, Dwight Zscheile deeply engages the unique history of the Episcopal Church USA to reframe its ecclesiology and polity in missional terms. In the second essay, Daniel Anderson explores what taking a missional approach would look like for understanding the three expressions of the recently formed (1987) Evangelical Lutheran Church in America — in congregations, in the synod, and churchwide. In the third essay, Kyle Small challenges the Evangelical Covenant Church to stay true to its historical roots, which he feels had many missional impulses implicitly embedded within it. He draws out these impulses and grounds them more explicitly in Trinitarian foundations. In the fourth essay, Todd Hobart retells the story of the Baptist General Conference and then reframes the identity of this denomination from a missional perspective. He offers specific examples of what changes might be made to its specific polity in order to more faithfully express this understanding.

The third section, an epilogue, provides insights into the journey that the Reformed Church in America has now been taking for over a decade in seeking to become a more missional denomination. Wesley Granberg-Michaelson, who serves as the general secretary of the Reformed Church in America, told this story in a special banquet speech to the participants in the 2006 Missional Church Consultation.

A MISSIONAL ENGAGEMENT WITH DENOMINATIONS AND DENOMINATIONALISM

Denominations are a fact of life in Christianity today, especially within the United States. But it is important to note that denominations as a form of the church of Jesus Christ in the world are of rather recent origin, dating from only about the mid- to late-1700s, which makes denominations less than 250 years old. Much has been written about denominations over the years. By the middle of the nineteenth century, writers such as Robert Baird, the father of American church history, had chronicled their value in representing a voluntary approach to church life. The denomination was celebrated for its ability to be entrepreneurial in reaching out and contextualizing church life for distinctly different groups of people. By the end of the nineteenth century, lengthy histories were being written by almost every denomination, and these books celebrated the denominations' significant growth, the expansion of their institutions, and their heroic leadership.

H. Richard Niebuhr developed a sharply contrasting view of denominations during the first decades of the twentieth century. Within the rising influence of the ecumenical movement, he critiqued denominations in his seminal book *The Social Sources of Denominationalism,* saying that they represented the ethical failure of Christianity. Niebuhr contended that race, social class, educational differences, and geographic disparities all stood as intervening variables that better explained the reality of denominations.

By the second half of the twentieth century, Martin Marty proposed another view of denominations within the context of the expanding ecumenical movement. In his important book *Righteous Empire*, Marty observed that many denominations, especially those in the mainline, were moving past their divisions and competitiveness and were seeking ways to worship and work in unity. Denominational distinctives were still valued, but those were now being framed as "gifts" that they had to offer to the larger church.

The dramatic changes in the U.S. context in the 1960s and 1970s significantly disrupted the ideals of the ecumenical movement. The mainline denominations simply quit growing, and many of them entered into what would become decades of decline. In contrast, many of the more conservative and evangelical denominations were showing growth. Dean Kelly captured all of this well in his seminal study *Why Conservative Churches Are Growing*, and then Finke and Stark reconceptualized the whole discussion of denominations at the beginning of the twenty-first century by placing their interpretation within a market economy of winners and losers in their book *The Churching of America 1776-2005: Winners and Losers in Our Religious Economy.*

Denominations — how should we understand them? Are they a blessing or a curse? One premise of the essays in this section is that, in trying to answer such questions, we need to give careful attention to both historical realities and biblical and theological foundations. Another premise is that using a missional church perspective to explore biblical and theological foundations throws fresh light on how to both conceive of and interact with denominations.

My opening chapter unpacks the historical DNA of denominations and offers insights into how to reframe this DNA from a missional perspective. David Forney picks up the critical issue of how polity shapes denominational identity, and he offers a biblical perspective by using the book of Hebrews to rethink denominational polity. Alan Roxburgh locates the formation of the present form of denominations — the corporate denomination — within the rise of corporations in the early twentieth century. He then offers suggestions for how denominations might navigate the disarray they now find themselves facing with the collapse of corporate culture. Finally, the essay by Wyvetta Bullock explores what a missional ecclesiology and polity for denominations might look like, and then she applies this perspective to the Evangelical Lutheran Church in America.

Denominations are not going to go away; however, they are going to continue to morph within our ever-changing cultural context. The essays in this section provide helpful perspectives and useful clues for bringing a missional imagination to bear on rethinking, reframing, and reclaiming denominations in the midst of the transition they are presently experiencing.

CHAPTER 1

An Ecclesiastical Geno-Project:
Unpacking the DNA of Denominations
and Denominationalism

Craig Van Gelder

Introduction

The denominational church is one of the primary expressions of the visible, institutional church in our context.[1] This kind of church institution began to be formally organized during the late colonial period, and by 1800 there were approximately thirty-six major denominations in the newly formed United States. Rapid expansion of this system took place during the nineteenth century, and by 1900 there were over 200 such organizational expressions of the church. Although the rate of expansion slowed somewhat during the twentieth century, the number of denominations has continued to multiply.[2] Today denominationalism is made up of a complex array of organizations in the United States. The challenge for people working in this context is to try to make sense of this diversity of denominational, organizational churches as being expressions of the church of Jesus Christ. Key questions concerning this challenge include the following: Where did they come from? How do we explain their origins? What do they have in common? How are they unique?

All of these questions, however, give rise to a still deeper question:

1. This essay takes the position that the visible, institutional church consists of a variety of forms, including congregations along with their judicatories and denominational structures, in addition to parachurch organizations, and various other institutions and movements.

2. Robert Wuthnow, *The Restructuring of American Religion* (Princeton, NJ: Princeton University Press), 20-21.

How are we to understand, historically and theologically, the reality of these denominations and the principle of denominationalism that undergirds them in relationship to the visible church of Jesus Christ that the Spirit of God has created and continues to create in the world? This is a question about ecclesiology: What is the church? It is also a question about polity: How should the church organize and structure its life? These are the issues I seek to explore in this essay. In particular, I will attempt to discern something of the DNA[3] that appears to be inherent in the denominational, organizational church, DNA that has come to be the normative expression of the church in the United States.[4] As we identify this DNA, some dimensions appear to be more common to all denominations, dimensions I will label as *foundational.* Other dimensions appear to be working within the overall genetic makeup, and they affect some but not all denominations — what I will label as a *strain.* Finally, I will here identify the inherent makeup of a missional understanding of the church and suggest ways in which this understanding may be used to rethink and reframe the ecclesiology of the denominational, organizational church.

Perspectives on Denominations and Denominationalism

Denominations are part of the air we breathe in our experience of the church. Interestingly, these denominations tend to function so much as a part of our worldview regarding the church that it is difficult for most of

3. Significant advances have been made in recent years in the field of genetics, where the mapping of the genetic makeup of living forms has become common. The field of genetic engineering has grown up alongside these developments. Here is a definition: "Genetic engineering, genetic modification (GM) and gene splicing are terms for the process of manipulating genes, usually outside the organism's normal reproductive process." This essay argues that the denominational, organizational church, as it came to expression in the United States, has a unique genetic makeup, or DNA, and that there is both the need and opportunity to bring the DNA of a missional ecclesiology into play in reframing this type of church in more missional terms. (Wikipedia, the Free Encyclopedia, http://en.wikipedia .org/wiki/Genetic_engineering [accessed Oct. 12, 2006].)

4. I use the concept of the "denominational, organizational church" throughout this essay to depict a particular kind of church that had its formative development within the colonial setting of what eventually became the United States. In this essay I argue that this is a unique kind of church that needs to be understood in terms of its inherent and constructed characteristics.

us to conceive of the church in different terms. This represents, as much by default as by design, our basic understanding of what it means to be the church in North America. But, as Martin Marty notes, denominations entered the ecclesiastical story line fairly late, coming into formal existence in the United States only in the late 1700s.[5]

It was in England, in the midst of the struggles to reform the Anglican Church during the 1600s, that the denominational conception of the church was first developed. The Dissenting Brethren at the Westminster Assembly in the 1630s-1640s, many of whom became Independents, used a new term to denote different organizational expressions of the church: to *denominate* these expressions. They were objecting, at that time, to the establishment of a national church on a Presbyterian model,[6] and they were guided by two major convictions: (a) to attempt to follow the primitive pattern and example of the Apostles; and (b) not to make present judgments and practices binding on the future.[7]

While affirming the principle of conscience, they also sought to find a way to practice unity in the midst of diverse expressions of the church. Inherent in their understanding was that the existence of multiple denominations was possible. This makes the denominational church different in intent from a sectarian church, or sect, that views itself as the only true church; it also mediates against seeing every schism that results in a new denomination as, necessarily, legitimate.[8] While the views of the Independents did not initially carry the day, a dramatic change in policy was adopted by the Parliament following the Glorious Revolution of 1688: it resulted in the passage of the Act of Toleration in 1689. This act provided for at least limited religious freedom for some denominations, such as the Congregationalists, Baptists, and Quakers, though Roman Catholics continued to be excluded. These developments in England during the 1600s served as an important backdrop for promoting the principle of religious freedom among the diverse churches that came into existence in the newly formed colonies that were eventually to become the United States.

5. Martin E. Marty, *Righteous Empire: The Protestant Experience in America* (New York: The Dial Press, 1970), 67-68.
6. Winthrop S. Hudson, "Denominationalism as a Basis for Ecumenicity: A Seventeenth Century Conception," in Russell E. Richey, ed., *Denominationalism* (Nashville: Abingdon, 1977), 24.
7. Hudson, 24-25.
8. Hudson, 39.

The more neutral understanding of the term "denomination," as conceived by its early proponents, was always commingled with theological and confessional understandings as the different denominations sought to distinguish their identities. However, inherent within their separate identities was an understanding that other denominations were also legitimate expressions of the church. The challenge of working out this understanding in a practical way became most evident in the American colonies during the seventeenth and eighteenth centuries. Here the discussions of the *theory* of the denominational church that were taking place in England interacted with the *pragmatic necessity* to come to terms with the patterns of immigration and the diverse churches that were the result.

The story line of the denominational, organizational church unfolds from the colonies to our day through several developmental phases, which I will discuss in more detail below. At this point, it will be of interest to note how denominations and denominationalism have been assessed by various church leaders and scholars. The following quotations illustrate the diverse views on this phenomenon as they have been expressed over the past several hundred years.

John Wesley (1703-1791): Denominations Viewed as Basically Being Neutral[9]

I . . . refuse to be distinguished from other men by any but the common principles of Christianity. . . . I renounce and detest all other marks of distinction. But from real Christians, of whatever *denomination,* I earnestly desire not to be distinguished at all. . . . Does thou love and fear God? It is enough! [italics added]

Gilbert Tennet (1703-1764): Denominations Representing a Functional Catholicity[10]

All societies who profess Christianity and retain the foundational principles thereof, notwithstanding their different denominations and diversity of sentiments in smaller things, are in reality but one church of Christ, but several branches (more or less pure in minor points) of one visible kingdom of the Messiah.

---

9. As quoted in Sydney E. Ahlstrom, *A Religious History of the American People* (New Haven, CT: Yale University Press, 1972), 381.

10. As quoted in John Corrigan and Winthrop S. Hudson, *Religion in America,* 7th ed. (Upper Saddle River, NJ: Pearson-Prentice Hall, 2004), 104.

Robert Baird (1798-1863): Denominations as a Result of the Voluntary Principle[11]

Baird devoted one of the eight sections of his book to explaining the voluntary principle . . . [and] concluded that the voluntary principle "has brought gospel influences to bear in every direction."

H. Richard Niebuhr (1919-1962): Denominations as the Ethical Failure of Christianity[12]

Denominationalism in the Christian church is . . . a compromise, made far too lightly, between Christianity and the world. . . . It represents the accommodation of Christianity to the caste-system of human society. . . . The division of the churches closely follows the division of men into the castes of national, racial, and economic groups.

Martin Marty (1928-) Denominations Rediscovering Their Essential Unity[13]

The Protestant churches in the nineteenth century are usually pictured as having a centrifugal momentum. By their missionary activity, every move they made seemed to spin them out from a spiritual center through a competitive principle to divisions all over the world. In the twentieth century their momentum has been centripetal: they noted the limits of their competition and division . . . and began to draw back together in the ecumenical, or Christian unity, movement.

Finke and Stark (2005): Denominations as a Market Economy of Christianity[14]

Some readers may shudder at the use of market terminology in discussions of religion, but we see nothing inappropriate in acknowledging that where religious affiliation is a matter of choice, religious organizations must compete for members. . . . The fate of these [denominations] will depend upon (1) aspects of their organizational structures,

---

11. As quoted in Roger Finke and Rodney Stark, *The Churching of America 1776-2005: Winners and Losers in Our Religious Economy* (New Brunswick, NJ: Rutgers University Press, 2005), 6.
12. H. Richard Niebuhr, *The Social Sources of Denominationalism* (New York: New American Library, 1929), 6.
13. Marty, *Righteous Empire*, 244.
14. Finke and Stark, 8-9.

(2) their sales representatives, (3) their product, and (4) their marketing techniques.

This diversity of interpretations illustrates the deep ambivalence that is a part of the heritage associated with denominational, organizational churches. We have them, and they are not going to go away, but how are we to understand them in relationship to their being expressions of the church of Jesus Christ?

The Emergence of the Denominational, Organizational Church

In general, the conception of the denominational church developed against the backdrop of the established church. In particular, it emerged within the context of the established state church of England. During the 1530s, Henry VIII followed the pattern of the other northern European countries by carrying out a magisterial reformation and establishing the Anglican expression of the Protestant church. By the late 1500s, every country in northern Europe, in addition to England, had adopted one expression of the Protestant church as its national church, whether Lutheran (Germany and the Scandinavian countries), Reformed (the Netherlands), or Presbyterian (Scotland). Inherent within these multiple established national churches was the key underlying principle of denominationalism: *diverse expressions of the church being accepted as legitimate.* However, each of these diverse national churches still exercised ecclesiastical dominion over a particular geographical area. In doing so, they were not required to develop a theological understanding of how to live alongside one another. This also allowed them to be quite aggressive in persecuting those they viewed as sectarian groups, such as the Anabaptists and Mennonites on the continent, and the Puritans, Independents, Baptists, and Quakers in England.

The understanding of the established church is quite different from that of the denominational church. In the *established church,* the church's self-understanding is that it serves as the primary location of God's presence on earth through which God can be encountered. The active work of God in the world is centered, in general, in the church as the gathered community and, in particular, in the ministry of the Word and Sacrament. In contrast, the denominational church, as it came to expression in the colonies, has a self-understanding that is more functional (or instrumental) in nature. It understands itself as being in existence to accomplish a purpose on behalf of God in the world. It is "unlike any previous 'church' in Christendom, it has no official connection with a civil power whatsoever," and therefore finds its organizational logic around an inherent "purposive" intent.[15] This follows the logic of organizational sociology that all organizations inherently seek to accomplish some goal.[16] The denominational church represents an organizational self-understanding around a purposive intent. The contrast between these two understandings is illustrated in the table below.

Established Church	Denominational Church
Self-understanding: Exists as the primary location of God's presence on earth through which the world can encounter God, with this authority being legitimated by the civil government.	Self-Understanding: Exists as an organization with a purposive intent to accomplish something on behalf of God in the world, with this role being legitimated on a voluntary basis.

The established church came into existence in the fourth century when Christianity was made the official religion of the Roman Empire. The situation that resulted has become known as Constantinian Christendom: this form continues to this day within many Catholic and Orthodox countries, as well as within a variety of Protestant national churches.[17] While these churches all have an organizational makeup, the key to their legitimacy within their self-understanding is that their presence represents

15. Sidney E. Mead, "Denominationalism: The Shape of Protestantism in America," in Richey, *Denominationalism,* 71.

16. Mary Jo Hatch, *Organizational Theory: Modern, Symbolic, and Postmodern Perspectives* (New York: Oxford University Press, 1997), 119-22.

17. Clearly, there are different understandings regarding the rationale for the established church among Roman Catholics, Orthodox, Lutherans, and Calvinists, but common to all is the core understanding that the established church represents the primary location of God's activity in that particular location since the boundaries of the church's domain are the same as the boundaries of the world that it possesses. For the specifics regarding the differences among established church views, see the helpful treatment provided in Ernst Troeltsch, *The Social Teaching of the Christian Churches,* vol. 2 (1912; reprint, Louisville: Westminster/John Knox Press, 1992).

the primary horizon of God's activity in the world, and this presence is legitimated by civil authority.[18]

The problems associated with this understanding became painfully evident in the wars of religion that raged throughout Europe from the late 1500s into the early 1600s. The eventual solution that was accepted at the Peace of Westphalia in 1648 — *whose realm, whose religion* — ended these hostilities but left unresolved the core self-understanding of the established church.[19] This is reflected in the continued efforts by most established churches to persecute other expressions of the church, what they labeled as *sects*.[20]

It is important that the discussion about the denominational church include at least two different organizational expressions. On the one hand, there are specific congregations that follow the logic of the denominational, organizational church. They are organized on a *voluntary* basis around a *purposive intent.* On the other hand, there are associations of such congregations, along with their judicatories and national structures, that have come to be known as "denominations." Independent congregations organized on a voluntary basis around a purposive intent are, in essence, expressions of the same inherent logic that is found in the denominational, organizational church. This has profound implications for the church in North America, where numerous *independent* congregations continue to be formed, since many define themselves as "nondenominational." While they may not be a denomination in technical terms, they are, in fact, denominational in functional terms relative to their inherent organizational logic.

It is now clear that the denominational, organizational church has undergone several phases of development over the past two hundred years and more, but the core genetic code of an organizational self-understanding

18. An example of this perspective is found in the Westminster Confession of Faith (1646) in Chapter XXV, *Of the Church,* sec. 2: "The visible church . . . is the kingdom of the Lord Jesus Christ. . . ." This connecting of Jesus' announcement of the kingdom (see footnote references to the confession in this section) makes the visible church and God's kingdom on earth the same entity.

19. The Peace of Augsburg in 1555 established this principle, but it was not until the end of the thirty years of religious wars and the Peace of Westphalia in 1648 that this principle became the accepted practice. See Eric W. Gritsch, *A History of Lutheranism* (Minneapolis: Fortress, 2002), 109-13.

20. Troeltsch, 461-94, 671-73, 691-94.

around a purposive intent remains at the center of its existence. This tends to place the emphasis more on matters of polity (how the church is organized and administered) than it does on ecclesiology (how the church's nature or essence is understood).

The European national churches had confessions that addressed the ecclesiology of the church, but these had been formulated from the perspective of a church exercising domain over its territory. The polities associated with this understanding of ecclesiology relied on magistrates for support. This did not fit the new reality facing the emerging denominations in the American colonies, where various churches occupied the same space geographically. Of necessity, the ecclesiologies and polities undergirding these churches came into question. But the emerging denominations, mostly out of pragmatic concerns for creating viable organizations, tended to focus more on redefining the church around polity in relationship to its purpose than in rigorously reexamining the assumptions of the ecclesiology that stood behind it.

This crucial distinction leads us to the important conversation that is now emerging regarding a missional understanding of the church. This understanding works primarily from the perspective of ecclesiology and understands the church's identity — its nature or essence — in relationship to the triune God and the mission of God in the world. I take up issues related to this conversation in the closing section of this chapter.

DNA of Denominations and Denominationalism

Purposive: developing a functional ecclesiology primarily around a
   purposive intent (foundational).
Organizational: developing an organizational self-understanding to
   support the purposive intent (foundational).

Formation of the Denominational, Organizational Church in the United States

It is interesting that immigrants from both the European state churches and many of the persecuted sects began to settle within the colonies of what eventually became the United States after 1600. Here they found that a different core identity was required to give legitimacy to the church. As I have noted above, this alternative conception came into existence as an organizational self-understanding around a purposive intent, what I am referring to here as the *denominational church.* By the mid- to late 1700s, the denominational view of the church in the colonies, soon to become states, became the normative understanding of the diverse associations of congregations that had formed. It is helpful to trace this development in a bit more detail in order for us to more fully unpack the DNA of denominations and denominationalism.

The Colonial Experience, 1600-1780

The formation of the American colonies was the result of diverse interests. Some were economic, some were political, and some were social; however, deeply religious motives were also embedded in the colonial experience. Many of the more radical sectarian groups in Europe immigrated to the colonies to secure their religious freedom, especially the Puritans, Baptists, Quakers, and Mennonites. Some of these groups, such as the Puritans in the New England colonies, attempted to set up their own version of what might be identified as a kind of state church, what some have inappropriately labeled a theocracy.[21] But dissenting groups within these colonies soon challenged this approach in the name of religious freedom, notably the Baptists in Rhode Island. The seeds of religious diversity had been planted in all the colonies by the mid-1600s, and they had begun to take deep root by the early 1700s.[22]

Religious Diversity

The religious diversity in the colonies included immigrants that represented the established churches of Europe, such as Lutheran, Dutch Reformed, Scottish Presbyterian, and Anglican. They soon found themselves living alongside other Christian faith traditions that had also emigrated from Europe, such as the Quakers and Mennonites, and new groups that emerged from within the colonies, such as the Baptists. During this period some colonies chose to have religious establishment: Anglicans in

21. Ahlstrom, *Religious History,* 146-50.
22. Corrigan and Hudson, *Religion in America,* 47-48.

the South (New York, Maryland, North Carolina, South Carolina, and Georgia) and Congregationalists in the North (Massachusetts, New Hampshire, Vermont, and Connecticut). However, in the middle colonies (Rhode Island, New Jersey, Pennsylvania, and Delaware) it was not possible for any one group to be dominant. It was in the middle colonies, therefore, that the tradition of religious freedom quickly gained currency.[23] Even in those colonies that established either the Anglican Church or the Congregational Church, the presence of denominational diversity soon came to expression based on the call for religious freedom.[24] While the Roman Catholic Church at that time functioned as an established church that expected to have domain, political realities in the colonies soon necessitated that the Catholic Church also had to function alongside other churches as simply another denominational expression of the church.

The de facto acceptance of religious diversity became common in all of the colonies by the early 1700s, even in those colonies that had established a particular church. This shared experience of religious diversity throughout the colonies required a new imagination for how to conceive of the church and how to organize congregations. The old formula of a state church with an establishment identity that allowed it the privilege of persecuting other Christian sects was obsolete almost from the beginning, though some vestiges of it lingered into the late 1700s.[25]

The Two Strains of Reformation and Restoration

It is important to note the two diverse strains that make up those organizations that became fully developed denominations.[26] One group represented denominations formed by the immigrants coming from the established state churches of the magisterial Protestant Reformation of Europe — churches from the *left*. These churches on the left worked from the premise of *ecclesia semper reformanda:* the church is always reforming (Reformation). In the new context of the colonies and emerging states, they had to recontextualize their European understandings of

23. Hudson, "Denominationalism," 62-63; Ahlstrom, *Religious History,* 200-13.
24. Hudson, "Denominationalism," 51-52; Ahlstrom, *Religious History,* 184-99.
25. Ahlstrom, *Religious History,* 151-65.
26. Mead, "Denominationalism: The Shape of Protestantism in America," 73-75.

ecclesiology, polity, and liturgy to fit the new setting. For example, the Anglicans (who became Episcopalians in 1785) found that they had to forgo the practice of parish boundaries that was familiar to them in England.[27]

In contrast to these denominations that represented churches on the left were other groups — churches from the *right*. They sought to create something new within the emerging nation and took their starting point from one of the principles emphasized by the Dissenting Brethren (Independents). This was the practice of going back to biblical foundations to restore the church to its original intent (Restoration). The denominations that represent this restoration impulse stand in contrast to those that represent the reforming impulse; they represent what might be called "made-in-America denominations."

There are numerous such made-in-America denominations, some of which came into existence during the colonial period, such as certain strains of Baptists, and others that came into existence during the revivals associated with the Second Great Awakening in the early decades of the nineteenth century, such as the movements of the Disciples of Christ and the Churches of Christ. And scores of other newly forming denominations followed this pattern throughout the nineteenth century. A variation of this pattern came to expression with the Methodists, who melded the role of bishops from Reformation influence through Anglicanism with congregational polity from Restoration influence and the emphasis on democracy in the American context.

Free-Church Ecclesiology

The formation of this new identity, what I am identifying here as the denominational church with an organizational self-understanding around a purposive identity, drew on a number of historical developments with regard to clarifying its ecclesiology and polity. One such development was using free-church ecclesiology as the norm for understanding the emerging denominations within the colonies. Free-church ecclesiology had emerged during the Protestant Reformation when the Anabaptists moved away from the concept of established European national churches. The Anabaptists conceived of the church primarily as a gathered social com-

27. Mead, "Denominationalism," 76.

munity of believers who possessed the freedom to associate and the right to govern their own affairs.[28]

More influential, however, for the development of free-church ecclesiology in the colonies was the work of English Baptists: they formulated their foundational principles in the Savoy Declaration of 1658.[29] An earlier representative figure of this tradition, John Smyth (1554-1612), had developed a free-church view of the church — first in England, and later in exile in the Netherlands. Smyth emphasized the importance of obedience and a biblical form of church organization as also being essential for the church — in addition to the Word, the sacraments, and the gathered assembly of God's people.[30] As I have noted above, even though many churches in the colonies brought with them the ecclesiologies and polities of their European state churches, the new context of religious diversity required adjustments almost from the beginning.[31] The primary adjustment all churches made toward the end of the eighteenth century — with the formal separation of church and state — was the adoption of free-church ecclesiology. They adopted this either as their formal ecclesiology or at least as an overlay on their former established, state-church ecclesiology.

Church as Voluntary Organization

A parallel development that fed into the conception of the denominational church during the colonial experience was the understanding that religious freedom required that the church be established on a voluntary basis. While the immigrants carried many patterns of European society into the colonies, new social constructions were also required. The recently arrived European immigrants, in attempting to construct a new social order, turned to the use of voluntary societies for much of this work.[32] The no-

---

28. See, for example, the Dordrecht Confession (1632), which was adopted by the Mennonites, esp. Article VII, "Of the Church of Christ."

29. Ahlstrom, *Religious History,* 94.

30. Miroslav Volf, *After Our Likeness: The Church as the Image of the Trinity* (Grand Rapids: Eerdmans, 1998), 23-24, 131-34.

31. A helpful discussion of the shift to the gathered church as a voluntary organization in the midst of the breakdown of the parish system is provided in Hudson, "Denominationalism," 52.

32. Hudson, "Denominationalism," 52, 162-65.

tion of the voluntary character of the church had been conceptualized by John Locke in 1689 in his *Letter Concerning Toleration.*[33]

> A Church I take to be a voluntary society of men joining themselves of their own accord in order to the public worshipping of God in such manner as they judge acceptable to Him. . . . I say it is a free and voluntary society. Nobody is born a member of the church; . . . since the joining together of several members into this church-society . . . is absolutely free and spontaneous, it necessarily follows that the right of making its laws can belong to none but the society itself; or at least to those whom the society by common consent has authorized thereunto.

Locke used the notion of social contract to conceive of the church similar to what he had done in regard to developing the social order of civil society. This view was ratified within the English experience that same year with the formal adoption of the Act of Toleration. The freedom to develop the church on a voluntary basis first became legitimated in England, but it came to its more prominent expression in the emerging colonies that would become the United States. It required only a small step to marry a voluntary society understanding of the church to a free-church ecclesiology. As a result, the emerging voluntary associations of congregations during the seventeenth and eighteenth centuries gradually became formal denominations by the late 1700s. The pattern of understanding church life in the United States as voluntary in nature came to be the normative expression of church life.

Divine Destiny or Civic Responsibility

Most of the immigrants to the colonies in the 1600s brought with them the expectation of being able to exercise religious freedom. But many of them, especially those representing churches on the right, also brought a keen sense that it was God's *providence* that was providing them with an opportunity to do so in this new land. This was especially the case for the Puritans in New England, though the Quakers in the colony of Pennsylvania

33. Locke, an English exile in Holland, wrote this letter to his Dutch friend Philip von Limborch in 1685: in it he calls for an end to the oppression of people who held unorthodox religious beliefs. The letter was published without Locke's permission after he returned to England following the Glorious Revolution of 1688.

held similar views. The voice of Puritan John Winthrop is illustrative of this viewpoint:

> God had "sifted a whole nation" in order to plant his "choice grain" in the American wilderness, but his purpose was more far-ranging. . . . Their role, John Winthrop had reminded them, was to be "a city set on a hill" to demonstrate before "the eyes of the world" what the result would be when a whole people was brought into open covenant with God. As part of God's program of instruction, they were to provide the nations with a working model of godly society and by contagion of their example were to be God's instruments in effecting the release from bondage of all mankind.[34]

This perspective represents a rather high view of God's unique blessing on what became known as the "American experiment." It also introduced a strain into the DNA of Christianity in the United States that is still very much alive.

However, not all of the newly emerging churches held this view; it tended to be more the case among the churches on the left, such as the Anglicans, Presbyterians, and Lutherans. But many from these emerging denominations did develop what might be called a strong sense of *civic responsibility,* especially during the mid-1700s, when tensions with England began to grow and calls for independence began to increase. The call for patriotic loyalty in supporting the revolutionary cause was nurtured by many of these churches, just as it was among churches from the right. The result, whether because of a view of divine destiny or of civic responsibility, was that churches took on the responsibility of supporting public policies particularly when matters of national security were at stake. This commingling of God and country from these different perspectives became important strains within the DNA of denominationalism, and these strains are also still very much alive today. Especially in times of war, both of these strains have been actively mined by political leaders among the churches.

The outlines of the denominational church were beginning to come clearly into focus by the mid-1700s. The call for independence and the Revolutionary War furthered its formation; and with the formal separa-

---

34. As quoted in Winthrop S. Hudson, *Religion in America: An Historical Account of the Development of American Religious Life* (New York: Charles Scribner's Sons, 1965), 20.

tion of church and state, this pattern became institutionalized. The first amendment of the Bill of Rights, as it was proposed in 1789, made a provision for the legal separation of church and state: no church would be established in the United States, and every church would be protected to practice religious freedom. This decision affirmed the organizing principle of denominationalism, and it gave impetus to the further development of the denominational, organizational church. Within the last two decades of the eighteenth century, representatives of numerous church bodies in the newly formed United States met to form national organizations: the Methodists in 1784, the Episcopalians in 1785, and the Presbyterians in 1789.[35]

These newly emerging denominations had to adapt themselves to the dynamic context of the colonies as the movement of those colonies toward becoming the United States began to unfold. In the midst of the constitutional decision to separate church and state, the churches on the left had to give up the practice, built into their European-shaped polities, that relied on the magistrate to favor the church within civil society. The churches on the right had to create new forms that would give the church shape within the democratic social order that was emerging. All of the emerging denominations, whether from the European left or right, had to recontextualize or contextualize themselves within the dynamic setting of the newly formed United States.

DNA of Denominations and Denominationalism

Religious Diversity: acceptance of religious diversity as a norm for church life (foundational).

Confessional Reforming or Biblical Restoring: relying on either confessional reformation or biblical restoration to help the church adapt to a new context (strains).

Free-Church Ecclesiology: developing a free-church ecclesiology within the practice of democratic ideals (foundational).

Voluntary: engaging in the formation of churches on a voluntary basis (foundational).

Divine Destiny or Civic Responsibility: the commingling of God and country in the support of national policies or purposes (strains).

35. Hudson, *Religion in America,* 138-46.

Further Development of Denominations and Denominationalism

Since the formation of denominations reflected the contextual realities of the colonial setting, it is not surprising that this expression of the church has been fairly dynamic over the past two hundred years. There are at least four phases of further development of the denominational, organizational church that can be observed during this period.[36]

The Denominational, Organizational Church, 1790-1870

Within the American setting, the denominational, organizational church was a unique creation that was largely the pragmatic result of a variety of circumstances and events that were usually rationalized biblically and theologically after the fact, if at all.[37] As I observed above, church historian Martin Marty views them as a turning point in the history of the church, one that departed from the previous 1400 years of the church's self-understanding.[38]

As the newly emerging denominations began to form, they had to adopt polities to guide their organizational development. Immigrants from the churches on the left brought with them confessional understandings of the church, as well as organizational polities that had been shaped by the assumptions of Constantinian Christendom and the established church. These polities assumed institutional domain and focused primarily on ordering the internal life of the denomination around a series of representative assemblies at the local, regional, and national assemblies. For the most part, the churches from the left adapted this organizational pattern into their new polities, in many cases by simply adopting with minor adjustments the European national church polity.[39] The churches on

36. These four phases are introduced as a framework for understanding denominations in Russell E. Richey's article "Denominations and Denominationalism: An American Morphology," in Robert Bruce Mullin and Russell E. Richey, eds., *Reimagining Denominationalism: Interpretive Essays* (New York: Oxford University Press, 1994), 77-90.

37. Richey, *Denominationalism*, 19-21.

38. Marty, *Righteous Empire*, 67-68.

39. We find, for example, the Presbyterians adopting and adapting the Book of Order, which was developed by the Westminster divines in the 1640s, and the Reformed Church in America adopting the polity of Dordt, developed in 1619.

the right tended to follow this pattern of developing a series of ascending assemblies at the local, regional, and national levels, though they tended to give much less authority to the regional judicatories and national assemblies. Most followed a more congregational approach to polity.

Developments during the colonial period challenged some of the underlying assumptions embedded in the assembly-structured polities, especially the notion that one's being born in the parish meant that one was baptized into the church. There were no structures in place for reaching those outside the church. The new situation of religious diversity, and the challenge of reaching vast numbers of unchurched persons, especially on the frontier beyond the Allegheny Mountains, led the newly emerging denominations to rely on the formation of special societies to engage in what came to be known as *home missions*.[40] This work on the frontier was paralleled by the formation of other societies to engage in what became known as *foreign missions*.[41] There were earlier precedents for these societies, such as the Anglican mission organizations of the Society for the Propagation of Christian Knowledge (SPCK, founded in 1698) and the Society for the Propagation of the Gospel (SPG, founded in 1701).[42] But more important was the work of William Carey, who in 1792 conceived of the independent *mission society* as a preferred structure for engaging in missionary work.[43] The formation of such mission societies in the early nineteenth century in the United States represented a remarkable organizational development in the life of the church, which paralleled in many ways the development of denominations.

By the early 1800s, de Tocqueville would identify this characteristic as one of the unique features of the emerging American society.[44] The rich fabric of voluntary associations within the colonies included many that were secular in origin, but also many others that were religious. While there were hundreds of such religious societies that were formed locally or

40. Hudson, *Religion in America,* 103-04; and Ahlstrom, *Religious History,* 382-83.

41. Hudson, *Religion in America,* 159-68.

42. Elwyn A. Smith, "The Forming of a Modern American Denomination," in Richey, *Denominationalism,* 111.

43. William Carey proposed the formation of a mission society as the way to fund the work of missionaries. William Carey, *An Enquiry into the Obligation to Use Means for the Conversion of the Heathens* (London: Hodder and Stoughton, 1892), 82-83.

44. Alexis de Tocqueville, *Democracy in America* (1835), as quoted in Ahlstrom, *Religious History,* 386.

regionally, seven of them managed to gain national prominence by the early 1820s: the American Board of Commissioners for Foreign Missions (1810), the American Bible Society (1816), the American Education Society (1816), the American Colonization Society (1816), the American Sunday School Union (1824), the American Home Missionary Society (1826), and the American Temperance Society (1826).[45] These structures, while reflecting the democratic principles that were being nurtured in the colonies, were also the natural extension of the logic of the voluntary basis of the church with regard to a free-church ecclesiology.

The formation of mission societies deeply impacted the genetic code of the emerging denominational church, with its organizational self-understanding concerning a purposive intent.[46] While many focused on evangelizing and reaching the unchurched, others were formed to promote specific moral agendas, such as the temperance and antislavery movements. These moral crusades sought to transform personal views of ordinary Americans as well as to shape public policy. The involvement of churches in such moral crusades was a common theme throughout the nineteenth and twentieth centuries, and it continues to this day. There is an expectation among most U.S. denominations that they are responsible to help shape public behavior, and they often seek to use the democratic political process to achieve this end.

Being developed alongside the interdenominational societies in the early 1800s were structures internal to the denominations that came to expression as committees and boards. They were established to function under the authority of the regional and national assemblies and became responsible to help manage the growing mission work that was taking place both at home and abroad. Representative of this trend were the Presbyterians: they formed a standing committee on missions in 1802, and then a Board of Missions in 1816. Initially, these structures sought to coordinate and integrate their efforts with the interdenominational mission societies.[47]

The challenges associated with bringing the gospel and the church to the frontier also led to the adoption of some different approaches to ministry. One of the more significant of these was the development of the *re-*

45. Fred J. Hood, "Evolution of the Denomination Among the Reformed of the Middle and Southern States 1780-1840," in Richey, *Denominationalism*, 145.
46. William W. Sweet, *The Story of Religion in America* (1930; reprint, Grand Rapids: Baker Book House, 1975), 155-71.
47. Sweet, 147.

vival (or camp) meeting, with its emphasis on nurturing personal piety. This approach to ministry became especially prominent during the Second Great Awakening. These events served as social gatherings as much as they did religious events: people in isolated settings took the opportunity to gather in order to experience community. However, the revivals soon took on a life of their own, and they became a regular part of denominational life, especially among the Baptists, Methodists, and the newly formed Disciples of Christ and Churches of Christ. The use of revivals to foster personal piety and to stimulate growth is a pattern that continues to this day in some denominations. The development of the revival also led to the adoption of a variety of new methods to reach people with the gospel, which included such innovations as the anxious bench, itinerate preachers, and the Sunday schools.[48]

The use of these new methods of ministry also contributed to the development of another key strain in the DNA of denominationalism: new denominations started up on the margins. The acceptance of religious diversity and the separation of church and state created greater freedom for the starting up of new denominations. Population segments that were not accepted by existing denominations, as well as newly arriving immigrant groups, often took the opportunity to form their own denominations, a pattern that continues to the present time. It is interesting to note that some of these upstart denominations during the nineteenth century (Baptists and Methodists) outpaced the Congregationalists and Presbyterians in growth, so that by the 1860s they had become the largest denominations in the country.[49]

In the unfolding story line of the denominational, organizational church in the United States, it is very important for us to note the emergence of one other type during this period: new denominations that were started from below, that is, denominations that involved the enslaved black population. Some from this population were included within existing white congregations as marginalized participants. But significant numbers of black slaves also developed their own forms of church in the midst of their bondage. These forms often followed the patterns of their white precedents, especially those of the Baptists and Methodists. Prior to the Civil War, these groups functioned as an "invisible church," but they quickly

48. See Marty, 68; Hudson, 150-57; Ahlstrom, 429-54.
49. Finke and Stark, 55-116.

took on institutional expression following that war.[50] We should not underestimate the importance of the black church that emerged from below, in terms of how it contributed to forming an identity and providing a voice for the freed-slave population, an identity and voice that came to full expression during the civil rights movement of the 1950s and 1960s.

It was not long before tensions began to surface within some denominations over the use of the new measures on the frontier. Conflict was especially evident among the Presbyterians, and it led eventually to a split between the Old School and New School Presbyterians in 1837.[51] This split led the Old School leaders to distance themselves from the interdenominational mission societies in order to form their own denominational boards and agencies that could be controlled by their national assembly. Other denominations soon replicated this pattern, so that it became the norm by the late 1830s.

The expanding work in managing missions and other support services had led to significant changes. What had earlier been committees or boards that were made up of active pastors and lay leaders became formal denominational agencies with permanent staff at the national level.[52] The purpose of these agencies was to plan for and coordinate the expanding ministries of domestic and foreign missions, along with emerging ministries, such as Christian education and publishing houses. With these changes, the basic structure of the modern denomination was now in place: a series of representative assemblies, which governed the work of denomination-specific boards, which in turn supervised agencies with professional staff.

The biggest question left unresolved in their formation was the relationship between the formal denominational boards and agencies and the previously formed assembly structures of the new national denominations. The initial logic of the denominational church vested its organizational self-understanding around a purposive intent in its representative assemblies at the national, regional, and local levels. Now a new organizational dimension was placed into the mix: the denominational agency with its representative board. Which would lead? Which would be subordinate?

50. E. Franklin Frazier, *The Negro Church in America* (New York: Schocken, 1974), 14, 35-51.

51. A helpful perspective on this conflict is provided by Elwyn A. Smith, "The Forming of a Modern American Denomination," in Richey, *Denominationalism*, 108-36.

52. See Smith in Richey, *Denominationalism*, 108-36.

It soon became clear that the assembly structures would maintain primary control.

By the mid- to late 1800s, the modern organizational, denominational church had become the norm for church life in the United States. Congregations of a particular denomination usually differentiated their existence from others primarily in terms of confessional distinctives, and these distinctives were related to the different polities of the congregational, presbyterian, and episcopal forms of church government. But underneath these confessional and polity differences lay the elements of a common genetic code as identified above. Being added to the DNA of denominations during this period were the following traits:

DNA of Denominations and Denominationalism

Representative Assembly Structures at the Local, Regional, and National Levels: denominations developed a representative assembly governance system (foundational).

Moral Crusades: the mobilization of churches to transform public behavior and shape public polity, often by using the political process (strain).

Revivalism and Piety: the inner life of denominations being continuously energized through the use of revivals and the call to a life of piety (strain).

Mission Societies: denominations partnering with specialized mission societies to carry out particular ministries (strain).

Boards and Agencies for Mission and Service: specialized ministries being organized around denomination-specific boards and agencies (foundational).

Upstart Denominations from the Margins: marginalized groups forming new denominations that provided identity and often access to the broader society given time (strain).

New Denominations from Below: enslaved population of blacks forming new denominations from below that provided both identity and voice in the midst of social, economic, and political restrictions (strain).

The Churchly Denomination, 1870-1920

Coming out of the Civil War, most denominations began to develop more elaborate infrastructure as the frontier rapidly filled in and cities began to grow. By the latter part of the 1800s, another phase in the development of the denominational, organizational church became discernible. Refined methodologies for developing new congregations were developed, especially in the West, with standardized plans for constructing church buildings; existing congregations adapted previous ministry approaches to new conditions, as illustrated in the development of urban revivalism.[53]

Most churches began to take on a more comprehensive, programmatic approach to their ministries during this time. The pattern they followed often found a denomination either copying or co-opting one of the ministries of an interdenominational society and then bringing that activity in house under the management of its own board and agency. In the field of education, this was especially evident in the mainstreaming of the Sunday school movement within denominational programming. As this ministry was brought in house by almost all denominations during the mid-1800s to late 1800s, standardized curricula for the expanding Sunday school systems were put into place by denominational publishing houses.[54] Similarly, denominational youth ministries began to appear by the late nineteenth century, often patterned after the parachurch ministry of Christian Endeavor.[55]

A comprehensive approach to ministry began to take shape in most denominations during this period. By the turn of the century, new urban congregations were engaged in fully implementing this ministry approach. One could begin to see congregations developing comprehensive programmatic activities, such as the building of extensive educational buildings that accommodated classes for instruction broken down by age and gender; the formation of robed choirs; the building of recreational facilities for family activities; and the establishment of church libraries. A comprehensive church program was being put into place that would, in effect, deal with its members from cradle to grave.[56]

53. Hudson, 246-54.
54. Hudson, 246-54; Ahlstrom, 741-42.
55. Ahlstrom, 858.
56. Mullin and Richey, *Reimagining Denominationalism*, 82-84.

Another development that emerged during this period was the fracturing of various denominations along liberal and conservative lines — what became known as the modernism-fundamentalism controversy. The result, more often than not, was the formation of new denominations by groups of conservatives who separated from their parent denominations.[57] Contributing to the theological debates that stood behind this fracturing were a variety of factors: the teaching of evolution; the introduction of higher criticism in biblical studies; the emergence of the social gospel; and rising levels of education among both pastors and parishioners within many denominations. This new dividing line between denominations added to the growing complexity of denominationalism for the churches in the United States as they took up the challenges of a new century.

DNA of Denominations and Denominationalism

Programmatic: denomination-specific programs were developed by the national church and delivered to the congregations for their ministry (foundational).

Comprehensive: the denominational programs put into place sought to address the whole of the life of the members — from cradle to grave (foundational).

Liberal and Conservative Denominations: denominations began to identify themselves in terms of their theological stance (strains).

The Corporate Denomination, 1920-1970

While the suggested date that divides the previous phase from this one is certainly somewhat arbitrary, a discernible shift became evident within denominational church life during the first decades of the new century. As I have noted above, the growing complexity of the churchly denomination required new ways for structuring and managing the church. Interestingly, this occurred at about the same time that the newly emerging field of organizational management was gaining influence. Though several sources were involved in the formation of this new social-science discipline, the most important for religious denominations in the United States was the

---

57. Ahlstrom, 805-24.

stream issuing from Frederick Taylor, what became known as Scientific Management.[58] This movement focused on bringing productivity and efficiency into the business organization, and it did so by de-skilling tasks, organizing similar work activities into functional units, and building command-and-control systems through the establishment of a hierarchical bureaucracy.

This movement found an early voice in the emerging world of complex churchly denominations via the work of Shailer Mathews, the dean of the University of Chicago Divinity School, who in 1912 published *Scientific Management in the Churches*. This book's focus was on treating the church as "something of a business establishment."[59] The increasingly rationalized world of the modern bureaucracy started becoming the norm for denominational church life. Boards and agencies at the national level increasingly adopted corporate forms of organization and management as the number of departments expanded and the number of staff members grew.

Also during this period, an increasing number of ministers were becoming seminary trained, and this led to a growing professionalization of the clergy, as well as the increased importance of seminaries within denominational church life. In the midst of all this, denominations were becoming complex organizational systems with multiple boards and agencies at the national level. Over time, these national-level structures began to find their counterparts at the regional level, and even to some extent at the local level, where organized committees tended to parallel the design of the national church.

By the end of World War II, when the rapidly growing suburbanization of the church took place, most denominations were well positioned to wage the campaign of starting new franchise congregations in cooperation with their judicatories. High birth rates for over two decades (the baby-boom generation of 1946-64), an expanding middle class, increasing levels of education, the mass-produced automobile, oil at $3 a barrel, a newly expanding interstate highway system, and the creation of the thirty-year fixed-rate mortgage were all key factors that contributed to the suburbs'

58. In the early decades of the twentieth century, at least three streams emerged: scientific management by Frederick Taylor (1911); administrative management by Henri Fayol (1919); and bureaucracy by Max Weber (1924).

59. Shailer Matthews, *Scientific Management in the Churches* (Chicago: University of Chicago Press, 1912).

emergence as the new destination of choice.[60] Migration from both the central cities and rural areas fed the growth of these suburbs. Continued high levels of denominational loyalty during this period allowed for the rapid growth of suburban congregations in almost all denominations.[61]

Thousands of congregations were started as local franchises by their particular denomination. The logic of the denominational church, with its organizational self-understanding around a purposive intent, was now coming to full expression as the good life of the American dream was packaged and commodified into the suburban ideal.[62] It was an ideal to which millions aspired, but it was mostly realized by the emerging white middle class. The darker side of this suburban success was what Gibson Winter labeled in 1962 the *suburban captivity:* with its profound success during the two and half decades from 1945 to 1970, the denominational, organizational, suburban congregation extended the logic of the organizational self-understanding around a purposive intent of the denomination to a new level.[63]

The primary logic of the previous city-neighborhood congregation had continued to be a mixture of intergenerational relationships that operated in the midst of an increasing programmatic structure that was fed by the denominational agencies. But in the suburban congregation, relationships became largely functional in the midst of high rates of mobility. Here a corporate identity came to be established primarily around shared programmatic activities.[64] It is interesting that the small-group movement began to emerge during this time to try to bring some sense of social community back into congregational life. The organizational and programmatic phase of the denominational church was now in full bloom. It is also interesting to note how rapidly this kind of congregation imploded in the

---

60. The dynamics of this new suburban growth are captured well by David Halberstam, *The Fifties* (New York: Villard Books, 1993), 131-43. In that section he discusses the beginning of mass-produced suburban housing as it was developed at Levittown, New York.

61. A Gallup poll in 1955 found that only 1 in 25 persons switched from their childhood faith as an adult, whereas by 1985 1 in 3 persons were found to have switched; reported in Wuthnow, *The Restructuring of American Religion,* 88.

62. Halberstam, *The Fifties,* 131-43.

63. Gibson Winter, *The Suburban Captivity of the Churches: An Analysis of Protestant Responsibility in the Expanding Metropolis* (New York: Macmillan, 1962).

64. Winter, 96-101.

midst of the dramatic cultural shifts of the 1960s and 1970s, which I will discuss in the next section.

DNA of Denominations and Denominationalism

Corporate: denominations took on a corporate character as they turned to modern management and organizational approaches to govern their internal lives (foundational).
Professional: ordained ministry in many denominations became increasingly professionalized (strain).
Franchise Model of Congregational Development: most denominations developed a franchise approach to starting and developing new congregations (strain).

Diversity: downsizing and regulation versus strategy, growth, and networking, 1970 to the present

As I have observed above, dramatic changes disrupted the growth patterns of the denominations in the 1960s and 1970s. A whole range of movements define the transition that took place: the civil rights movement, the youth/counterculture movement, the feminist movement, the ecological movement, and the antiwar movement. What is important to note is the rapid collapse of institutional identity among the emerging generation, a shift that had huge consequences for the denominational church.[65] The baby-boom generation left the church in greater numbers than had any previous generation, and they came back in fewer numbers. The start-up of new congregations by denominations as franchise models came to a screeching halt by the mid-1970s.[66] Standardized, denominational educational curriculums went into decline, and most were out of business by the 1980s. In the midst of these dramatic changes, the denominational, organizational church entered yet another phase of development, one that is particularly marked by increasing diversity and divergence.

The increased cultural diversity evident in the broader society in the 1960s began to become evident within denominations by the 1970s. Associ-

65. Wade Clark Roof and William McKinney, *American Mainline Religion: Its Changing Shape and Future* (New Brunswick, NJ: Rutgers University Press, 1987), 48-57.
66. Lyle E. Schaller, *44 Questions for Church Planters* (Nashville: Abingdon, 1991), 13-36.

ated with this diversity was an increasing divergence of theological view-points, illustrated well in how persons viewed the role of women or re-garded abortion. Liberal and conservative views that had previously divided denominations from one another now began to divide denomina-tions internally.[67] This pattern has continued in denominations, and it is currently being played out regarding the issue of human sexuality. New al-liances of conservative or liberal groups made up of like-minded people from among a variety of denominations are now common. In addition, the formation of coalitions and the exercise of advocacy politics has in-creasingly become the primary format for internal denominational decision-making regarding matters affecting theological policy.

Another dimension of the diversity that developed within denomi-nations during this time is an increasing divergence on matters of theolog-ical policy between national church leaders and the local congregations. Many local congregations within denominations continue to be more theologically and socially conservative than what they perceive their na-tional church body to be. In the face of this, national church leaders often cast their roles in terms of taking prophetic stands, and they often label the resistance they encounter as a form of insipid congregationalism, espe-cially when financial resources for denominational ministries are not forthcoming. In the meantime, many congregations are involved in trying to recontextualize their ministries in the midst of substantial changes. It is not unusual for them, as they do so, to turn to outside groups for inspira-tion or ideas, because denominational programming no longer exists, or they view it as less relevant. It is also not uncommon for them, as they pur-sue their local ministries, to use more of their financial resources to de-velop programming, upgrade buildings, or hire additional staff.

Overall, the revenue coming in to national church offices is dramati-cally down. This, in turn, has led to the continued downsizing of national agencies and churchwide staff for many of the former mainline denomina-tions.[68] The median age of members of most mainline denominations now exceeds the national median age, in many cases by twenty or more years

67. Dean R. Hoge, *Division in the Protestant House: The Basic Reasons Behind Intra-Church Conflicts* (Philadelphia: Westminster Press, 1976).

68. The Evangelical Lutheran Church in America, newly formed in 1987, is a case study of the continuing pattern of denominational downsizing at the national level as churchwide revenues continue to decline. Most other mainline denominations follow a sim-ilar trend.

(55+ vs. 35).[69] These shifts have led some of the former mainline denominations to attempt to create internal versions of approaches pioneered by evangelical denominations or independent congregations, that is, becoming seeker-sensitive, developing small groups, using contemporary worship, and so forth. But in the end, these denominations have tended to become more *regulatory* in character. When denominational loyalty is lost, one option available is to turn to rules and procedures to seek compliance.

In contrast to what is happening in many former mainline denominations, there are scores of more conservative or evangelical denominations that are showing positive growth trends, such as the Southern Baptists, Assemblies of God, Christian Missionary Alliance, and the Church of God (Cleveland).[70] In addition, there has been a rapid expansion of the number of independent congregations.[71] Many of these denominations and independent congregations have been influenced by what might be labeled as market-driven or mission-driven models of church.[72] The seeker-church phenomenon pioneered by Willow Creek is probably the most influential, especially as it has come to be operationalized into the purpose-driven model of Saddleback Community Church under the leadership of Rick Warren.[73]

Usually at the heart of these various market-driven and/or mission-driven models is a theology of the Great Commission, where mission is understood primarily as something the church must do. This follows the inherent logic of the denominational church as having an organizational self-understanding around a purposive intent. Accompanying this development has been the emergence of the association network. These networks are comprised of congregations that are self-selecting in their participation. A good example is the Willow Creek Association, which was formed in 1992 by the Willow Creek Community Church.[74] It is interesting

69. Roof and McKinney, 152-55.

70. Roof and McKinney, 150.

71. Roof and McKinney, 148-51.

72. Craig Van Gelder, *The Essence of the Church: A Community Created by the Spirit* (Grand Rapids: Baker, 2000), 20-21.

73. Rick Warren, *The Purpose-Driven Church* (Grand Rapids: Zondervan, 1995).

74. From the Willow Creek web site http://en.wikipedia.org/wiki/Willow_Creek _Community_Church (accessed August 30, 2006). "In 1992, the Willow Creek Association was created as a way to link together churches for the purpose of 'reaching increasing numbers of lost people.' The WCA develops training and leadership conferences and resources

that this association network is not identified as a denomination; but it may very well be, in reality, a new expression of the denominational form.

Clearly, we are in a period of transition in the life of the denominational church. From the 1960s to the present time, new movements have continued to emerge to give direction in the midst of the changes taking place. All of them follow the inherent logic that the denominational church has an organizational self-understanding around a purposive intent. In this regard, all of them tend to treat the church in primarily functional or instrumental terms. The church renewal movement of the 1960s and early 1970s focused on trying to make existing structures more relevant to a new generation in the midst of a rapidly changing context. The church-growth movement of the 1970s and early 1980s placed emphasis on evangelism and focused largely on pragmatic technique. By the 1980s and early 1990s, the church-effectiveness movement brought the wider range of a social-science, organizational perspective to bear on trying to manage and lead congregations through renewal and growth in the midst of change.[75] This latter movement has recently morphed into what is now the church-health movement.[76] Parallel to it is the emphasis now being placed on pastoral excellence.[77]

Continuing efforts are being made to renew the church and transform denominations. But the core genetic code of the denominational church as having an organizational self-understanding around a purposive intent has yet to be sufficiently examined to allow for this. Those who have gone this route tend to still work within the same assumptions of a functional approach to ecclesiology and polity, a view that gave birth to the denominational church to begin with.[78]

---

for its member churches. The WCA is often confused with Willow Creek Community Church, or mistaken for a denomination; however, it is a distinctly separate organization which has close affiliations with Willow Creek Community Church. There are more than 11,000 member churches, which come from 90 denominations, and 45 different countries."

75. Darrell Guder et al., *Missional Church: A Vision for the Sending of the Church in North America* (Grand Rapids: Eerdmans, 1998), 72-73.

76. Many denominations have adopted this approach by using the program of Christian A. Schwarz, *Natural Church Development: A Guide to Eight Essential Qualities of Healthy Churches* (St. Charles, IL: ChurchSmart Resources, 1996).

77. Grants being made available over the past few years by the Lilly Endowment, Inc., for developing and sustaining pastoral excellence are illustrative of this.

78. See, for example, the recent book by Episcopal Bishop Claude E. Payne and Hamilton Beazley, *Reclaiming the Great Commission: A Practical Model for Transforming Denominations and Congregations* (San Francisco: Jossey-Bass, 2000).

DNA of Denominations and Denominationalism

Internal Diversity: many denominations are now divided internally between competing interests often rationalized around diverse theological commitments (strain).

Retrenchment by Some and Growth by Others: many former mainline denominations are in decline while some more conservative denominations are showing growth (strains).

Organizational Efforts at Renewal: many denominations and congregations use organizational renewal strategies to pursue growth and develop health (strain).

New Networks and Associations: what appears to be a new denominational form is emerging as networks or associations (strain).

Rethinking Denominationalism from a Missional Church Perspective

The past several decades have seen a seemingly endless obsession with trying to discover strategies to help denominations and congregations become more effective or successful. Consistent with the DNA of denominationalism, these strategies are usually defined with respect to carrying out the purpose of the church. To put it simply, in attempting to renew the church, you can't get there from there. It is essential to probe deeper beyond the mere attempt to reclaim the purposive intent of the church.

The argument I am proposing is that the denominational, organizational church has focused more on matters of polity than on ecclesiology. This ends up making the operational ecclesiology of the denominational church more functional, or instrumental, in character. In contrast, the missional church conversation has reintroduced a discussion about the very nature of the church, its essence. This conversation no longer understands "being missionary" primarily in functional terms, as something the church *does,* as is the case for the denominational, organizational church; instead, it understands "being missionary" in terms of something the church *is,* as something that is related to its nature. This represents a change of kind in the conversation about the church where ecclesiology is, once more, front and center.

Returning to this fuller discussion of ecclesiology is crucial if we are to break the impasse created by the functionalism that has come to be associated with the denominational, organizational church. But returning to this discussion from a missional perspective is even more critical if we are to live into all that God intends regarding the church created by the Spirit. This discussion has been popularized largely by the publication in 1998 of a book entitled *Missional Church: A Vision for the Sending of the Church in North America,* which is fast becoming a seminal work. This volume explores how the discipline of missiology, understanding God's mission in the world, is interrelated with the study (ology) of the church (ecclesia). The result is the construction of a missional ecclesiology, or, in shorthand, the concept of the "missional church."

In the missional church conversation the focus shifts to the world as the horizon for understanding the work of God, and God's redemptive work in the world as the basis for understanding both the nature and purpose of the church. In taking this approach, the *organizational self-understanding around a purposive intent* of the denominational church is replaced by an understanding of the church as being *created by the Spirit and thus missionary by nature.* The table below illustrates this contrast of perspectives.

Denominational Church	Missional Church
Self-understanding: exists as an organization with a purposive intent to accomplish something on behalf of God in the world, with this role being legitimated on a voluntary basis.	Self-understanding: exists as a community created by the Spirit that is missionary by nature in being called and sent to participate in God's mission in the world.

The missional church conversation brings together two streams of understanding God's work in the world. First, God has a mission within all of creation — the *missio Dei.* Second, God has brought redemption to bear on all of life within creation through the life, death, and resurrection of Jesus Christ. This redemptive work of God through Christ is best understood in terms of its announcement and inauguration of Jesus as the presence of the kingdom of God in the world.

A missional understanding of God's work in the world from this perspective is framed as follows. God is seeking to bring God's kingdom, the redemptive reign of God in Christ, to bear on every dimension of life within the entire world so that the larger creation purposes of God can be fulfilled. The church's self-understanding of being missional is grounded in the work of the Spirit of God, who calls the church into existence as a gathered community, equips and prepares it, and sends it into the world to participate fully in God's mission.

This missional church perspective understands that congregations are created by the Spirit and that their existence is for the purpose of engaging the world in bringing God's redemptive work in Christ to bear on every dimension of life. In being true to their missional identity, they can never function primarily as an end within themselves, the tendency of the self-understanding of the established church. In being true to their missional identity, they can never be satisfied with maintaining primarily a functional relationship with their contexts and communities, the tendency of the self-understanding of the denominational church. The missional church has a different genetic code.

The kingdom of God, the redemptive reign of God in Christ, gives birth to the missional church through the work of the Spirit. Its nature, ministry, and organization are formed by the reality, power, and intent of the kingdom of God. The church participates in God's mission in the world because it can do no other; it was created for this purpose. This purpose is encoded within the very makeup of the nature of the church: it is missionary by nature.

In the biblical framework outlined above, the missional church is identified as living between the times. It lives between the now and the not yet. The redemptive reign of God in Christ is already present, meaning that the power of God is fully manifest in the world through the gospel under the leading of the Spirit. But the redemptive reign of God is not yet fully complete, because the church looks toward the final consummation, when God will remove the presence of sin and create the new heaven and new earth.

Summary

This chapter has attempted to identify characteristics of the DNA that are present within denominations and denominationalism as they came to expression in the United States. An organizational self-understanding about a purposive intent was the primary logic identified that seems to characterize the denominational, organizational church. From this baseline, I have examined other foundational characteristics as well as particular strains of DNA. In contrast to this DNA of denominationalism, I have proposed that the growing missional church conversation, especially with its increased emphasis on framing a missional theology, offers a more fundamental approach to rethinking and reframing the ecclesiology and polity of denominations and their congregations in our context. Most of the essays in this volume provide specific insights into what the DNA of being missional might look like in reframing the ecclesiology and polity of particular denominations in light of their unique faith traditions. We invite and encourage readers to engage in thinking through what their denominations might look like if they were to take seriously the DNA that is inherent in a missional understanding of the church.

CHAPTER 2

Living in the City — Journeying outside the Gate:
A Missional Approach to Polity

David G. Forney

> *Therefore Jesus also suffered outside the city gate in order to sanc-tify the people by his own blood. Let us then go to him outside the camp and bear the abuse he endured. For here we have no lasting city, but we are looking for the city that is to come. Through him, then, let us continually offer a sacrifice of praise to God, that is, the fruit of lips that confess his name. Do not neglect to do good and to share what you have, for such sacrifices are pleasing to God.*
>
> (Heb. 13:12-16)[1]

The focus of this volume is on using a missional church perspective to reframe the ecclesiology and polity of denominations. This essay contrib-utes to this focus by exploring what a missional approach to polity might look like by using the Epistle to the Hebrews, especially Hebrews 13, as a guide. Given the contextual nature of polity and the varied ways in which we anticipate and participate in God's mission, this exploration is inten-tionally suggestive. My aim here is to provide denominational and congre-gational leaders with a substantive metaphor by which to think about their respective polities missionally. Given its direct connection to the word *pol-ity,* this essay begins with a survey of the Greek root for city. In the second

---

1. All biblical references are from the New Revised Standard Version.

section, the liturgical understanding of the city in Hebrews guides the conversation for thinking about polity theologically. In light of this reading of Hebrews, I want to suggest in this essay some implications of the city metaphor for polity today.

A Survey of the Meaning of City

Greek Meaning of Polis

Polis translates as "city," thus the English use of it in city names such as Minnea*polis*. In the Greek world, *polis* also meant "city-state," "capital city," or "main city" — in contrast to the desert (e.g., Mark 1:45).[2] We derive from *polis* such words as "politic" (c. 1420 CE), "political," "policy," "politician," and "polity" (meaning civil organization or civil order, c. 1538). In 1594, Richard Hooker connected polity with church governance:

> The necessitie of Politie, and Regiment in all Church may bee held, without holding any one certayne forme of politie, much less politie ecclesiasticall should be good, vnlesse God himself bee authour of it.[3]

From Hooker's ecclesial connection, polity has subsequently referred to the particular forms or systems of church government (e.g., congregational, presbyterian, episcopal).[4] Because of this historical connection between *polis* and polity, I will focus in this essay on the city as an instructive metaphor for approaching polity.

Structured human communities, such as cities, municipalities, towns, villages, camps, and so forth, obviously play an instrumental role in their members' lives. Fundamentally, the city is the embodiment of human

2. Walter Bauer, *A Greek-English Lexicon of the New Testament and Other Early Christian Literature*, trans. William F. Arndt and F. Wilbur Gingrich (Chicago: The University of Chicago Press, 1979), 685.

3. Richard Hooker, *Eccl. Ol.* iii.ii.i, in *The Oxford English Dictionary*, vol. 11, J. A. Simpson, ed. (Oxford: Oxford University Press, 1989), 36.

4. These three elementary forms of government place authority in different locations. Theoretically, congregational polity places the authority in the congregation; presbyterian polity places the authority in a group of elders (or presbyters, from the Greek *presbuteros*); and episcopal polity places the authority in the highest-ranking bishop *(episkopos)*.

community — both righteous and sinful. For some, the city is a place of excitement and prosperity; for others, the city is a place of dislocation, hardship, and violence. Between those two poles are many and varied experiences of the city; yet, whether we enjoy or loathe the city, our local centers of community impact our lives regularly. Therefore, each of us brings to the metaphor our varied experiences of the city. It is these particular experiences, both the encouraging and discouraging ones, that bring richness and complexity to the metaphor.

Historical and Biblical Understandings of Polis

A biblical understanding begins with a Hebraic conception of city.[5] In 1 Kings 8, we learn about Zion, the city of God where Solomon dedicates the temple.[6] "Then Solomon assembled the elders of Israel and all the heads of the tribes, the leaders of the ancestral houses of the Israelites, before King Solomon in Jerusalem, to bring up the ark of the covenant of the LORD out of the city of David, which is Zion" (v. 1). While biblical scholars are not certain about the precise Hebrew meaning of "Zion," we know that it clearly refers to Jerusalem, the city of David (see 2 Sam. 5:6-10), and that an important tradition (or theology) developed for Zion.

Four basic motifs constitute the "Zion tradition" in the Old Testament. "(1) Zion is the peak of Zaphon, that is, the highest mountain; (2) the river of paradise flows out of it; (3) God has defeated the assault of the waters of chaos there; and (4) God has defeated the kings and their peoples there."[7] The Zion tradition, or Zion theology, is marked consequently by (among other things) God dwelling on earth, a fidelity to the covenant, and the blessings that are afforded those who trust in God. From these we see that God is deeply concerned about public policy and practice, as J. J. M. Roberts observes:

5. In this essay there are two types of cities: the first type is the provisional (or the historical and contemporary cities, municipalities, towns, villages, and camps) in which we live; the second type is the city of God, Zion, the New Jerusalem.

6. I use various names (such as New Jerusalem, Zion) for the city of God that arrives with consummation. While there are important historical and theological differences between these names, I use them synonymously here.

7. J. J. M. Roberts, "The Davidic Origin of the Zion Tradition," *Journal of Biblical Literature* 92, no. 3 (1973): 329.

Faced with such a public policy with its inevitable social dislocations and hardships, which Judah's leadership probably justified as necessary evils to achieve security, peace, and well-being for Jerusalem, Isaiah responded with a prophetic critique of both poetic and theological depth. Metaphorically drawing on the ancient temple ideology of the Zion tradition, Isaiah contrasted the solid foundation Yahweh was laying to the government's flimsy fortifications, hastily built on inadequate foundations. Those fortifications would be measured for alignment with Yahweh's foundation, and, found wanting, they would be swept away, clearing the ground for Yahweh's new structure.[8]

Therefore, we learn from Isaiah 28:16 about Yahweh's new structure and the foundation that will not shake for those who trust.

> Therefore, thus says the Lord Yahweh:
> Look, I am about to lay in Zion a stone,
> A massive stone,
>   a cornerstone valuable for a foundation,
> A foundation which will not shake
>   for the one who trusts.[9]

The old is swept away precisely because the city's rulers do not bring righteousness and justice.

Following Isaiah, the Psalms repeatedly echoed the centrality of Zion to Judaism (and later for early Christianity). Zion is God's "holy hill" (Ps. 2:6), or "the holy habitation of the Most High" (Ps. 46:4), where we "sing praises to the LORD" (Ps. 9:11). "Out of Zion, the perfection of beauty, God shines forth" (Ps. 50:2). Jerusalem is "Mount Zion, which he loves. [God] built his sanctuary like the high heavens, like the earth, which he has founded forever" (Ps. 78:68-69).

The intersection of Judaism's Zion with the Greco-Roman *polis* produces the New Testament imagery of the Holy City, Jerusalem, as (1) "the assembly of the firstborn who are enrolled in heaven" (Heb. 12:22), (2) the gospel message of Jesus Christ, the "living stone" (1 Pet. 2:1-6), and (3) the dwelling place of the Lamb (Rev. 14:1). Compared with Western cities of our

---

8. J. J. M. Roberts, "Yahweh's Foundation in Zion (Isa. 28:16)," *Journal of Biblical Literature* 106, no. 1 (1987): 43-44.

9. Translation by J. J. M. Roberts, in "Yahweh's Foundation in Zion," 37.

time (e.g., Paris, Berlin, New York), Jerusalem's history is unparalleled, and it continues to be an important political and religious focal point.[10] Jerusalem began a relatively obscure place, but under the monarchies of David and Solomon it became the unifier of the nation and the place God lifted up in Israel's theological life (Ps. 68:15-16). In 587 BCE, however, Jerusalem was leveled by Babylon (2 Kings 25:10). Later it welcomed the return of exiles (Ezra 1), became the center for preserving Judean purity (Neh. 13:28-30), came under Roman rule (63 BCE), and was again devastated (70 CE).[11]

In the Greco-Roman world the cultural significance of the city was highly important. *Polis* was the government, the city-state. The government varied from city to city, of course; but as a rule, a city's *citizens* had the right to engage in its government. However, residing in the city did not confer citizenship. In fact, citizens only constituted a minority of a city's population: women and slaves, as noncitizens, composed the largest part of the population, and a small remainder of a city's population was typically foreigners. Citizenship meant power, wealth, and education. Consequently, after Alexander the Great would conquer an area, he would establish the citizenry from his Macedonian veterans and their families. "A city was built, with a gymnasium, and land was confiscated and assigned to the veterans; however, it was not farmed directly by them but by slaves or, as was often the case in Asia, by serfs who were bound to the land."[12] In this way, citizenship was the identifier for those in power.

The function of the city in the Greco-Roman world gave its citizens their sense of identity to a much larger degree than our cities do today. A citizen's identity was tied directly to his city. Both Greco-Roman and Jew-

---

10. A significant example is the diverse population of today's Jerusalem and the Israeli-Palestinian conflict. From the Jewish-Muslim reality within its walls today, Jerusalem is a place like no other. "Think of Jerusalem as a holy place, and at least two images spring to mind. One is the towering slab of yellow-white, pockmarked stone at the foot of which Hebrew prayers are softly uttered. The other is the dazzling golden dome that commands the skyline. These images are different views of the same structure: the western wall, a focal point for Jewish prayer and pilgrimage, is one of the supports for the elevated stone platform that is known to Jews as Temple Mount and to Muslims as Haram al-Sharif, or the Noble Sanctuary." *The Economist*, "The Heart of Holy War: Jerusalem's Holy Places," April 12, 2006.

11. "Jerusalem," in Paul J. Achtemeier, ed., *Harper's Bible Dictionary* (San Francisco: Harper & Row, 1985): 463-73.

12. Lester L. Grabbe, "The Hellenistic City of Jerusalem," in John R. Bartlett, ed., *Jews in the Hellenistic and Roman Cities* (London and New York: Routledge, 2002), 9.

ish literature attest the importance of the city to provide its citizens their "primary reference group."[13] In addition, the city extended its reputation to its citizens if they were sojourning elsewhere. For instance, when Paul makes his defense for his life in Jerusalem, he persuades the tribune to let him speak to the angry mob by saying, "I am a Jew, from Tarsus in Cilicia, a citizen of an important city; I beg you, let me speak to the people" (Acts 21:39). Tarsus, one of the great ports of the Mediterranean, was the terminus of a road that crossed the length of Asia Minor. Tarsus also claimed one of the greatest gymnasiums; Paul also boasts of being brought up "at the feet of Gamaliel" (Acts 22:3). At his first opportunity to speak to the tribune, he declares his citizenship to gain legitimacy: Paul is a citizen of a great city. For the ancients, the city's reputation conferred identity on its citizenry, and thus Paul's mistaken identity is corrected by his citizenship. As a citizen of Tarsus, he could not be one of the ". . . Egyptians who recently stirred up a revolt and led the four thousand assassins out into the wilderness" (Acts 21:39). Accordingly, the tribune allows Paul to speak to the mob, and again Paul begins by telling them his identity: "I am a Jew, born in Tarsus in Cilicia . . ." (Acts 22:3). Paul's struggle in Acts is an example of the important function of the city for structuring life and community in the Hellenistic world.

The New Testament writers and the early church knew well the powerful social realities of the city and appropriated this image in their writings.[14] The authors of Galatians, Hebrews, and Revelation presume that their readers understand the significance of "Jerusalem" as both a contemporaneous city and an analogy precisely because it carried a multitude of associations. According to Paul Minear, the three associations of city in these New Testament books are *genealogical, geographical,* and *liturgical.*[15] Minear ascribes the genealogical association to Galatians, where the image of the city follows Paul's allegory between free (Sarah) and slave (Hagar).[16]

---

13. David A. deSilva, *Perseverance in Gratitude: A Socio-Rhetorical Commentary on the Epistle to the Hebrews* (Grand Rapids: Eerdmans, 2000), 394.

14. It should also be noted that in the Bible the cities are both places of holiness (e.g., the City of David) and wickedness (e.g., Sodom, Gomorrah, Nineveh, and Babylon).

15. Paul S. Minear, *Images of the Church in the New Testament* (Louisville: Westminster John Knox, 2004), 96.

16. An example of genealogical association is in Galatians, where Paul harkens to Genesis to illustrate the needlessness of circumcision by lifting up the freedom provided by Christ. Specifically, in Gal. 3:6-29, Paul draws on the OT narrative of Abraham, Sarah, and

Revelation uses the geographical association for the city — where the physical manifestation of the New Jerusalem is to come.[17] An example of a liturgical association for *polis* is found in Hebrews, where the author calls readers to an approach, or way, that is created by the one who is crucified outside the gate.[18]

Hagar to answer his opponents who have apparently argued that only the circumcised are truly Abraham's heirs to the promise of salvation. In Gal. 4:21-31, Paul returns to the Genesis narrative with the allegory of Sarah and Hagar. This passage is part of a larger argument about freedom in Christ (Gal. 4:8–6:10). In typical rabbinical fashion, Paul interprets the account of Sarah and Hagar allegorically and presents it as evidence to support the importance of freedom (see Gen. 16:15; 21:1-21). In 4:24-27, Paul identifies the two women with two different covenants, presumably an "old" and a "new" covenant, and with two different Jerusalems in parallel — one present and earthly, the other above and heavenly. The one Jerusalem is the realm of bondage; the other is the realm of freedom. In Gal. 4:27, Paul quotes from Isaiah 54:1, which speaks of Jerusalem before and after the exile. With her people gone into captivity, New Jerusalem (Sarah) has more cause for rejoicing than before, since after the ordeal her prosperity will exceed that of former times. Thus Paul insists that the New Jerusalem (freedom) offers far more than the old (slavery), the gospel far more than the law. For an excellent discussion of God's promise and Christian freedom in Gal. 4, see Charlie B. Cousar, *Galatians* (Atlanta: John Knox, 1982), 102-10.

17. One example of geographical is John's apocalypse, which is sent to the churches geographically located in seven large cities, several of which comprised a where's where of Asia Minor. Beyond the geography of the present cities of Asia Minor, Revelation maps the important geographical contours of the city that is to come. The New Jerusalem is holy and will come from out of heaven from God. This city will be the home of God among us and will be the place where God wipes every tear from our eyes. Here crying, mourning, and even death will be no more, "for the first things [will] have passed away" (Rev. 21:1-4). Absent from this city's skyline, though, is the temple (Rev. 13:6). New Jerusalem does not have a temple because the city itself is filled with God and God's people, the twelve tribes of Israel and twelve apostles of the church (Rev. 21:15-17). See M. Eugene Boring, *Revelation* (Louisville: John Knox Press, 1989).

18. In Hebrews, the notion of "approach" is an important theme and is used specifically six times in reference to our approach to God. An important distinction the Preacher argues for is that, in the new reality of Jesus Christ, all are able to approach God, whereas in the former covenant the regulations for worship prevented all but the priests from approaching the holy place, and only the high priest himself could approach the holy of holies. With Christ as the forerunner, the Preacher encourages us to "approach the throne of grace with boldness, so that we may receive mercy and find grace to help in time of need" (Heb. 4:16).

Hebrews as Our Guide

Our polity discussions would benefit from a thorough examination of each of the three city associations — genealogical, geographical, and liturgical. I find the liturgical association from the book of Hebrews to be a particularly pertinent guide because it contains four important components for thinking about polity missionally.[19] The first component is the book of Hebrews' picture of Christian hope that is inextricably connected to God's revelation in Jesus Christ. "We have this hope, a sure and steadfast anchor of the soul, a hope that enters the inner shrine behind the curtain, where Jesus, a forerunner on our behalf, has entered" (Heb. 6:19-20). The author of Hebrews, or the Preacher, understands that long ago "God spoke to our ancestors in many and various ways by the prophets" (Heb. 1:1), and that God's last messenger is the Son (Heb. 1:2).[20] Christian hope is thus rooted in God's promise — in the life, death, resurrection, and coming again of Jesus, the forerunner. This promise governs our vision. The Preacher calls us to a Godward orientation by the promise's "once-for-all-ness" that is the final word — then, now, and forever.[21]

The second component is that Hebrews redirects our attention so that we see our relationship to and participation in the biblical narrative. Hebrews 11:4-40 traces the people of God, from Abel to the desert and mountain wanderers, through their sufferings of torture, mockery, imprisonment, destitution, persecution, torment, and death by stoning and the sword. This is our community, and these are our people. They surround us as "so great a cloud of witnesses" to encourage us to "run with perseverance the race that is set before us" (Heb. 12:1). The Preacher exhorts us to take a longer view in order to perceive the ways in which God's mission creates, redeems, and sustains. Even if we do not see God's mission pres-

19. These components are found, of course, throughout the Bible. In the book of Hebrews they are focused to address an audience that is anxious, apathetic, and expressing bitterness (Heb. 12:15). I believe that these three adjectives are increasing in our context and that we would significantly benefit from attentively listening again to the Preacher.

20. Following the convention that Thomas Long incorporates in his commentary, *Hebrews* (Louisville: John Knox, 1997), I will be referring to the author of Hebrews as the Preacher because the Epistle is a "word of exhortation" (Heb. 13:22) and "bears all the marks of an early Christian sermon" (p. 2).

21. Ernst Käsemann, *The Wandering People of God: An Investigation of the Letter to the Hebrews,* trans. Roy A. Harrisville and Irving L. Sandberg (Minneapolis: Augsburg, 1984), 27.

ently, the Preacher urges us to have faith, which is "the assurance of things hoped for, the conviction of things not seen" (Heb. 11:1), despite whether we are anxious, apathetic, or bitter. The sermon preached in Hebrews is a hopeful one[22] in which we live in the city and are sent outside the camp actively to "bear the abuse he endured" (Heb. 13:13).[23]

Third, the book of Hebrews takes sin seriously for both unbeliever and believer. Each of us has a real possibility of possessing an "evil, unbelieving heart that turns away from the living God" (Heb. 3:12). We are in danger of neglecting the message spoken by Jesus and attested by God (Heb. 2:3) and can even fall away after tasting "the goodness of the word of God and the powers of the age to come" (Heb. 6:5-6). Few of us live up to what the Preacher expects from mature believers (Heb. 5:12). Sin clings to us closely, it distracts us easily (Heb. 12:1). We grow weary and lose heart (Heb. 12:3). The Preacher knows full well what the human condition is and what is at stake. This realism is important for rethinking polity given humanity's propensity for idolatry and tyranny, both within and beyond the church, because it dispels the illusion that we can predict, control, and command the mission of God.

Finally, Hebrews uses the city as a liturgical metaphor to help us persevere in this in-between time — the time between Christ's first and second appearances (Heb. 9:28). The Preacher uses *polis* as a powerful ecclesial image on three different occasions toward the end of the sermon (in chapters 11, 12, and 13). Indeed, the one sentence that applies to the entire book of Hebrews, according to Ernst Käsemann, is 13:13: "For here we have no lasting city, but we are looking for the city that is to come."[24] Therefore, grappling with the city metaphor brings us to the heart of the Preacher's approach.

Some Complexities of the In-Between Time

Before focusing on the Preacher's approach, however, we need to have a short discussion of two complexities for thinking about polity and the role

22. See Hebrews 3:1-6; 6:11-19; 7:18-19; 10:19-23; 11:1-3.

23. One liturgical example of actively bearing the abuse Christ endured is the Eucharist. A central refrain in many traditions (from 1 Cor. 11:26) is that "every time you eat this bread and drink this cup, you proclaim the saving death of the risen Lord, until he comes."

24. Käsemann, *Wandering People*, 23.

of authority. Polity from a missional perspective takes seriously the two important complexities of this in-between time. The first complexity is one central to the Christian life, both corporately and individually, namely, the Holy Spirit's ongoing work in our processes of discernment and decision-making. This work is both harder and richer than we might like or expect. Culturally, we prefer the instantaneous and disposable; we prefer to send short e-mails and to leave voice messages rather than writing a letter by hand, and we would like our church work and polity to follow suit. Yet salvation history narrates journeys of forty years in the wilderness and trials of forty days in the wilderness. The work of the Holy Spirit is deeper and more substantive than any pager, fax machine, or e-mail can deliver. In the Nicene Creed we read: "I believe in the Holy Spirit, the Lord and Giver of Life, who proceedeth from the Father (and the Son), who with the Father and the Son together is worshiped and glorified, who spoke by the prophets."[25] From this creed we affirm that the Holy Spirit gives life, acts in creation, and continues the work of God the Creator and God the Redeemer. The Holy Spirit is our guide and advocate in all facets of life, including polity issues. Therefore, while we might desire a polity prescription, we are to lead a life together that is more substantive and complex because our life in the Spirit is relational.

The second complexity is the contextual character of church governance and God's mission. Church governance is created out of and for specific contexts. Salvation history is replete with examples of different forms and functions of governance, given their specific contexts: from Moses' need for judges (Exod. 18:13-27) to Israel's desire for a king (1 Sam. 8:1-18); from the casting of lots to decide who will replace Judas (Acts 1:26) to the selection of the seven to serve food to the widows (Acts 6:1-6); from the appointment of elders in every town (Titus 1:5-9) to the church fathers' selections of bishops (e.g., the bishop of Rome); from the convening of church councils (e.g., the Council of Nicaea in 325) to Pope Gregory's manual on

25. The Council of Constantinople, 381 CE. The Nicene Creed is the most ecumenical of creeds: Eastern Orthodox, Roman Catholic, and most Protestant churches affirm it. Nevertheless, in contrast to Eastern Orthodox churches, the Western churches declare that the Holy Spirit proceeds not only from the Father, but from the Father and the Son (Latin, *filioque*). To the Eastern churches, saying that the Holy Spirit proceeds from both Father and Son threatens the distinctiveness of the person of the Holy Spirit. To the Western churches, the *filioque* guards the unity of the triune God. This issue remains unresolved in the ecumenical dialogue.

the duties of the clergy (c. 600); from papal decrees (e.g., the one in 1059 establishing papal elections by cardinals only) to the writing of confessions (e.g., the Confession of Augsburg in 1530); from the development of denominations to our present-day practices of governance.[26] In all these places and times, God's mission has taken numerous forms. Paradoxically, God's mission is changeless *and* ever-changing.

> And the one who was seated on the throne said, "See, I am making all things new." Also he said, "Write this, for these words are trustworthy and true." Then he said to me, "It is done! I am the Alpha and the Omega, the beginning and the end." (Rev. 21:5-6)

It is changeless because Jesus Christ is the alpha and omega; it is also ever-changing because it meets us precisely in our particular contexts, for God makes all things new in Jesus Christ. These two complexities — discernment and context — encourage us to abandon our solution-oriented drive and to embrace the dynamic relationality of a life of faith. We are not called to a solution but to an approach.

Another reason a polity prescription is not tenable concerns *authority*.[27] Congregations, denominations, and other ecclesial groupings experience, struggle, and work with a tapestry of authorities: for example, the Bible, tradition, church governance, and the pastoral office. With the ending of functional Christendom in the United States, we are becoming aware of Christianity's volunteer aspect, where people are culturally freer to take it or leave it. Therefore, we are beginning to function similar to the Roman law's notion of *auctoritas*, which was "the capacity to produce consequential speech, quelling doubts and winning the trust of the audiences whom they engage."[28] In other words, Protestant churches in the United States are no longer granted general authority, but they increasingly hold only the authority that particular audiences (congregations, denominations, consortia) agree on.

---

26. See Craig Van Gelder's essay, chap. 1 above.

27. Authority is a broad concept that is difficult to fully develop, especially in a short space. The literature on authority is enormous: philosophy, sociology, ethics, history, political science, theology, and psychology provide conceptualizations of authority, each offering a wide array of specific definitions. In this chapter I have used the helpful analysis of Bruce Lincoln, *Authority: Construction and Corrosion* (Chicago: University of Chicago Press, 1994).

28. Bruce Lincoln, *Authority,* 4.

Our polities are provisional systems where we intend to use authority responsibly to help us navigate our way to the city of God, where the authority is the triune God. On Mount Zion, God is the builder, host, and resident; but on our way to Zion, we encounter many authorities who are prophets and pretenders, sages and fools. Some authorities are the principalities, the cosmic powers of this present darkness, or the spiritual forces of evil (Eph. 6:12). Other authorities are messengers of God, and we may even be entertaining angels without knowing it (Heb. 13:2).

The discernment and proper use of authority ought to be a fundamental concern of our provisional polities, because polity deals with what the congregation is, what its mission is, what it believes, who its members and leaders are, how decisions are made, and what proper liturgy is. In large part, polity concretizes our values and sets our expectations when we gather, and therein lies the issue. Authority is the intersection of (1) a particular effect, and (2) our capacity to create that effect, and (3) the commonly shared opinion that a person or group of people has the capacity for producing that effect.[29] When these three converge, authority is then exercised in that particular time and place.

Hebrews and a Missional Approach

In both the Old and New Testaments, Mount Zion is the desired and ultimate destination for humanity. As Isaiah testifies concerning Zion:

> In days to come the mountain of the LORD's house
> shall be established as the highest of the mountains,
> and shall be raised above the hills;
> all the nations shall stream to it.
> Many peoples shall come and say,
> "Come, let us go up to the mountain of the LORD,
> to the house of the God of Jacob;
> that he may teach us his ways
> and that we may walk in his paths."
> For out of Zion shall go forth instruction,
> and the word of the LORD from Jerusalem.

29. Lincoln, 10-11.

He shall judge between the nations,
and shall arbitrate for many peoples;
they shall beat their swords into plowshares,
and their spears into pruning hooks;
nation shall not lift up sword against nation,
neither shall they learn war any more. (Isa. 2:2-4)

As fellow sojourners, we long for the city that shall not be moved, says the Preacher, from Abraham to today. Abraham was able to endure as a foreigner; he "willingly embraced a lower status in terms of the world's estimation" because of his hope for the city of God.[30] Abraham "looked forward to the city that has foundations, whose architect and builder is God" (Heb. 11:10); Abraham's faith was steadfast because of the unshakable foundations of that city.[31] However, that city is not fully here and now: we continue to struggle, hurt, and die. Like Abraham, we "desire a better country, that is, a heavenly one" (Heb. 11:15). Until then, we create polities that are contextually driven and provisional, polities in which to live in the city and journey outside the gate.

I vividly remember the first time I heard that the church is *not* the reign of God. I remember it because that fundamentally reoriented my ecclesiology. That simple statement broke open for me an internal struggle that had been churning within me. The people I knew and loved in the church were often petty, insincere, and hurtful to one another and themselves. Moreover, from my perspective, the church's organizational structures were (are) flawed and, at times, terribly misguided. Nevertheless, it is among these gathered people that I experienced God's mission. Therefore, learning about the now-and-not-yet reality of God's reign within the church freed me to live with the provisional realities of this in-between time. Until "the Day" (Heb. 10:25), we need provisional dwelling places and temporal governances so that we might "provoke one another to love and

---

30. DeSilva, *Perseverance*, 394.

31. This is similar to Isaiah's vision of the city: "The nature of [Zion's] measurements, however, is the real key to Isaiah's meaning. His identification of the divine builder's line and plummet as justice and righteousness shows that Isaiah was not referring to the foundation of an actual physical temple, whether contemporary or future. The temple symbolized Yahweh's presence in Jerusalem, and, according to the Zion tradition, it was Yahweh's presence that provided the city's security, that constituted its real walls and towers (Ps. 48:2, 6, 8, 12; 48:4)." Roberts, "Yahweh's Foundation in Zion (Isa. 28:16)," 44.

good deeds" and not neglect to worship together (Heb. 10:24, 25). Since these dwelling places are provisional, we should expect them to change, grow, retract, and even discontinue. Our polities are not the New Jerusalem: they cannot encapsulate God's reign, but they are here to help us navigate this in-between time.

To help the hearers better understand the liturgical approach, the Preacher juxtaposes Mount Sinai with Mount Zion. In Hebrews 12:18-29, we learn that we have not come to something tangible but to God. The route we take is no longer that of the spoken law issued from a blazing fire, a tempest, and a voice whose words make the hearers beg not to hear another utterance from it (vv. 18-19). We come to Mount Zion by a more joyful way: our approach to the heavenly Jerusalem is with the firstborn and the spirits of righteousness, with the mediator of the new covenant through blood that speaks a better word than the blood of Abel (vv. 23-24).

The Preacher uses the former approach of Mount Sinai as a negative image to juxtapose a religious establishment that is severed from those who are suffering and, consequently, longing for a word of comfort. The new approach radically removes the religious barriers to the Holy of Holies through Jesus Christ, whose sacrifice tore the curtain from top to bottom. In this new approach, everyone is given access to worship God directly, to sing with the angels to the ruler of the unshakable kingdom (Heb. 12:18-29). Worshiping the one crucified outside the gate is the approach that the Preacher commends to us, and it is the association of *polis* that ought to command our attention.

The city is our place of residence: we live, work, and dwell in the city. Of course, the geographic and demographic makeup of our communities varies widely. But unless we find ourselves solitary on a desert island, we are part of a community where we (usually) benefit from one another. From law enforcement and firefighting to markets and hospitals, we live in communities where we share similar values of how to live together. In other words, the structures of the city provide for us a place to practice our livelihoods (again, this is usually the case). In the case of the church, its structures (rituals, governance, practices) — both formal and informal — help shape what the community believes and what its expectations and values are. Consequently, our cities are ever changing; they are at best provisional.

Yet, while we live in our cities, the Preacher pushes us outside the gate to the one who is crucified. Drawing on an Old Testament understanding of outside the gate (or camp), the Preacher points to our justification and sanctification outside the walls of the city: "For the bodies of those animals whose blood is brought into the sanctuary by the high priest as a sacrifice for sin are burned outside the camp. Therefore Jesus also suffered outside the city gate in order to sanctify the people by his own blood" (Heb. 13:11-12). Like Moses, we go to the tent of meeting located outside the camp: "Now Moses used to take the tent and pitch it outside the camp, far off from the camp; he called it the tent of meeting. Everyone who sought the LORD would go out to the tent of meeting, which was outside the camp" (Exod. 33:7; cf. Num. 11:16-30). When we leave our camps to go to the Holy of Holies, we venture to the place were unclean persons were cast, such as lepers, those with discharge, or someone who had touched a corpse (Num. 5:2-4); where all those requiring purification waited (Num. 12:14-15; 31:1-20); and where lawbreakers were put to death (Num. 15:32-36). This is the place that the Preacher pushes us toward, for it is the place where Jesus was crucified; consequently, it is the place we go to worship God.

One observation about the role of the city and the importance of going to the crucified outside the gate is about their *proximity:* the city and the trash heap are connected; Jerusalem and Golgotha are inextricably linked. Jesus is condemned in the city by the powers and principalities, and he is subsequently marched outside Jerusalem's gates to be crucified (Matt. 27:11-54; John 18:28–19:19). This close proximity points to the important relationship between the city and the crucified. Our journey to the crucified is within walking distance, and we readily offer our praise to God through Christ (Heb. 13:15) within hearing distance of the city. Moreover, from Golgotha we have a clear vantage point from which to view our provisional cities with all their vigor and indolence. In fact, the Preacher urges us to pass regularly through the gate to strengthen our buckling knees and make straight our paths, "so that what is lame may not be put out of joint, but rather be healed" (Heb. 12:12).

The close proximity of the gate and Golgotha also guards us against unqualified power and authority. "Unqualified power is *per se* the power of negation, destruction, and dissolution. The [one] who is obedient to the command of God self-evidently cannot and will not desire this power."[32] Our provisional cities help qualify our exercise of authority, while the city's authority is qualified by the one hung at Golgotha. With only the city, we

---

32. Karl Barth, *Church Dogmatics*, III.4, ed. G. W. Bromiley and T. F. Torrance (Edinburgh: T&T Clark, 1990), 391.

destroy ourselves with rampant idolatry; with no city in sight, we destroy ourselves with uncontrolled tyranny. In either case — gates closed for travel or no gates at all — we perish when we have lost sight of Golgotha.

Living in the city and journeying outside the gate to Golgotha can be described as a "permanent liminality," where we "inhabit the fringes and interstices of the social structure."[33] This is what Victor Turner believes Saint Francis urged the friars to do: he wanted to keep them "in a permanent liminal state, where, so the argument of this [Turner's] book would suggest, the optimal conditions inhere for the realization of communitas."[34] It is this urging to liminality that the Preacher advocates: he encourages us to live liminally by living in the city *and* journeying outside the gate.

In my initial thinking about the metaphor, I related the city to polity. In this conceptualization, I consigned polity to the city's governance and detached it from our journeys outside the gate. Of course, metaphors collapse when they are pushed to the extreme. But I wonder whether the metaphor can function more broadly than this simple representation. What if polity serves to guide both our city living and our journeys outside the gate? In this way, polity would promote the cooperation (rather than competition) required for both living in the city and our journeying outside the gate by establishing a faith community's expectations, values, and role demands in both places.

Examples of this broader view of polity are actually found in many denominational standards for worship. For example, the *Book of Order* of the Presbyterian Church (USA) is divided into three parts: the form of government, the directory for worship, and the rules for discipline. When considered metaphorically by this extended view, the first part sets the standards for city living, the second part presents norms for journeying outside the gate, and the third part provides the process for discipline (with its restorative intent) when correctives are needed. This broadened view of the metaphor, though, does not encapsulate the Christ whom we worship; rather, it points us toward the dynamic approach that the Preacher advocates.

33. Victor W. Turner, *Ritual Process* (Ithaca, NY: Cornell University Press, 1969), 145.
34. Turner, 145.

Worship as the Approach

The Preacher urges us to worship, to "continually offer a sacrifice of praise to God, that is, the fruit of lips that confess his name [and to] not neglect to do good and to share what you have, for such sacrifices are pleasing to God" (Heb. 13:15-16). Worship is the approach advocated by the Preacher; it is the central location for offering praise, confessing Christ, learning what is good, and practicing generosity. These are the sacrifices that are pleasing to God and the ones that help us navigate our way faithfully to Zion in this in-between time.

The theme of sacrifice runs throughout the Preacher's sermon (used nineteen times in the NRSV) and is central to understanding Jesus as the High Priest "after the order of Melchizedek" (Heb. 5:6). The Preacher points to the fact that "every high priest chosen from among mortals is put in charge of things pertaining to God on their behalf, to offer gifts and sacrifices for sins" (Heb. 5:1). He then goes on to show us that Jesus' main gift is that he affords everyone unrestricted access to God.[35] Jesus' self-sacrifice (Heb. 2:17) affords us face-to-face access to God (cf. Heb. 8:1-13); consequently, the Preacher urges us (the hearers) to take advantage of this access to God by drawing near in assembling ourselves together for worship. "He establishes the Christian assembly as the hub or center of their lives in this world. Motion away from this hub (i.e., defection or 'shrinking back') signals motion away from the divine center of the cosmos."[36]

Not only does the Preacher directly encourage us to praise God; he also uses a sermon to communicate this message. Throughout this chapter I have called the author of Hebrews the "Preacher" because the Epistle to the Hebrews functions more as sermon than a letter; indeed, most commentators view the book as a sermon and even believe that it is "unfortunately named" a letter.[37] In this sermon the Preacher models proclamation while encouraging us to offer to God our praise. The dramatic representation of this heavenly and unrepeatable liturgy will have a profound effect on the addressees: it will remind them of the holiness that has been conferred on them by the water of baptism and the blood of Jesus (Heb. 10:22),

35. I use the masculine for the Preacher following deSilva: "The author's use of a masculine ending for the self-referential participle [in 11:32] would rule out Prisca or another female author" (p. 25).

36. DeSilva, *Perseverance*, 333.

37. DeSilva, 6.

and of the access to God, which they have been able to enjoy in congregational worship and private prayer. They have been consecrated, perfected in terms of the conscience. Thus their impulse will be to preserve what is holy from desecration (which comes through the "willful sin" of apostasy, distrust, shrinking back).[38]

The space from which we are made holy (sanctified) is both living in the city and journeying outside the gate. And this holy space is worship. In worship we learn what is good: we are consecrated and perfected in terms of the conscience. Worship creates the space where the city's seemingly orderly walls and the messiness of Golgotha meet, and in this space we learn to do good and to share what we have (Heb. 13:16).

Jesus' selfless act on Golgotha calls and leads us directly to generosity. Our gratitude for the sacrifice of the one outside the gate is fully expressed in practicing generosity. Throughout the sermon the Preacher urges us to draw near to God's presence through the pioneer and perfecter, and then to go out and serve. From our encounter with the crucified one, we are sent to "let mutual love continue" (Heb. 13:1), "to show hospitality to strangers" (Heb. 13:2), and to "remember those who are in prison" and "those who are being tortured" (Heb. 13:3).

Generosity is a vital expression of the love of the believers for one another; in fact, generosity provides the basis for our life together. "The author of Hebrews reinforces this connection between showing gratitude to God and giving assistance to one's sisters and brothers, between honoring God and serving others."[39] When we journey to Jesus outside the gate in worship, the encounter sends us back to our cities to serve all in need. Therefore, we dare to approach the throne of grace with boldness (Heb. 4:16; 10:22), to hold fast to our confession (Heb. 4:14; 10:23), and to imitate the generosity of those who, through perseverance, have inherited the promises of God (Heb. 6:12).

Moving toward a Missional Polity

In Ernst Käsemann's *The Wandering People of God*, we read from an imprisoned biblical scholar in 1937 Nazi Germany about how the book of He-

38. DeSilva, 70.
39. DeSilva, 506.

brews "intends to show the Christian community the greatness of the promise given it and the seriousness of the temptation threatening it."[40] That is, the church has faced, is facing, and will face serious temptations until Zion's consummation by God. In Hebrews, the Preacher encourages a liturgical association for city living and journeying outside the gate as essential for our life until consummation, and I believe that this liturgical association helps us avoid two temptations we face in the denominational church: *institutional idolatry* and *antinomianism*. As we are encouraged by the Preacher, the metaphor of the city affords us a constructive approach (living in the city, journeying outside the gate) in the face of our tendencies to either entrench ourselves in our respective cities or to pack up our bags and evacuate.

Institutional Idolatry

In 1989, the year I began the ordination process in the Presbyterian Church (USA), the governing body of the congregation I grew up in presented me with a copy of the denomination's constitution. This guide, Part Two of the constitution called the *Book of Order,* was a rather thin volume at that time. Today, as candidates for ministry begin their ordination journeys in the PCUSA, their guidebook is nearly twice as thick. There are many reasons for this tremendous expansion of the *Book of Order,* one of which is a response to our increasingly litigious climate. United States law, such as compliance with the American Disability Act, necessitates some of the increases in church polity. But other increases are the result of harmful motivations, such as a false understanding of polity's role. Denominations at times believe that, if they solidify a policy or procedure by vote (or other decision-making process), then their problems, issues, or struggles will be resolved. But this is rarely the case, especially when it concerns deeply divisive issues. Yet sometimes we expect our polities to deliver such deliverance, and we act in accordance with that expectation. When we place our hope principally in a polity rather than in God, then we are in danger of practicing institutional idolatry.

This misplaced allegiance comes, in part, from a legacy of Christendom. Darrell Guder observes:

40. Käsemann, *Wandering People,* 17.

> Neither the structures nor the theology of our established Western tra-
> ditional churches is missional. They are shaped by the legacy of Chris-
> tendom. That is, they have been formed by centuries in which Western
> civilization considered itself formally and officially Christian. . . . Even
> when the legal structures of Christendom have been removed (as in
> North America), the legacy continues as a pattern of powerful tradi-
> tions, attitudes, and social structures. . . .[41]

These traditions, attitudes, and social structures are so systemic that many
members of the Western traditional churches believed that their specific
ecclesiologies are *the* right or only faithful ones.

When Christendom's legacy is coupled with modernity's scientific
management, the idol becomes all the more alluring. Fundamentally, scientific management at the beginning of the twentieth century postulated
that there is an optimal way (measured by efficiency) for operating organizations.[42] The premier twentieth-century example of this scientific management comes from the distinguished German social theorist Max Weber,
who made the term "bureaucracy" famous by advocating it as a means of
rationally managing organizations.[43] Weber's bureaucratic model prescribed detailed rules, regulations, and procedures; job specialization that
connected a job's function with the worker's skill base; selection and promotion based on objectively measured criteria (rather than subjective fa-
voritism); a strict chain of command; and the consolidation of power at
the top of the organization. The confluence of the scientific management
philosophy with Christendom's legacy of powerful traditions, attitudes,
and social structures creates a ripe environment for institutional idolatry
to flourish. Many religious leaders came to believe that the correct man-

41. Darrell L. Guder, "Missional Church: From Sending to Being Sent," in Darrell L.
Guder, ed., *Missional Church: A Vision for the Sending of the Church in North America*
(Grand Rapids: Eerdmans, 1998), 5-6.

42. Scientific management is the classical organizational theory that advocated using
research to determine the optimal way to standardize work tasks and specialization. It began
in the early 1900s with Frederick Taylor, who was primarily concerned with job design and
the manufacturing flow. See Frederick Winslow Taylor, *The Principles of Scientific Management* (New York: Norton, 1967). For a summary of earlier scientific management theorists
and relevant references, see Daniel A. Wren, *The Evolution of Management Thought,* 4th ed.
(New York: Wiley, 1993).

43. Max Weber, *The Theory of Social and Economic Management,* trans. A. M. Hender-
son and T. Parsons (New York: Free Press, 1974).

agement of the church's mission would resolve many of the problems that afflict us.

David Bartlett calls our attention to the danger of this rationalized institutional structure in his book *Ministry in the New Testament*.

> More than the facing of eschatological hope or the recurrent threat of heresy, the movement toward rationalized institutional structures in a complex world causes the church legitimately to call some people to provide leadership in teaching, administering, enabling care, and preaching. . . . The danger is that those of us who are paid for churchly jobs will so lose touch with other Christians that we will think ecclesiastical issues are the main issues and the bright new paraments a sign of redemption for the pain of the world.[44]

In response to this misplaced focus, Bartlett provides a thoughtful analysis of church structures as understood in the New Testament and believes that these ought to shake "us from our careful institutional rigidity lest we miss the moving of the Spirit and the reality of our fellow Christians."[45]

Of course, institutions are necessary to provide the structures for our life together. But when we put our central trust and primary focus in the maintenance of our polity, and/or the denomination's survival, then we will lack the time, energy, and resources to anticipate God's mission and participate in it, or we will simply neglect God's activity altogether.

Antinomianism

One helpful corrective to our temptation to place our ultimate trust in institutions is remembering and celebrating the freedom given us in Christ Jesus. "For freedom Christ has set us free. Stand firm, therefore, and do not submit again to a yoke of slavery" (Gal. 5:1). However, if we understand this freedom as a rejection of the law, then we are in danger of practicing what Martin Luther called "antinomianism." From its literal Greek etymology, antinomianism means "against" *(anti-)* "the law" *(nomos)*. Historically, Christians who dismissed obedience — because it was legalistic — were branded antinomians: they believed that they as Christians had

---

44. David Bartlett, *Ministry in the New Testament* (Minneapolis: Fortress, 1993), 188.
45. Bartlett, 188-89.

been freed from the strictures of the Mosaic law and were, through grace, guided by the inner workings of the Holy Spirit. Following this line of thought, some even believed that grace meant freedom from the law and thus meant freedom for licentious behavior. A formal decree of the Roman Catholic Church in 1312 denounced antinomianism as heretical in three distinct ways: (1) the belief that we can attain sinlessness; (2) that we can dispense with all the rituals and structures of religion; and (3) that we are no longer subject to the law of God or the church.[46] However, this decree by the Council of Vienna did not end the use of the brand or practice of antinomianism.

Others who have been labeled "antinomian" are Luther's collaborator Johann Agricola; the left-wing Anabaptists for opposing the cooperation of church and state; the Separatists in the seventeenth century; the Familists, the Ranters, and the Independents in England. In the Massachusetts colony, Anne Hutchinson challenged church authorities by arguing (rather successfully) that a believer possessing the Holy Spirit is not subsequently bound by the requirements of the law. One reason this heresy continues to appear is because of the now-and-not-yet reality of this age. We are, all at once, freed from and in need of the Decalogue; therefore, we continue to grapple with the tension between the freedom we have in Christ and the necessity of the law. Taken to the extreme, a congregation that believes it is completely free from any governance structure is moving toward an *antinomian polity.*

Of course, the term "antinomian polity" is an oxymoron. The term intends to convey the reality that, when people gather for sustained worship, service, and mutual encouragement, a polity is formed — whether it is recognized or not. There is an increased need for structure and rules, for decision-making processes and the exercise of authority, as larger numbers of people gather, regardless of their stated purpose. Moreover, we need more structure as the complexity of the effort increases. But even small and informal groups create structures and conventions for organizing themselves.

The danger of an antinomian polity is an idealism that stems from the mistaken idea that rules, regulations, or laws — especially those of organized religion — are antithetical to the freedom afforded in Christ. This

46. See Williston Walker et al., *A History of the Christian Church,* 4th ed. (New York: Charles Scribner's Sons, 1985), 362.

idealism fails to take seriously the various ways, benevolent and malevolent, in which authority is used in all human interactions. "A confidence that a benevolent will can bring together love and the facts in each decision-making moment precludes the intrusion of moral laws."[47] Such a confidence disregards the fact that we have a propensity toward idolatry and tyranny. It seems that our foretaste of God's reign gives us an anticipation of the freedom that is to come with Zion's consummation: in Zion we will have no need for church polity. But today, as we wait, we still practice the very things we hate. "For we know that the law is spiritual; but I am of the flesh, sold into slavery under sin. I do not understand my own actions. For I do not do what I want, but I do the very thing I hate" (Rom. 7:14-15). Paul knows the goodness of God and of the banquet that is to come; even so, he does the very thing he hates. He is a forgiven sinner. Likewise, when we gather, we want to live in harmony, peace, and goodness; but eventually we become fearful, we compete for seemingly scarce resources, and we are violent to one another.

These two temptations — institutional idolatry and antinomian polity — are at the heart of the challenge, the now-and-not-yet. As the author of Hebrews says, "We have no lasting city, but we are looking for the city that is to come" (Heb. 13:14). In Jesus Christ we know what Zion will be like, the city whose architect and builder is God (Heb. 11:10). Through faith (Heb. 11:1) we come to know about this city because it is revealed to our minds and sealed on our hearts through the work of the Holy Spirit.[48] But Zion has yet to be consummated.

The first temptation is institutional idolatry, where we believe and act as if there is one correct polity for all people, places, and times.[49] This temptation is not surprising, however, since we have a foretaste of what the reign of God is. We know what justice, kindness, and humility are in Jesus Christ. Like Peter, James, and John on the mountain where Jesus was transfigured, we want to concretize our foretastes of God's reign, of Zion. However, we are not called to build dwelling places on the mountaintop, but rather to travel with Christ back to the people in the valley (see Mark 9:2-13). The sec-

47. Gabriel Fackre, "Antinomianism," in Alan Richardson and John Bowden, eds., *The Westminster Dictionary of Christian Doctrine* (Philadelphia: Westminster, 1983), 27.
48. See John Calvin's definition of faith, *Institutes of the Christian Religion*, 3.2.7.
49. One Old Testament passage that exemplifies the futility of this idolatry is the Tower of Babel (Gen. 11:1-9), which tells of our inability to build for ourselves a structure that is ultimately stable and intrinsically valuable.

ond temptation that clings to us is an antinomianist polity in which, we believe, our freedom in Christ means we are free from commonly agreed-on procedures. From an organizational-theory perspective, these two temptations stand on the opposite ends of the spectrum; but from a theological perspective, they stem from the same root cause, that is, our propensity to sin. If we lose sight of Jesus, the forerunner of our faith, either because our city walls are too high and rigid or because the city is nowhere in sight, then we will fall away.

Early in his teaching career, Martin Luther lectured on the subject of *simul iustus et peccator* — that we are, at the same time, both righteous and sinners. To illustrate this point, he asked, When a physician declares that a sick man will recover,

> [c]an one say that this sick man is healthy? No; but he is at the same time both sick and healthy. He is actually sick, but he is healthy by virtue of the sure prediction of the physician whom he believes. For the physician reckons him already healthy because he is certain that he can cure him, and does not reckon him his sickness as death.[50]

With this same confidence, we should anticipate and participate in God's mission now, even as we recognize that the city of God is not yet fully revealed. Therefore, our provisional cities[51] should not be confused with the main issue of *missio Dei,* where the "mission is the result of God's initiative, rooted in God's purposes to restore and heal creation."[52] To illustrate the approach offered by the Preacher, let us consider an example from Germany in the 1930s.

Example of Living in the City, Journeying outside the Gate

One example of this missional approach comes from the struggle of the Confessing Church of Germany in the 1930s. A group of church members, pastors, and theologians who lived in the city journeyed outside the gate when some "German Christians" proclaimed that they did not believe there

---

50. Martin Luther, quoted by J. C. O'Neill, *"Simul iustus et peccator,"* in Alan Richardson and John Bowden, eds., *The Westminster Dictionary,* 538.

51. I use the plural deliberately because the cities we live in are diverse and changing.

52. Guder, *Missional Church,* 4.

was a conflict between God's claim for us in Christ and Hitler's National Socialism. As a result of their journey, they offered the Theological Declaration of Barmen[53] to help all Christians in Germany persevere amid the incredible challenges of Hitler and his government. Among this group were Hans Asmussen, Karl Barth, Karl Iraruer, Karl Koch, and Martin Niemöller.

Under the leadership of Hitler, Germany had begun operating as a totalitarian state in 1933, and this resulted in oppressive restrictions on political and human rights, on the rights of assembly, and the imposition of Hitler's handpicked judges in the entire court system. In the first six months of the National Socialist Government, the two largest church bodies in Germany were integrated (by the government) into one through the National Church for the Protestants and the concordat with the Roman Catholic Church. Most German Christians were not alarmed by these rapid and dramatic changes, precisely because they believed that the Christian faith and nationalism were in accord. In May 1934, however, 139 delegates met at the Gemarke Church in Barmen, Germany, to work toward a faithful way forward. This group included ordained ministers, fifty-three church members, and six university professors from Lutheran, Reformed, and United churches in Germany. This gathering approved a six-proposition declaration, which became known as the Barmen Declaration of 1934.

The conference's aim was to encourage the evangelical churches not to accommodate National Socialism. Using Scripture as its base, the Declaration interpreted the biblical passages for their situation, and thus they showed the false doctrines of the German Christians. Thus, for example, using John 10:1, 9 and John 14:6, the Declaration states in proposition 1:

> Jesus Christ, as he is attested for us in Holy Scripture, is the one Word of God which we have to hear and which we have to trust and obey in life and in death.
>
> We reject the false doctrine, as though the church could and would have to acknowledge as a source of its proclamation, apart from and besides this one Word of God, still other events and powers, figures and truths, as God's revelation.[54]

---

53. See Rolf Ahlers, *The Barmen Theological Declaration of 1934: The Archeology of a Confessional Text* (Lewiston, NY: Edwin Mellen Press, 1986); hereafter, Declaration.

54. "The Theological Declaration of Barmen," Proposition 1, in Ahlers, *The Barmen Declaration*, 40.

This extraordinary example offers several important modern-day acts of living out the approach that the Preacher encourages. The first issue is to highlight that the synod was not fighting about the polity process used at the integration (*gleichschaltung,* literally "synchronizing") of the churches. Germany's two churches (the National Church for the Protestants and the Roman Catholic Church) were "proper" with respect to their polities. The two cities' structures allowed for such changes to be made. Given the imperfections of our cities, we make decisions that are in line with our prescribed processes but that can be actually contrary to the gospel. In this particular instance, members of the three denominations ventured outside their respective cities to the one outside the gate.

The journey of the synod's members was outside, per se, the Lutheran, Reformed, and United churches, but it was not a departure from their respective traditions (i.e., a schism). Instead, it was an act of faith and obedience as encouraged by the Preacher. Their journey brought them together to do good and share what they had (Heb. 13:16). They deliberately did not gather to start a new church (or city) that stood against the new integrated church (German Christians); rather, they gathered to listen to the one who is outside the gate and who bears the abuse Jesus endured (Heb. 13:13). Well-known examples of those who endured abuse for standing against the Nazi tyranny include Dietrich Bonhoeffer, Martin Niemöller, and Ernst Käsemann.

One example that indicates the Barmen gathering's desire not to form a new city comes from the synod's discussion of what the Declaration means in *quality* compared to the Heidelberg Catechism or the Augsburg Confession. The synod agreed on the presupposition that "the declaration did not have the quality of a confession such as the Heidelberg Catechism and the Augsburg Confession."[55] In other words, the primary focus of this synod was to learn how to serve all believers in Germany by solely following Christ. The outcome of this focus took the form of the Declaration.

Another aspect of how the synod's journey exemplifies the Preacher's approach is the return of the synod members to their respective denominations. They were sent back by God to serve the German Christians as brothers and sisters by encouraging them not to drift away (Heb. 2:1) because of the corruption of the Nazi government. Hitler understood well that if he

---

55. Ahlers, 27.

were to succeed in his quest, the church would need to be contained by — if not aligned with — his government. Thus it is not surprising that he orchestrated *gleichschaltung* within the first six months of his newly formed government. Interestingly, it has been reported that he was surprised that the churches followed along as willingly as they did with the integration. However, those in the synod recognized that *gleichschaltung* was not intended to help the church but was instigated by the government to help Hitler consolidate his authority. Therefore, the synod rejected the Nazi party's positions. The synod members understood God's mission to the churches, which is reflected in the Declaration's threefold structure: "(1) ministering to the spiritual renewal of ministers; (2) development of the confessing congregation; and (3) the mission of the confessing congregation."[56]

The Declaration concludes with a closing passage from Matthew's Gospel and a verse from 2 Timothy. The sixth proposition, like the other five, first claims a truth and then declares the false doctrine to be rejected. This final proposition also adds an invitation for readers to join in the Declaration's "acknowledgment of these truths and in the rejection of these errors" so that all may "return to the unity of faith, love, and hope."[57] This was their prayer, then, and it continues to be a prayer for the church today.

> 6. "Lo, I am with you always, to the close of the age" (Matt. 28:20). "The word of God is not fettered" (2 Tim. 2:9).
>
> The church's commission, upon which its freedom is founded, consists in delivering the message of the free grace of God to all people in Christ's stead, and thus in the ministry of his own Word and work through sermon and sacrament.
>
> We reject the false doctrine, as though the church in human arrogance could place the Word and work of the Lord in the service of any arbitrarily chosen desires, purposes, and plans.
>
> The Confessional Synod of the German Evangelical Church declares that it sees in the acknowledgment of these truths and in the rejection of these errors the indispensable theological basis of the German Evangelical Church as a federation of confessional churches. It invites all who are able to accept its declaration to be mindful of these

---

56. Ahlers, 35.
57. "The Theological Declaration of Barmen," Proposition 6, in Ahlers, 40.

theological principles in their decisions in church politics. It entreats all whom it concerns to return to the unity of faith, love, and hope.

Verbum dei manet in aeternum[58]
[The Word of God abides forever]

Conclusion

The challenges we face as mainline denominations are extremely important. They are vital to address not because denominations need saving, but because they provide us with opportunities to participate in and anticipate God's mission. Sadly, though, we proceed as if there are really only two polity options to consider — entrenchment or evacuation. The entrenchment option typically rings of nostalgia: this is where we somehow return to the golden days (typically thought of as the 1950s) through legislated revitalization programs. The evacuation option is typically expressed in a wholesale adoption of *culturally relevant* liturgical practices that all but remove the Christ whom we worship from the liturgy. But I believe that neither of these options is trustworthy, nor will either one achieve its expressed outcomes. Rather, we need to take seriously the approach the Preacher advocates, namely, enduring this present context by approaching the throne of grace with boldness (Heb. 4:16; 10:22), holding fast to our confession (Heb. 4:14; 10:23), and imitating the generosity of those who, through perseverance, have inherited the promises of God (Heb. 6:12).

The Preacher uses the city image to help us persevere in our present struggles until Zion comes. The Preacher is concerned with the anxiety, apathy, and the root of bitterness that springs up in Christian communities (Heb. 12:15), and thus he draws our attention to worship. In fact, he implores us to "approach the throne of grace with boldness, so that we may receive mercy and find grace to help in time of need" (Heb. 4:16). Worship is the approach that the Preacher believes will keep us in the race that is set before us (Heb. 12:1); in worshiping we will be enabled to reach Mount Zion.

If we believe, however, that either evacuation or entrenchment is the way forward, then we in essence believe that Zion has already come (either inside or outside our cities). Often our anxieties are raised to new heights

58. "The Theological Declaration of Barmen," Proposition 6, in Ahlers, 42.

when the church does not act, live, and function as Zion does, and thus we look for polity solutions to fix it. But this expectation of Zion is not what the Preacher imagines; he assumes that this in-between time is an endurance race to be run. The Preacher does not advocate living in the city and journeying outside the gate because Zion is to be found in either location; rather, he believes that this is the way to be faithful until God consummates Zion. Therefore, the Preacher wants us to "consider how to provoke one another to love and good deeds, not neglecting to meet together, as is the habit of some, but encouraging one another, and all the more as [we] see the Day approaching" (Heb. 10:24-25). The Preacher shifts our focus away from our current provisional structures and "the city that has foundations, whose architect and builder is God" (Heb. 11:10).

Particular to the Preacher's approach is the liminal space that is created in worship. At Golgotha our self-centered perspectives are changed to ones of gratitude: Jesus' selfless act redirects our attention from ourselves to a call to render gratitude in equal measure (Heb. 13:13) to the other. "Gratitude should compel the hearers not to flinch from the cost of being loyal, reverent, grateful beneficiaries of Jesus' benefits . . . in short, to make this response of gratitude the most important agenda for their lives, which no other consideration will mute or diminish."[59] Indeed, we are summoned to "go to him outside the camp and bear the abuse he endured. For here we have no lasting city, but we are looking for the city that is to come" (Heb. 13:13-14). We need to make a sacrifice of praise to God, and thereby to learn what is good, and to practice generosity. It is here — in this liminal place of living in the city while journeying outside the gate — that we can "run with perseverance the race that is set before us" (Heb. 12:1) and thereby anticipate God's mission and participate in it until Zion comes.

59. DeSilva, *Perseverance*, 501.

CHAPTER 3

Reframing Denominations
from a Missional Perspective

Alan J. Roxburgh

Introduction

The conversation with a denominational executive had a familiar ring that illustrates a common concern of denominational leaders. He rehearsed the story of his faith community. This story had its roots in movements of reform in the nineteenth century that shaped the religious life of a community of European immigrants. These roots reflected their commitment to what they perceived as fidelity to the biblical imagination of God's kingdom in the United States. That imagination birthed local communities across the country, binding them together as a denomination that thrived through much of the twentieth century. But in the closing decades of the last century, pastors, members, and denominational leaders began to awaken to the strange awareness that the narratives and practices that had once shaped their identity as a social community were no longer cohering. These narratives could no longer form the emerging generations.

This is now a familiar story in our time, but it is one that also resonates with another time and place. The Southern Kingdom in the early sixth century BCE was centered around the imagination of the Temple. It thrived amidst a deep sense of having an identity as being God's people, faithfully framing God's work for their time. Then, in about 586 BCE, came the fall of Jerusalem and the destruction of the Temple, and along with that the destruction of all that symbolized Israel's identity, followed by their deportation to Babylon. This was a time of massive dislocation that would last for several generations. It would in the end reshape the identity of God's people and require the creation of new structures for framing their life as a community. During this time Israel was compelled to reassess some of its most basic assumptions about the nature of God and their identity as God's people.

The captivity fostered among many Israelites a desire to recover the former times of Jerusalem with the Temple, when their world seemed to be in place and the systems worked well. But in Jeremiah 29, the prophet brings a letter from God, a letter calling God's people to settle into Babylon with all its threats, confusion, and dislocation. It appeared that only by living within this liminal place would it be possible to discover and imagine an alternative future, one that God was shaping among them. Babylon became the location for reframing Israel's identity and sense of mission as God's people. The loss of identity and coherence that the aforementioned denominational leader expressed suggests that a missional reframing of denominational life today will only come as we live into accepting the loss of our former identity. It is only in a place of dislocation that we can reimagine the one who has called us and who is (re)forming us as God's people.

There are multiple indicators of the loss of coherence in denominations today: loss of membership, precipitous drops in financial resources, staff cuts, and conflict over issues of authority, purpose, and practice. But its most evocative expression is found in the single sentence I heard from this executive: "We're struggling with the question of identity — who are we today?" That has the familiar ring I hear over and over from denominational leaders: they are struggling with questions of identity. Like the characters who populate a Margaret Atwood or Don DeLillo novel, denominational leaders sense that their organizations are adrift, not just in practice or programs but at their very core. The question of identity is at the center of this malaise, and it will not be addressed merely with more tactics, money, or visionary programs. But the notion of identity is a complex concept to get a handle on in the context of denominational systems.

Denominational Identity

Operationally, identity is not primarily the definition that a group has been given; it is more a sense of who we are (or of who we are not). There are several interrelated dynamics that contribute to this sense of who we are. A group possesses a *content narrative*, which explains its most basic convictions about meaning and existence. For example, this might be its understanding of the gospel as found in Scripture as it is developed within its tradition of the Christian faith. Then there is a *shared history*, in which a particular group's identity is shaped by where it began, for instance, an immigrant community with stories of the homeland it left behind for a multitude of reasons. Stories such as these are formed over time against the backdrop of historical events. These contribute to a *common memory*, which tells the group who they are on the basis of what they have gone through. There is also the *structural side*, in which the group creates organizational forms and roles to give concrete, material form to its sense of identity as a particular community.

Church bodies combine these elements by developing a self-understanding around a set of institutions that give them — both internally and externally — a unique identity that is different from all other groups. Identity is the elaboration of this "knowing who we are" as a group. It is both time-bound and geography-shaped. The denominational executive I quoted at the beginning of this chapter expressed his disorientation in terms of the language of identity. He meant that the certainties that once provided them with the sense of who they were on the map of the wider culture no longer held them together. The ways his group had located the gospel and the meaning of God's activities in the world were now being called into question.

Many of the specific histories of faith communities no longer serve as a glue to hold the people of those communities together. The structures and roles created to concretize their life as a community in the wider culture no longer function in that way. The way these core elements were put together to form the overall sense of ourselves is now failing. This is why that denominational executive couldn't find ways to explain what is happening. The challenge for the reframing of denominational systems is more complex; it requires more than a technical change. It requires an adaptive change, and Jeremiah 29 provides a rich, if disorienting, imagination for how we might engage such complexities.[1]

Denominations remain a critical part of the North American reli-

---

1. See Ronald A. Heifetz and Marty Linsky, *Leadership on the Line: Staying Alive Through the Dangers of Leading* (Boston: Harvard Business School Press, 2002), 15.

gious scene. But they increasingly find themselves lost in the outworking of massive shifts within the systems of legitimation that came to shape the culture through most of the twentieth century. Today they are like a house built on a high cliff overlooking an ocean that has had a position of prominence. They view the sweep of the horizon from their balcony, but they are unaware that the waves of change have undercut the ground on which they were built. These houses now tilt on precipitous ledges because most of their support has been eroded. Regarding denominations, we must note that they were built on forms of legitimation shaped mostly in the early decades of the last century, and it is these very forms of legitimation that have now been undercut. The result is that the systems of identity that gave denominational cultures the experience of "this is who we are" no longer hold people's imaginations as they did at one time. Thus denominations face questions of identity and legitimacy.

The Importance of Denominations
for a Missionally Shaped Church

Denominations are an abiding element of the North American religious landscape. They are not going away; however, they are in a process of major transformation. We see multiple kinds of experiments today that seek to shift the work and patterns of denominational life, but no clear answer about identity, ethos, and roles has emerged as yet. Denominations represent the particular ways in which churches adapted themselves to the North American context. They are a primary form of association and social formation for thousands of local churches. Whether they call themselves "movements," such as the Disciples and Churches of Christ, or claim the label "mainline denominations," such as Presbyterians (USA), Episcopalians, Lutherans, and Methodists, or refer to themselves as conservative denominations, such as the Christian Reformed Church and Presbyterian Church in America, they have been the means of social and theological organization for the majority of local churches, and as such they are systems of integration and development. They hold powerful clues as organizational and social systems regarding how broad change occurs within a culture.

Multiple congregations have demonstrated their ability to go it alone in terms of evangelism, growth, and mission. But it is also true that only within an extended system of congregations that have created some kind of tradition is it possible to form environments that result in a systemic change of DNA. If our concern is for a multigenerational innovation of missional life among local congregations, then the locus of energy and engagement is not primarily in an individual, local church. Rather, it is in the systems of relationships that sustain and nourish the common narrative life among a set of congregations. This is what denominations provide and will continue to provide. Furthermore, sustained social transformation does not occur at the periphery. Elements of unrest, critique, and experimentation toward change often originate from this location, but long-term cultural change usually comes from within existing social systems as they adapt to and internalize innovation from the edge. This means that denominational systems have a critical role to play in the formation of missionally shaped congregations.

Findings about Denominations from Previous Research (2002 to 2005)

In September 2002, the Gospel and Our Culture Network, supported by a major grant from the Lilly Endowment, undertook a three-year study of denominational systems that was called Resources for Discerning Missional Innovation in Congregations and their Denominational Systems.[2] The purpose of this study was to identify points of intervention and innovation within denominational systems in order to develop a model for action by members of a church system that would support the development of a missional church. Several key findings were common to the five systems studied:

- With low understanding of requirements for transformation, there is a need for significant adaptive change.
- Missional language is helpful for theologically framing the conversation.
- Technical and tactical changes dominate the primary imagination.
- "Missional" and "mission" language are often confused, with "missional" language regularly co-opted to mean any activity.
- Denominational leaders are already overextended and have a ten-

2. See http://www.gocn.org/main.cfm (accessed Dec. 15, 2007).

dency to add new missional and adaptive processes to already busy
schedules.

- A pervasive functional rationalism obstructs the reframing of denominational life.
- Performative habits prevail over theological imagination.

This study suggests that the formation of missionally shaped denominational systems requires a fundamental reframing of imagination. But in
order to address this issue, we need to address the question of legitimacy.

How do denominational systems cultivate missionally shaped
ecclesiologies and polities in this strange new context? Without a clear
understanding of the legitimacy issues that are now at stake, denominations will find it difficult to reframe themselves from a missional perspective. In David Forney's essay (chap. 2 above), the metaphor of the city,
polis, suggests social organizations that have clearly defined identities:
they know who they are and how they operate. The invitation to go "outside the gate" is to experience a liminality that recognizes that the assumed narratives can no longer map the geography of experience. In
Craig Van Gelder's essay (chap. 1 above), the denominational DNA of "organizational self-understanding around a purposive intent" is no longer
sufficient to cultivate identity. In both cases the indications are that significant cultural change is now being required of denominations. In my
essay I will argue that such an adaptive change must be understood from
the perspective of a legitimacy crisis similar to what the 586 BCE captives
must have experienced.

Legitimating Frameworks

What do I mean by *legitimacy?* We make sense of our particular moment
in time by placing interpretive frameworks around periods and events; we
create meaning from a storehouse of narratives, metaphors, and myths.[3]
The narrative frameworks that shape a culture at a particular time exist be-

---

3. This is an important element of Alasdair MacIntyre's argument in *After Virtue*
(Notre Dame, IN: University of Notre Dame Press, 1981), which Lesslie Newbigin represents
in *Proper Confidence: Faith, Doubt, and Certainty in Christian Discipleship* (Grand Rapids:
Eerdmans, 1995).

cause people find in them the resources to shape their lives in relationship to the surrounding context.[4] The legitimacy of a narrative involves its ability to provide an explanatory framework that addresses a group's basic understanding of life and that provides them with a means of successfully ordering that life. Organizations such as governments or denominations lose legitimacy when they cease to hold sufficient loyalty, commitment, or authority from people. This loss has been happening across denominational systems: they are confronting a legitimacy crisis and will be unable to become missionally shaped systems unless they understand the dynamics of this crisis.

Jürgen Habermas's book *Legitimation Crisis* analyzes what happens to social systems that are confronted with a crisis of legitimacy.[5] People form social systems within which they express the meaning of their cultural assumptions: these systems include political institutions, schools, churches, families, professional associations, and so forth. Over time they form traditions and habits that become the taken-for-granted environment. Members of these systems indwell the environment so that it becomes their tacit backdrop of life. Thus a social group is composed of a symbolically integrated meaning system for its members, relative to their internal and external relationships. People formed in a narrative community develop a specific kind of organizational culture that embodies their implicit values and commitments. These organizational cultures, in turn, produce leaders, experts, and managers whose role it is to *perform* those

---

4. *Culture* is a multivalent idea; see Kathryn Tanner, *Theories of Culture* (Minneapolis: Fortress, 1997); Charles Taylor, *Modern Social Imaginaries* (Durham, NC: Duke University Press, 2004); Graham Ward, *Cultural Transformation and Religious Practice* (Cambridge, UK: Cambridge University Press, 2005). For an interesting engagement with issues of culture and our perceptions of narrative, see also Justo Gonzalez, *The Changing Shape of Church History* (St. Louis: Chalice Press, 2002), and Kathryn Tanner, ed., *The Spirit in the Cities: Searching for the Soul in the Urban Landscape* (Minneapolis: Fortress Press, 2004). This essay cannot give space to the variety of interpretations and definitions of culture available. Because the focus of this work is the organizational culture of denominational systems, it will use the particular description developed by Edgar Schein in his book *Organizational Culture and Leadership* (San Francisco: Jossey-Bass, 1992), 12, where he offers this definition: "A pattern of shared basic assumptions that the group learned as it solved its problems of external adaptation and internal integration, that has worked well enough to be considered valid and, therefore, to be taught to new members as the correct way to perceive, think, and feel in relation to those problems."

5. Jürgen Habermas, *Legitimation Crisis* (Boston: Beacon Press, 1973).

activities that are deemed important and appropriate for the maintenance of the organizational environment. This is achieved as they provide:

- overarching narratives, told and retold, that locate people and interpret their lives;
- direction, purpose, and future for the social system;
- environments for shaping the values, beliefs, and practices of the community;
- mechanisms for living out the purpose of the social system;
- passed-on habits and roles that sustain social integration;
- boundary recognition that maintains identity; and
- rituals of belonging.

The combination of these elements in complex interactions over time gives an organization identity and provides a system of meaning for those inside. Legitimacy is strong when sufficient numbers of people place their tacit trust, confidence, and belief in the identity, meaning, and practices of the organization. A nation, corporation, family, congregation, or denomination is not an abstraction: it exists because it has provided successful adaptation within a larger cultural environment through its organizational structures and codes of meaning. Such groups function within an overarching cultural matrix. An example of such an organizational structure is that of the corporate organization formed in the United States in the early part of the twentieth century, which was an adaptive response to the rapid industrialization, technological innovation, and economic transformation of the second half of the nineteenth century. This legitimation, however, has its historical roots in the rise of modernity.

The Rise of Modernity: A New Form of Legitimation

Modernity in the West has been bookended by two events: (a) the first Thirty-Years War, which resulted in the Peace of Westphalia in 1648, and (b) the second Thirty-Years War (World Wars I and II), from 1914 to 1945.[6] Westphalia legitimated the formation of a coherent, interconnected politi-

---

6. Stephen Toulmin, *Cosmopolis: The Hidden Agenda of Modernity* (Chicago: University of Chicago Press, 1992), 156ff.

cal, religious, and intellectual imagination in the West. But by the end of the twentieth century, these same Western societies were again being transformed with respect to other forms of political, religious, and intellectual life.[7] The following summarizes the forms of legitimacy that emerged after Westphalia.

Political Formation

Westphalia established the sovereign state that was ruled by prince or king as the legitimate form of government. These states, by treaty, agreed on defined borders; in addition, to guarantee a stable, manageable political situation, they agreed not to interfere in each other's internal life. Thus began the first phase of the development of the modern state. It did not remain static, but it transmuted from kingly states, to state-nations, and finally to nation-states, each having its own form of legitimacy and social organization.[8]

Religious Formation

Westphalia established the principle of *cuius regio, eius religio:* the state had one form of the church and persecuted any other expressions of the church within its borders. This was not an early form of denominationalism. Post-Westphalian Europe had little patience for religious groups that challenged its new clarity, certainty, and ordered world.

Intellectual Formation

The political and religious elements of Westphalia were based on intellectual transformations represented in Cartesian rationality, Baconian empiricism, Kantian reason, and Newtonian physics. Enlightenment thinkers

7. The following is a summary of the complex forces reshaping modernity. A variety of thinkers provide varying explanations for the massive dislocations and transformations in modernity. This section is an angle of interpretation, a schematic attempt at locating some of the reasons denominations are in a deep crisis of legitimacy.

8. See Philip Bobbitt, *The Shield of Achilles: War, Peace, and the Course of History* (New York: Knopf, 2002), 69-205.

sought a new axial point of knowing from which to build a secure house of truth, giving humanity the power to manage and control its life and determine its future. Reason, from within the self, could discover Truth. This new perspective was welcomed as a profound breakthrough in human imagination for guaranteeing predictability, certainty, and control.

Post-Westphalian Modernity

This enlightened perspective created a dichotomy between the universal and the local/temporal, which was seen as an unreliable source of knowledge. This resulted in a diminishing trust in the local and temporal, because they were based on erroneous and irrational opinions that were destructive to social harmony; they were also contrary to the clear universal laws of nature revealed by reason. The local and particular had led to the terrible strife and awful uncertainty of the previous period, of which the clearest example was religious convictions and the strife that resulted. During the terrible wars of the sixteenth century, conflicting religious groups claimed to have the truth, which led them to kill those who would not align with that truth. Reason ended dependence on the local and removed experience from the equation.

The idea of a *rational government* constituted a new conception and practice: society was manmade, and thus the state could actually make society through the appropriate application of scientific and technical rationality. For post-Westphalian Europe, creating a rational society was not a utopian dream but a viable possibility. The *rational individual* became the ideal, a novel and revolutionary understanding of the self. It was a concept of the self whose actions are shaped entirely by his or her own self-knowledge. Modernity wagered that it could make, form, and control life through the internal rational life of individuals without reference to a transcendent authority. This new self was malleable: it was possible to redirect thought and behavior through knowledge and expert technique. Newly emerging experts became high priests of modern culture.

These political, social, religious, and intellectual movements did not have to fight for a place after the first third of the seventeenth century. The old world lay exhausted by 1648, with its political, religious, and intellectual frameworks being called into mortal question. New forms of political, religious, and intellectual life were creating an alternative form of social life and looking for a different form of social organization to provide legitimation. Together these three elements — the political, religious, and intellectual — formed a new social legitimation, whose distinct forms of organizational life are summarized as follows:

- *bounded, set systems* of rationality that tolerated no challenges;
- *top-down systems* that were ruled by a firm hierarchy;
- *a performative world of manageability, control, and linearity* with an endless search for certainty.[9]

People created organizational systems to act as their forms of cultural legitimation. Through the eighteenth and nineteenth centuries a series of forces developed around this legitimating myth to form, by the late nineteenth century, the apex of modernity's organizational life — the corporation.

The Corporation: Legitimating Organizational Culture of the Twentieth Century

The corporation became the normative form of organizational culture in the early part of the twentieth century. It was the result of technological innovations that provided the ability to mass-produce goods and services to meet the rising expectations created by the state. It proved to be a key structure for meeting these needs and guaranteeing the welfare of citizens. The twentieth-century corporation was a work of immense creative genius that combined (a) the centralization of work through the innovation of the production line; (b) the development of extensive and efficient transportation systems; (c) organizational practices that created hierarchies of experts to manage the mass production of brands; and (d) the creation of branch plants and sales outlets to sell the goods and services produced at the central plant.

The state's role in supporting corporations was: (a) to regulate relationships with other states to protect its corporations and extend their markets; (b) to manage the supply of money; (c) to ensure the development of management elites through education; and (d) to ameliorate the

9. See the argument of Adam B. Seligman in *Modernity's Wager: Authority, the Self, and Transcendence* (Princeton, NJ: Princeton University Press, 2000).

effects of economic cycles by creating safety nets that guaranteed people's security (e.g., health-care insurance, social-assistance programs, and unemployment benefits). These corporate organizations were staffed by elites with expertise that would produce the goods and services expected by people. These elites were well paid and stood at the apex of the organizational hierarchy as they passed down the benefits of their oversight. The elites knew best: they understood how to produce expanding prosperity.

Twentieth-century corporate organizations had to interrelate three key dimensions: environment, organizational culture, and leadership functions. This was to have a profound influence on the development of the denomination as a corporate organization.

The Environment

The *environment* in which these organizations emerged was very stable. North America's oceanic isolation initially protected it from the eruptions of the old world. Immigrants escaping the insecurities of the homelands came seeking the American dream. They came to work, formed communities, and built new lives based on the dream of freedom, prosperity, and a better future. In order to realize these opportunities, they became loyal to their new state and its institutions. People's primary loyalty was not to themselves but to the promised future and the organizations that would deliver it. It was an environment of consensuality. Following Word War II, as the United States shifted its massive economic engines from wartime to peacetime production, the legitimating ethos became one of rebuilding and recommitting. From the late 1940s into the 1960s, people still committed themselves to the classic virtues of self-sacrifice, which included the subordination of their own needs for the sake of the greater good and the security of the whole.

Organizational Culture

This was built around hierarchies of responsibility and accountability that moved from the top down, or from the center to the periphery. Elaborate bureaucratic structures managed complex systems and chains of command to develop efficiencies of production that minimized costs and guaranteed quality. These organizations were run by experts and managers. Organizations functioned as linear, top-down systems that worked phenomenally well at delivering the goods and services people expected. A core conviction was that, through an overall plan that aligned resources, workers, and managers toward a defined goal, the goods and services would be produced that would meet the needs of the population. This approach worked incredibly well for a very long time.

Leadership Functions

The organizations mentioned above were primarily *performative* in character. What was rewarded was the capacity to manage or carry out predefined functions with excellence. Managers were people who had learned the job well and could carry out its requirements in a performative manner. Their function, like all workers in the system, was to operationalize their role in the plan. Emphasis was on the manageable, predictable control of continuous outcomes. Managers who performed well moved up the hierarchy.[10]

The Twentieth-Century Corporate Denomination

Organizational systems address specific legitimacy needs in a culture by establishing the mechanisms, roles, and structures through which groups structure their values and goals.[11] Through much of the twentieth century, Protestant America moved in a direction that would structure its life toward the cultural environment of a corporate denomination. Its mechanisms and structures had a high correlation with the forms of organizational life people experienced in business, commerce, education, and

10. A brief glance at the many books on leadership and organizational culture that have been written over the past twenty-five years will reveal that a primary theme in this literature is how to function in an environment that no longer provides the kind of stability, predictability, or continuity that supports the kinds of organizational cultures and leadership summarized here.

11. This section summarizes a variety of the arguments in Coalter, Mulder, and Weeks, *The Organizational Revolution: Presbyterians and American Denominationalism* (Louisville: Westminster/John Knox, 1992).

politics. The corporate denomination was a highly successful adaptation to the challenges of organizing religious life in late-industrial society. It entered mainstream Protestant life quickly and effectively by providing a ready means of identity and legitimation for members, many of whom worked and managed within these systems on a daily basis.

Denominations were shaped around this legitimating narrative during most of the twentieth century. The corporate denomination focused the energy of its members in congregations toward the overall goals of corporate identity and the reproduction of brand loyalty across the nation through the effective, centralized production of the goods and services — the denominational program. These represented the loyal name brand of the denomination on, for example, publishing houses, expert services, and training schools.

In *The Organizational Revolution*, Coalter, Mulder, and Weeks argue that, by the late nineteenth century, bureaucracies were displacing more informal, loose familial forms of organizational life as a wider search for order emerged throughout the culture.[12] The new corporate bureaucracies brought order. But with them came new values that shaped the culture of denominations and congregations in terms of a priority on efficiency and a rationalizing functionality within increasingly centralized organizations. Various committees working away at particular needs or issues increasingly gave way to the complex, hierarchical enterprise in which the *manager* emerged as the important figure: one who coordinated and provided

---

12. Coalter, Mulder, and Weeks, *Organizational Revolution*, 37-54. This search for order has remained a hallmark of the modern experiment as it continually seeks to provide ordered, predictable forms with which to control and define life. The metaphor of the machine dominates this search, as does that of predictive and controlling laws used to design, manage, and control production. The genius of Fordism is that it raises the search for control to the level of a highly complex, managed system capable of providing the promised goods and services to the state's citizenry. In the modern industrial corporation, Fordism thus provides a powerful legitimating method to the nation-state. This theme of control as applied to the corporate organizations is also seen in Demming's application of time and study techniques as a means of optimizing the corporate organizational culture's productivity from the center out and the top down. The metaphors of control, management, and predictability are at the heart of the modern, corporate culture that developed during the 20th century. They enabled it to efficiently provide the goods and services that became the hallmark of society. See Toulmin's discussion about the drive toward rational intelligibility within modernity in the chapter entitled "Economics, Or The Physics That Never Was" in his *Return to Reason* (Cambridge, MA: Harvard, 2001), 47-66.

oversight of centralized planning and the production and distribution of resources and programs.

North American religious institutions shaped their organizational lives around these methods and structures. The language of the corporation became the culture of the denomination. The corporation, with its centralized departments staffed by experts and managers, became the legitimating form of the denomination. As Louis Weeks points out, a direction was set at the beginning of the twentieth century that has persisted until the present. "One might even argue that the incorporation of American Presbyterians has become more thorough and determinative throughout the twentieth century and that subsequent decisions on structures and personnel have proven the point time and again." He continues: "Managers predominated in all the major streams of what has become the Presbyterian Church (USA), and governing bodies in the years since 1983 have relied heavily on a corporate model in selecting 'executives' and designing 'flow charts.'"[13] This corporate denomination was a highly successful organizational culture for much of the twentieth century, and it enjoyed a high social legitimacy among its members. But now this very form of denomination has become a barrier to innovating missional life.[14]

The post–World War II era was a period that experienced the early stages of the pluralization of the culture and the denomination's theological base. The reorganization of structures and hierarchies became the normal means used in an attempt to address these tensions. But the legitimat-

---

13. Coalter, Mulder, and Weeks, *Organizational Revolution*, 48.

14. In the introduction to *The Organizational Revolution*, the authors argue that a series of organizational revolutions have been moved through denominations such as the PCUSA at critical points in the twentieth century. I do not disagree with the premise that these denominations have been involved in *organizational* change; rather, I argue that most of these organizational changes have not been revolutionary. They were variations on the basic paradigm of the centralized, corporate organization and, in fact, never question the assumptions of this paradigm. It was not until sometime during the late 1970s and early '80s that the paradigm of the twentieth-century corporation moved through a revolutionary transition in North American business corporations. But this revolution did not affect the functionality of denominational systems as centralized, branch-plant corporate structures. The moves in the PCUSA to decentralize decision-making to presbyteries did not really address the underlying corporate model that lay deeply embedded in the organizational culture of the system; it shifted the locus of that imagination but did not challenge or transform the imagination itself. In this sense it was a tactical move from within a paradigm rather than the transformation of the paradigm itself.

ing forms of the culture itself were shifting from one of loyalty to an organization to that of loyalty to the self and the *individuation of needs*. In the place of a central focus on a shared denominational mission, there emerged the challenge of a plurality of foci: the shift to suburbanization (1950s forward), the challenge of the inner city (1960s forward), racial and ethnic reconciliation (1970s forward), and so forth. Today there is a continuing fragmentation of denominational life because of competing issues and demands. Simply put, strategies of reorganization will not address these challenges because they do not address changed legitimacy.

Denominational Legitimacy

Denominations in the early part of the twentieth century consciously took on the forms of the emerging corporate organization by developing social environments that reflected those of the broader culture. Behind the structure and function of the denomination as a corporation was a whole set of assumptions about the purpose, goals, and values of life — in other words, a legitimating framework. The flourishing of denominational systems through the twentieth century resulted from their capacity to adapt themselves to the legitimating forms of the wider culture.

In such a situation, an organization's leaders, managers, experts, and ordinary people were able to make sense of their lives because identity and meaning were effectively congruent with, or opposed to, the environment. A denomination's attitudes and beliefs, the assumed knowledge base, the appropriate skills, and the habits that could be passed on had high levels of congruence with the larger environment in which it was embedded. The organizational polities, practices, and agencies in this setting to which people belong had a high level of legitimacy because they structurally created stability and function as a powerful source of social integration and patterning. The organizational denomination, therefore, met the human need for stability, continuity, consistency, and meaning.

Legitimation Crisis for Denominations

But the forms of legitimacy that shaped the twentieth century have been disappearing in a process of rapid and discontinuous change. This goes a long way toward explaining the crisis the denominations are now encountering. But by the mid-1980s, the state and its attendant organizational culture entered rapid, discontinuous change; denominational systems, to a great extent, failed to understand or address these transformations. Their only recourse was to continue to try to function out of the corporate structures formed earlier in the twentieth century.

A crisis of legitimacy occurs when discontinuous change occurs in the overall environment and is not matched by corresponding responses within the organization. The identity of the organization is then called into question by both its constituency and the wider culture, and if this continues for any length of time, leaders are confronted with questions regarding assumed competencies and roles. The confusing element is that roles, practices, and assumptions that served these leaders so well for so long no longer function well. This is because the attitudes and beliefs, the knowledge base, the skills, and habits of the system were shaped interactively within a specific cultural environment, but they fail to adapt when the environment encounters major discontinuity. The system thus loses its capacity to provide an explanatory framework or an appropriate response to a context of rapid, discontinuous change: in this way, both the organizational forms and the tradition on which they have been formed are called into question by growing numbers of members. Its interpretive systems "lose their social integrative power," which "serves as an indicator of the collapse of the social system."[15]

The argument I am making in this essay is about the kinds of issues now confronting denominations, which form a legitimation crisis of significant proportions. The more a denomination responds with programmatic strategies for organizational change, the faster the loss of legitimacy. The diagram below shows three levels at which a system functions: culture, organizational structure, and leadership roles.

Discontinuous change happens at the level of culture. Instead of recognizing this, denominations tend to address the crisis at levels of organizational structure and role identity, both of which are drawn from the cultural level. Changing them will not address the legitimation crisis. The core issue facing a group is at the level of culture, or identity. Structure and leadership roles are expressions of how that culture is actually worked out in an environment. Currently, a significant portion of the energy in denominations is directed toward:

15. Habermas, *Legitimation Crisis*, 4.

- structural reorganization, policy and procedure manuals;
- programs to address growth, evangelism, or new church development;
- leadership development and role redefinition;
- personnel reductions because of falling budgets.

Such responses simply do not address the issues of legitimacy, identity, and transformation in an environment of discontinuous change.[16]

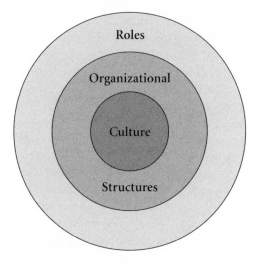

Culture is about the basic underlying assumptions that involve the traditions, narratives, values, and beliefs of a group.

Organizational structures and systems are the ways the espoused values, goals, and philosophies are concretized into the life of the group. This involves elements such as hierarchies, managers, experts, bureaucracies, programs, strategies, and planning.

Roles are the leadership functions that the organization creates to run the organizational system.

16. Heifetz and Linsky, *Leadership on the Line*, 15.

Transformations at the Beginning of the Third Millennium

The rise of denominations as corporate organizations in the early twentieth century, as I have suggested above, was located within a larger framework of cultural transformation. Their rapid loss of legitimacy in the last quarter of the twentieth century is part of a larger dynamic of transformation in the West. Denominations no longer have legitimacy for most people because the denominations have based their legitimacy on forms of social and organizational life that have become increasingly obsolete. What follows is an overview of what brought this about. It is based, in part, on the writings of contemporary thinkers who are wrestling with questions of social systems within: (a) environments of discontinuous change, and (b) the epistemological frameworks out of which social systems in modernity have operated.[17]

Manual Castells argues that, by the end of the second millennium of the Christian era, a series of changes and events of historical significance transformed the social landscape of the world. While global in effect, these changes emerged primarily in the West, their impact on social systems and organizational cultures has been profound, and congregations and denominations are not exempt from their influences. Some of these changes are:

1. *technological revolution* involving a rapid diffusion of information technologies;
2. *transformed economies* in an interdependent globalized economy;
3. *capitalism and globalization* undergoing profound restructuring;
4. the *role of the state* as a primary player in the transformation of capitalism;
5. *flexible management* that is flattening hierarchies;
6. *decentralization* of production and manufacturing around the globe;

---

17. Sources for this section come from Manual Castells, *The Rise of the Network Society*, 2nd ed. (London: Wiley-Blackwell, 2000); Philip Bobbitt, *The Shield of Achilles: War, Peace, and the Course of History* (New York: Knopf, 2002); Stephen Toulmin, *Cosmopolis: The Hidden Agenda of Modernity* (Chicago: University of Chicago Press, 1992), and *The Return to Reason* (Cambridge, MA: Harvard University Press, 2003); Ulrich Beck, Anthony Giddens, and Scott Lash, *Reflexive Modernization: Politics, Tradition, and Aesthetics in the Modern Social Order* (Stanford, CA: Stanford University Press, 1995).

7. *networking* as the primary form of information exchange and communication;

8. *changing forms of individualization.*[18]

Those who write from the perspective of a classical critical theory argue that modernity has its own contradictions built into it, and they undermine the basis of its functionalities. The forces of capitalism thus disembed people from primary relationships within social systems to create radically individual selves.[19] The result is that people feel cast upon themselves: they sense that the social contract between government and people is essentially torn up; and thus they feel increasingly in the grip of unnamed and unseen forces that determine their lives, over which they have little control.

These forces converged in the last decades of the twentieth century, shifting our society into massive disruption and destabilization in which social organizations were transformed.[20] Anthony Giddens puts it in the following terms: "We live, as everyone knows, at a time of endings. . . . We are in a period of evident transition — and the 'we' here refers not only to the West but to the world as a whole."[21] These transitions fundamentally affect denominations, not just in terms of their organizational structures, role, functions and programs, but also in terms of their identity as social systems.

The Shifting Forms of Legitimation

What is the nature of the legitimating narratives for denominational systems at the beginning of the twenty-first century? In stark contrast to the post-Wesphalian worldview, we face a dramatically changed alternative.

18. This point is made over and over by writers such as Castells, Beck, and Giddens.

19. See Zygmunt Bauman, *Liquid Modernity* (Cambridge, UK: Polity, 2000), and Jürgen Habermas, *Legitimation Crisis,* for this argument regarding an individualization that disembeds people from their life worlds.

20. Castells's view is not a minority position. There is consensus across a broad spectrum of intellectuals to build on the notion of change described by Castells. John Lukacs reflects this perspective: "For a long time I have been convinced that we in the West are living near the end of an entire age, the age that began five hundred years ago" (*At the End of an Age* [New Haven: Yale University Press, 2002], 3).

21. Beck, Giddens, and Lash, *Reflexive Modernization,* 57.

Political Formation

The nature and purpose of the state has changed. The *nation-state* has increasingly become the *market state*. With the emergence of new, globalized forms of political and economic life, we are in a period of great flux, and we have little clarity about what might emerge in this new form of the state.[22]

Religious Formation

Any notion of cultural domain that so many denominational systems had enjoyed is now over. These organizational systems had been built on the assumptions of domain and brand loyalty; but this has ended and is now creating anxiety and confusion within these systems. Denominations are in a liminal situation: they are seeking to understand how their organizational systems function in a context "outside the gate" (see chap. 2 above).

Intellectual Formation

The certitude of an abstract, universal rationality has been largely demolished.[23] Reason is again being understood from within the local, temporal, and sensual realities of everyday life. The narratives of local, particular peoples become the rich texture for the formation of understanding. A universal and abstract rationality, with its metaphors, symbols, and myths of experts functioning in distantiated hierarchies and bureaucracies, has ended. In its place is the reemergence of the local and the particular, where networks and gatherings of people with local knowledge are the elements of social learning. A result of these enormous and rapid shifts is a morphing in organizational culture, and we need to explore these changes a bit further in order to grasp their implications for forming missional denominations.

---

22. See Beck in *Reflexive Modernization*, 1-52; see also John Ralston Saul, "The Collapse of Globalism and the Re-birth of Nationalism," *Harper's*, March 2004, 33-43.
23. See Toulmin, *Return to Reason*.

The Implications for Denominational Systems

What do such massive changes mean for denominational systems? This section can merely provide a series of pointers, all of which require much more elaboration. Legitimating frameworks are, over time, sedimented into specific grammars of life that are concretized into organizational and leadership functions. This is a normal process of cultural formation. Specific vocabularies, formulas, roles, habits, and ideas become the taken-for-granted world of a group, and in this way an organizational system embodies a tradition. But these traditions are not fixed and stable. They continually undergo "new orientations towards future states as reflective negotiations with the past occur within the present."[24] Both *sedimenting* and *reorientation* are given processes for any group within a culture: they can neither be chosen nor rejected; they are simply the basis of social formation. But the question is how a group with a tradition engages these two elements when discontinuous change is the environmental reality? This requires deliberation and choice, but there is nothing necessarily determinative about the way a group responds.

In the language of David Forney's chapter above, a denomination can choose to engage this question by remaining "in the city" or choosing to go "outside the gate." This choice has implications for the kind of *grammar of interpretation* a denomination will use to make sense of its experience. The grammar of Jerusalem, for example, was radically different from that of Babylonian captivity. Different grammars forge different imaginations about the nature of God's activities in the world and about the vocation of the people of God.

Denominations have critical choices to make at this time: to either remain inside the city gates or to risk the liminal experience that lies outside the walls. Each contains its respective grammar of interpretation, its different strategies and different structures. Each expresses a different imagination about what God is about in the world and the vocation of the church. In Van Gelder's language, the choices involve a grammar of an "organizational self-understanding around a purposive intent" in contrast to a "missional grammar of a community created by the Spirit called and sent to participate in God's mission in the world." An important question to explore is how a denomination will renegotiate its tradition

24. Ward, *Cultural Transformation*, 80.

amid numerous other influences to evaluate its practices and actions in the light of these choices.

Pointer One: Liminality

When the legitimating frameworks that provided stability and predictability are disrupted, cultures are propelled into periods of crisis. Accepted forms of legitimacy disappear, while new ones are not yet fully on the horizon.[25] This is the liminal context that I have been describing: an ordered, performative world within the city no longer provides a system of meaning for increasing members, and there is no clarity about what might take its place. Here the narratives of Jeremiah 29 assist us: the loss of Jerusalem in Jeremiah is interpreted as something far more significant than an act of geopolitical displacement requiring adjustment, the restatement of purposive intent, or the restructuring of organizational processes.

It is an act of the sovereign Lord that invites the people of God to remember their founding narratives so that they might join again with God in the shaping of a new creation. To be taken outside the gate into a place of immense de-legitimation by God is to be invited to reframe our self-understanding as a people. This deeply challenges the legitimating frameworks of Jerusalem, where there was a world of well-structured and well-organized functionality.

The emerging structures, practices, and forms that reframe legitimation for a people can actually remove the possibility of remembering the original mystery and calling for which many of these structures and institutions were initially formed. Jeremiah gets at this issue by framing one of his primary judgments against the leaders as loss of memory: they have forgotten the Lord in the midst of all their religious structures and institutions. In such a situation, a form of social life can emerge in which it no longer seems necessary to live in the tension and openness of how the Spirit is at work disrupting the community out toward God's future.

This is part of David Bosch's argument in the first section of *Trans-*

---

25. This is part of the intent of both Bauman *(Liquid Modernity)* and Ulrich Beck, *Democracy Without Enemies* (Cambridge, UK: Polity, 1998). It is another way of expressing Marx's oft-quoted and -borrowed phrase: "All that is solid melts into air." The point is that the solid forms of social interaction that functioned over a period of time suddenly lose their legitimacy.

forming Mission.[26] For Bosch, Luke-Acts is a narrative engagement addressing the question of why things had not turned out as expected for the young churches. The response of the Luke writer, argues Bosch, is that the Spirit continually disrupts the settled assumptions and structures of God's people when these assumptions and structures come to define the extent and shape of God's kingdom. These disruptions are the work of the triune God who, through the Spirit, is inviting the church into a new direction by moving it "outside the gate." Such disruptions are always experienced as surprising, and as an unwanted breaking up of the legitimating frameworks of an assumed world.[27]

Pointer Two: Internal Culture

An organizational culture has legitimacy to the extent that those within it trust its veracity and tacitly authorize its functionality.[28] A denomination has legitimacy because people trust its systems of explanation and meaning. Vaclav Havel, for example, argues that the communist regime in Czechoslovakia had hegemony for so long because the citizens knew of no other system, and because the organizational culture of communism was not external to people but existed inside them. They were born into it, it was in their head, and thus it was a powerful — albeit negative — legitimating system. Communism fell because people stopped believing its narrative; they came to see it as a massive lie.[29] It then lost its legitimacy and could not survive.

A similar loss of legitimacy can be detected in denominations. In the PCUSA, for example, increasing amounts of funds from congregations to the denomination are directed to specific agencies, projects, and groups, and there is an increasing withdrawal of funding for the general budget.

26. David Bosch, *Transforming Mission* (Maryknoll, NY: Orbis, 1991).

27. See Bosch, *Transforming Mission,* chap. 3.

28. See Adam Seligman, *The Problem of Trust* (Princeton, NJ: Princeton University Press, 1997).

29. Havel's explanation of why this happened is a fascinating study in the possibility of transforming an organizational culture. The change came from below and from the edges of citizens, first the poets and prophets. Here we observe both critical rationality and prophetic imagination at work in a secular state that was undergirded by a Christianity that had to operate as a subversive movement.

This represents a tacit statement that the organizational culture has lost legitimacy. Those leading denominations often view such challenges in organizational terms and fail to grasp the deeper legitimating issues pressing on them. Internally, these legitimating structures become so sedimented that they actually close a community off from the disruptive imagination of the Spirit. As it was with Jerusalem, so it is with the legitimating narratives of denominations. Only by choosing to go outside the gate can we find the imagination, energy, and partnership to discern the disruptive purposes of God.

Pointer Three: External Environment

An organizational culture has legitimacy to the extent that other organizations and cultural systems perceive it to be an important element within a larger community of systems and organizations. At the beginning of the Industrial Revolution, the system of open land and commons, a core element of agricultural/feudal societies, ceased to be a legitimate form of social organization because these impeded the rapid diffusion of new technological developments in manufacturing. During the second period of the Industrial Revolution, the development of the steam engine, the railways, and electricity shifted the locus of economic life from the extended family to the factory. This shift in populations resulted in new social groups and organizations, which effectively ended the legitimacy of a whole way of life, since it was no longer seen as having a significant or useful purpose in the emerging industrial world.

The legitimacy of a denomination's organizational culture, both externally and internally, occurs within a *developmental* period. This refers to a period when the social environment is relatively stable, so that changes are made within existing, accepted, and well-understood frameworks. When such a period lasts for several generations, it comes to be assumed as the primary vehicle for delivering a predictable way of life. The imaginative possibility of a future beyond the current frameworks is pushed to the fringes, cordoned off from the possibility of affecting the system's homeostasis.

Assumed legitimacies are deeply challenged when they are confronted by *discontinuous* change. They are deeply challenged because the habits, outlooks, skills, and competencies that functioned in the developmental period cease to work in the new context. As leaders of denominations, we were formed in an organizational culture that was deeply sedimented in our imaginations, its grammars having become the accepted way of interpreting the world. Few of us were prepared for the revolutionary transitions that we are now encountering.

Conclusion: Moving Forward

Most leaders in denominational and congregational positions were trained for a stable, predictable corporate world of loyal customers/consumers. They were mentored in skills for performing well in that world. What are some ways forward?

First, the question of emerging frames of legitimacy at this time is open; it cannot be answered. I believe that the more we try to set new definitions in place, the more we close down the space for listening and discernment. We are in the midst of liminal change and will be for some time to come. We can name the forms of legitimacy that we have known in the recent past, but we now live in this in-between time, a time when it is simply impossible to name the nature of our context. All the current language of "post" and "emergence" are symbols and metaphors for this current situation rather than descriptions of what is forming and shaping the context. We use these words as if they were actually defining a reality that has taken the place of the world we once knew. But these words are only placeholders in a time of imprecision and ambiguity. Rather than being beguiled by this language and giving it more legitimacy than it deserves, we should hold it lightly and assume that it is a tentative language for a liminal time.

We need to learn and practice the skills of leading in a time of liminality and high ambiguity. Certainly, this will involve the skill of being *with others* — sitting among people and together discovering ways of discerning what the Spirit is saying to our churches. This is an act of discernment, or as an actor friend of mine once described it, it is about listening to the narratives beneath the narratives. And these are acts formed in worship and liturgy. But the primary skill in this place is that of learning to listen again to the ways the Spirit might be at work in and among the people of the congregations. Simply asking questions of pastors and church leaders, such as "What should we do?" will usually result in a cry for programs that once seemed to work but are currently on the shelves. In liminality, forms of engagement must change.

Second, there is no strategy or process that will quickly change this situation or provide a new and clear definition of a legitimating framework for the foreseeable future. This is what the communities of captives in Babylon needed to learn first and foremost: "How do we sing the Lord's song in a strange land?" God's invitation through Jeremiah was to learn the skills and attitudes of living into a liminal place without the need to fix it or solve it. In such acts, it becomes possible to listen to the grammar of the Spirit. Forms of faithful life emerge from this time and space, and it is in such a location that the identity question can be reengaged and can begin to be addressed through the recovery of memory concerning the founding narratives and the shaping of a worshiping people outside the gate.

These narratives will be about the nature of the *missio Dei* and the kingdom of God in this time and place. Therefore, one element of engagement with our liminal context is how we reenter our specific traditions and stories as God's people in order to reinterpret from within them the ways the Spirit is calling congregations to bring God's redemptive purposes in Jesus Christ to their worlds. This is one of the encouraging signs emerging from our situation; yet one can detect weariness with yet another set of tactics or programs promising new hope. There is recognition of the need to reenter the narratives of our tradition in order to discover the resources for developing a new imagination.

Third, the frameworks of liminality within our environment provide the most generative way of understanding and ordering ourselves as leaders. The basic meaning and forms of liminality are now well known. I am still surprised that, while the language is used in multiple contexts of leadership and change in the church, its principles are still not being integrated into the ways church systems function. This may point to a lack of clarity about what is required in a liminal context; in addition, it points to the power of our default leadership positions and the forces of inertia and stasis built into the policies, procedures, and structures of current systems.

A denominational system that understands the need for a changed DNA will require processes for engaging liminality and assistance in designing ways to practice the habits of a liminal community. My experience with numbers of judicatories suggests that this is a learning process that most will find difficult to accomplish by themselves. There will need to be some level of external assistance, coaching, and accountability to identify and cultivate the changes in imagination, habits, and skills among staffs and boards.

Fourth, a significant shift in the current locus of legitimation is occurring with the reemergence of the local. This is a critical element in grasping the ways in which denominations might engage liminality. One of the most helpful theorists in this area is Michel de Certeau, a Jesuit anthropologist who was asked by the French government to do research on the reasons behind the student and worker protests in Paris in the late 1960s.[30] What is relevant in his research is the way he turns away from explanations of culture change that are located in managers and producers of organizational, political, and religious life in the latter part of the twentieth century. Instead, his interpretation revolves around what happens among ordinary people who live with the sense that they are shaped by forces beyond their control and simply have to "make do."

Certeau's category of "making do" is an explanation of the everyday cultural response of ordinary people in local contexts as decentered participants in a time of dislocation and fragmentation. The assumption is that all the processes of de-legitimation are already present and are being experienced at the level of the local. But among ordinary people there is little sense of being able to effect any change; it is simply out of their control. Furthermore, there is usually little capacity to give language to their experience of loss and powerlessness.

It is this process of *making do in a liminal situation* that actually generates the tactics from which emerge new forms of cultural legitimacy. These shifts in legitimacy often come from unexpected and surprising locations. Here we sense that the intuition and research of de Certeau is pointing us to something the church has long experienced but too easily forgets: it is the disruptive, surprising movement of the Spirit among those who are deemed incapable or without imagination that God's future emerges. How else do we account for the church or, for that matter, Israel?

With our own self-understanding as Christians, as with de Certeau's research, God's future emerges from the disruptive lives of people who experience themselves "outside the gate." There we are all invited to name and attend to the anxieties and ways of making do that shape our lives. There we reenter the biblical stories from a new location, to hear the dis-

---

30. Michel de Certeau, *The Practice of Everyday Life* (Berkeley: University of California Press, 1988). This is also an element of Toulmin's argument in *Return to Reason* (2002).

ruptive directions of the Spirit of the God whose kingdom is shaped by the *missio Dei*. All of this will require the discernment and practice of new attitudes about leadership and new skills of formation and practice. It is in such environments that a missional imagination can emerge.

Fifth, the most generative means for developing these activities is found in that part of liminality that anthropologists call *communitas*.[31] The term describes a second phase of liminality. It is about what can happen to the relationships among a divergent group that is undergoing radical, discontinuous change. *Communitas* is about the creation of an open space, where hierarchies level out and the notion of expert/professional no longer makes sense. In this context members of a group learn from one another in powerfully innovative ways. *Communitas* is somewhat like the old practice of the "commons," where spaces (land, ideas, values, relationships) are open to ordinary people.[32] In the early industrial age in Europe, the commons were enclosed: privatized, traded in the market, turned into a commodity for the use of some group. Today there is a rediscovery of the idea of the commons as a way of dialoguing about issues that are important for all of us — a place of both immense opportunity and risk.

The potential of *communitas* is for imagination and innovation to emerge from the local congregations that can affect the identity and shape of a denomination. *Communitas* is the power of people to enter a new kind of commons where they can journey together as God's pilgrim people to somewhere very different. The creation of these spaces, these new commons, needs to become a primary role for denominational leaders. Finally, in all of this disruptive change of the Spirit, denominational staffs serve in the midst of huge challenges in terms of time demands and performative expectations. A process of negotiation within denominations about the allocation of staff time for this kind of work is essential. The energy, time, and commitment demanded in these proposals cannot be met by adding this adaptive work to already existing workloads.

---

31. See Alan Roxburgh, *The Sky Is Falling — Leaders Lost in Transition: A Proposal for Leadership Communities to Take New Risks for the Reign of God* (Eagle, ID: ACI Publishing, 2006).

32. Note examples of this today in such phenomena as Wikipedia and open-source software; indeed, the internet creates a form of *communitas* that invites innovation and creativity from a bottom-up process. The early seasons of the television series *Lost* suggest a little of what this might mean.

CHAPTER 4

The Challenge of Developing Missional Denominational Agencies and the Implications for Leadership

Marion Wyvetta Bullock

Introduction

> *[M]ainline denominations will get better if they do things that fulfill their mission purposes within the framework of their long and well established and clearly articulated identities.*

(Bacher and Inskeep, 2005)

God's missional activity in Jesus Christ is central to Christianity. God sent Jesus into the world with the purpose of reconciling the world to God; through Christ, God called the church to participate in God's mission; empowered by the Holy Spirit, the church engages God's mission. The church's relationship with God makes the church missionary: this is at the heart of an understanding of a missional ecclesiology.

> The church is missionary by nature. Just as God is a missionary God, so the church is to be a missionary church. This is the fundamental meaning behind the four attributes of the church confessed to in the Apostles' Creed: one, holy, catholic, and apostolic.[1]

The church's identity is given to it by a triune, sending God. This sending God is also relational and is reconciling the world to God through

---

1. Richard Bliese, "The Mission Matrix: Mapping Out the Complexities of a Missional Ecclesiology," *Word and World* 26, no. 3 (Summer 2006): 239.

Jesus Christ. The church's identity is always understood through its relationship with God. This gift of identity includes being sent into the world to participate in the *missio Dei*. In "Called Out of Our Comfort Zone," I argue this way: "Congregations are the creation of the Triune God and find their identity and purpose in their relationship with God."[2] The identity of God's called-out people *(ecclesia)* is found in the life, death, and resurrection of Jesus Christ. It is in Christ that the church has its being. The church's *being-ness* is inextricably tied to its *being sent* into the world. The Holy Spirit empowers the church for living out its "sent-ness." This being sent into the world is the church's calling and vocation, its assignment and its purpose. The church's purpose for being on this planet unites it with the hosts of heaven. And the *misso Dei* into which the church is called to participate requires some organization: it requires structures and forms that engage with the world. Therefore, how the church is organized is directly linked to identity and purpose.[3]

In *Chasing Down a Rumor,* Bacher and Inskeep declare that the relationship between identity and mission is the key to unlocking the future for mainline denominations.[4] They argue that, in order for mainline denominations to become better at denominational ministry, they will need to focus on mission purposes within clearly articulated identities. Therefore, a denomination will need to discern deeply and reflect on what it means to be the church — its ecclesiology — while attending to how it forms and engages structures and agencies for mission — its polity. I agree with the Bacher and Inskeep proposition, and in this essay I build on their understanding to make the case that in an ecclesial ecology, a church's

2. Wyvetta Bullock, "Called Out of Our Comfort Zone," in Richard H. Bliese and Craig Van Gelder, eds., *The Evangelizing Church: A Lutheran Contribution* (Minneapolis: Augsburg Fortress, 2005), 71.

3. National denominational church organizations have traditionally existed to serve with and on behalf of congregations. An example is the Evangelical Lutheran Church in America, which has an understanding of its denomination as the whole church in three primary expressions: congregations, synods, and churchwide organization (ELCA Constitution, chap. 1.01.01; 8.11). For the ELCA, its churchwide expression is "church." From an anthropological perspective, the churchwide organization plays a critical role in the common ecclesiastical culture called the ELCA. There is a need for the ELCA to further explore this understanding. In the midst of changing contexts, there is a lack of clarity of the role(s) for each expression.

4. Robert Bacher and Kenneth Inskeep, *Chasing Down a Rumor: The Death of Mainline Denominations* (Minneapolis: Augsburg, 2005), 18.

identity and purpose serve as the center and source of its energy. Therefore, a church's authority and agency function in networks and fields of
ministry for participating in God's mission in the world.

An Ecclesial Ecology[5]

An ecclesial ecology includes a church's congregations, institutions, agencies, judicatories, and related partnerships. For the church universal, this
ecology includes all expressions of the church; for denominations, their
ecology locates them in their particular environment. A denomination's
particularity is shaped by how it responds to what God has done and is doing in its environment in the world.

"Ecclesial" comes from the Greek word *ekklesia*, which means "to be
called out of" and implies being called out for a definite purpose.[6] Therefore, we can translate church as the *called-out purposive assembly.* Denominations, then, exist as organizations with a purposive intent, which flows
from the Spirit that created and empowers it to participate in God's mission in the world.

Ecology is the study of living organisms and the interrelationships
between organisms and their environment. In an ecclesial ecology a
church's sense of identity and purpose is foundational to the health and
development of the system. When the church's identity is unclear, its exercise of authority is weakened.[7] When the church's purpose is unclear,
its agency is reduced. Once there is an understanding of the church's
purpose as participating in God's mission, there is a core ecclesiology
from which to form particular denominational identities that can be renewed by returning to what God is doing for the sake of the world. The
God-given identity of a missional church is a constant for all Christian
denominations. However, the way a denomination understands and lives

5. The idea of an ecclesial ecology is developed from comments about the Evangelical
Lutheran Church in America by Craig Dykstra, senior vice president of the religion division
of the Lilly Endowment, Inc.

6. Bullock, "Called Out of Our Comfort Zone," 71.

7. Alan Roxburgh connects the issue of identity with legitimacy in his essay
"Reframing Denominations from a Missional Perspective," chap. 3 above. I agree with his
construct of linking these two. Here I am using "authority" in much the same way as he uses
"legitimacy."

out its purpose (vocation/assignment) in different times and contexts does change.

When I speak of the church in this essay, I am referring to the body of Christ in its visible form in the world today and in relationship to the church throughout the ages. When I speak of denominations, I am referring to how the church has organized itself into various theological expressions and particular political characteristics. Of course, the church has organized and structured itself since its beginnings — to fulfill its purpose. The first signs of this organization appear in the book of Acts, where the disciples cast lots and assigned tasks to different members. As the *missio Dei* unfolded and became clearer to the church, there was more organization. One significant result was the church's sending of Barnabas and Paul, along with others, to the gentiles: here an implicit ecclesiology and explicit polity were being born. The early leaders labored to be open to the purpose and calling of God as the church faced both internal and external challenges to its delivery of the gospel. The internal challenges usually took the form of questions about doctrine in relationship to authority: they began with who could receive the gift of the Holy Spirit (Acts 10), and they included in whose name one was baptized (1 Cor. 1).

This early ecclesial ecology was infused with disputes and disagreements. Paul's letters to the churches record examples of the growing pains. However, while there were internal disagreements, for the most part the (visible) church remained *one* church through the time of Constantine and up to the eleventh century. During that earlier period the church tried to create unity by labeling those with differing expressions as heretical and calling for their excommunication, for example, the Nestorians (431). In the fifteenth and sixteenth centuries, reformers such as Tyndale, Zwingli, Calvin, and Luther forged a movement that opened up Scripture and the structures of the church. A new ecclesial ecology began to emerge, the results of which appeared in North America as church denominations. These new denominations have European roots, but they are an expression of the American ethos that shaped them.

In this essay I explore the challenges for denominations in the United States to sustain and develop missional agencies for participating in God's mission. I begin with a brief review of the history of the development of denominations in the United States; I then point to shifts in the environment for mission in the United States during the latter half of the twentieth century; and I use the Evangelical Lutheran Church in America as a case study to consider responses to the resulting opportunities. I conclude this chapter with suggestions for the kind of leadership necessary for denominational agencies in light of an understanding of the missional church and its participation in God's mission in the world.

Historical Development of Denominational Agencies in the United States

Protestant denominations in the United States came into being primarily during the eighteenth and early nineteenth centuries. The early developmental stage of national denominations was characterized by a dissolution of cooperative benevolent societies.

> The modern American denomination emerged in a series of steps between 1790 and the breaking up of the great cooperative benevolent societies sponsored by Congregationalists and Presbyterians. The first step was the founding of the executive and promotional missionary societies. Conversion of the Indians lay heavily on the consciences of the founders of Plymouth. . . . Scots and Moravians also organized societies for mission work in the eighteenth century but it was late in that century before the action society for missions and church extension developed on a general scale in the United States among Baptists, Congregationalists and Presbyterians.[8]

These societies had emerged from the Pietist movement to renew the church.

> Since the church was restrained and often negative in its attitude towards the organization of mission work, there were few other options available. Activities needed to be organized in one way or another within the church, but bypassing the church leadership. In this connection the Pietists offered a model for the organization of mission work, that of voluntary activities and voluntary missionary associations.[9]

8. Elwyn A. Smith, "The Forming of a Modern American Denomination," in Russell E. Richey, ed., *Denominationalism* (Nashville: Abingdon Press, 1977), 111.

9. Risto A. Ahonen, *Mission in the New Millennium* (Helsinki: The Finnish Evangelical Lutheran Mission, 2006), 130.

The separation of church and state, religious freedom, and the emergence of voluntary societies in the United States provided the building blocks for the propagation of religious denominations. Groups such as the American Home Mission Society (1826), the American Board of Commissioners for Foreign Mission (1810), the American Bible Society (1816), the American Education Society (1816), the American Sunday School Union (1824), and the American Temperance Society (1826) are examples of what composed the early interdenominational voluntary societies.[10]

During the post–Civil War era, a diversity of cooperative and organized efforts continued. One example of an interdenominational effort was the revitalization of the Sunday schools with a new kind of youth organization in 1881. Within six years of its founding, this effort grew to more than 7,000 local societies, with a half-million members, boasted international conventions, and inspired emulation in almost every nonparticipating denomination.[11]

Relief associations for freed slaves were part of interdenominational efforts, such as the Relief of the National Freedman in 1863 and the American Freedman's Union Commission in 1866 (Ahlstrom, 694). It is important to note that churches remained divided along racial lines during this period; but black denominations were formed out of the conflict of race relations. The black Baptists were the first to organize in the South, and then the African Methodist churches in the North. During the latter half of the nineteenth century, the black church of the South, which had been invisible, became visible. Organization of the Baptist churches took the shape of state conventions and associations. "Colored" churches were formed out of the white denominations, for example, the Colored Methodist Episcopal in 1870 (Ahlstrom, 707-08). These denominations chose institutionalized structures much like those of their white counterparts; they also established schools, publications, social agencies, and foreign mission agencies.

The involvement of early white denominations with blacks had much the same mission motivation as did their involvement with the American Indian: they viewed these communities primarily as heathens to

---

10. Mark Chaves, "Denominations as Dual Structures," in N. J. Demerath III, Peter Dobkin Hall, Terry Schmitt, and Rhys H. Williams, eds., *Sacred Companies: Organizational Aspects of Religion and Religious Aspects of Organizations* (New York: Oxford University Press, 1998), 179.

11. Sydney E. Ahlstrom, *A Religious History of the American People* (New Haven: Yale University Press 1972), 858.

be saved. The evangelical impulse was paternalistic at best and culturally oppressive at worse.

> Until the Civil War, Christian missions had been almost the only American institutions to deal constructively with the [Indian] situation, although even they, like the Spanish and French, had always unabashedly sought to convert the Indian to Christianity and, in varying degree, to reshape his way of life according to Western norms. (Ahlstrom, 861)

Along with the home mission efforts among newly freed blacks and American Indians, denominations in the United States came to be formed out of the new immigrant ethnic groups. The denominationalism of immigrant or ethnic groups, Timothy Smith suggests, has the same basic features as that of the largely Anglo-Saxon evangelical mainstream:

> [T]he primacy of the congregation, denominational structures that were basically voluntary organizations, polity or ideology as a cohesive agent, division and organizational rivalry occasioned by ideological conflict, competition which in appealing to ethnicity (particularity) increased ethnicity (particularism) and sectarianism. . . .[12]

The mass immigration to the United States from Europe resulted in a strong ethnic clustering of denominational mission activities. Many of the activities began in response to the needs of the newly arrived immigrants. As denominations continued to develop in the nineteenth and twentieth centuries, they added the role of *agency* to their *administrative* (regulating authority) role, which mainly consisted of standards for religious professionals and teaching the faith. The agency function in some denominations included "gathering of independent, voluntary, mission societies. In others, those mission activities were always a more integrated part of the denomination's work."[13]

Mark Chaves proposes the answer to the question of why denominations created their own agency structures and moved away from cooperative voluntary societies by citing Primer's (1979) analysis shown below:

---

12. Timothy L. Smith, "Religious Denominations as Ethnic Communities: A Regional Case Study," in Russell E. Richey, ed., *Denominations* (Nashville: Abingdon, 1977), 183.

13. Bacher and Inskeep, *Chasing Down a Rumor*, 44-45.

1. the 1837 depression and the resulting resource shortage;
2. ever-present tension along denominational lines exacerbated by the resource strain;
3. direct access of denominational authorities to resources of congregations to fund their own initiatives.[14]

Denominational Identity and Purpose
Related to Authority and Agency

In the decade review of evangelism for the years 1991-2001 conducted by the Evangelical Lutheran Church in America, the report concluded that congregations that had a sense of mission and purpose and were open to innovation and change were the most effective in evangelism over the long term.

(ELCA Report "Toward a Vision
for Evangelism," 2001, 13)

How does a denomination keep a balance between a clear sense of identity rooted in a self-understanding of being created by God to participate in God's mission and an openness to the changing environments for mission? Equally important, how does the denomination's sense of identity and purpose relate to its authority and agency?

It has been documented in the Evangelical Lutheran Church in America that congregations that have a clear sense of identity and purpose have been among the most vital in the denomination. The groundedness of those congregations in who and whose they are supplies energy for their ministry and vision for the future. This moves beyond a functional understanding of purpose and calls for a rethinking of the core ecclesiology in the congregation. It requires asking questions about God's purpose and intent, and it reframes a response that is focused on God's activity in the world. Like congregations, denominations and their agencies need clarity of purpose to stay healthy and vital.

Purpose and identity are closely linked. Identity is the character, personality, uniqueness, and distinctiveness of a person or an organization. In organizational theory, an organization's identity is often referred to as its

---

14. Chaves, "Denominations as Dual Structures," 181.

"brand." Brand identity is about differentiation: branding combines who you are with whom you are directed toward — compared to whatever else. The church has been "branded" by being marked with the cross of Christ forever. This branding sets the church apart from other organized bodies and identifies it with a missionary God. So the church's core identity is God-given. That is *who* the church is — because of *whose* the church is. Denominations are known for their theological and political distinctiveness (e.g., their confessional and sacramental understandings; whether or not they ordain women; whether or not they have bishops), and their service in the world (e.g., Catholic Charities, Lutheran Services of America, etc.). In the reality of its operations and the delivery of its ministry, a denomination may express multiple facets of its identity. The chart below illustrates the categories of these facets.

Facets of Identity	Brief description
Actual	Who we *really* are (what are our values?)
Communicated	Who we *say* we are (image)
Conceived/perceived	Who people *think* we are
Ideal	Who we *should* be
Desired	Who we *want* to be

The expressed identity of a denomination is a combination of its perception of the mission to which God has called it, the vision it holds for getting there, and the values it demonstrates on the way. A denomination's worthy goal would be to have all five of the operational facets of identity functioning inextricably in its ecosystem as it participates in God's mission.

Today's organizational literature points companies to building performance relative to purpose. In *Good to Great and the Social Sectors,* Jim Collins says this: "In the social sectors, the critical question is not 'How much money do we make per dollar of invested capital?' but 'How effectively do we deliver on our mission [purpose], and make a distinctive impact, relative to our resources?'"[15]

In *Leadership and the New Science,* Margaret Wheatley talks about process structures that sustain their identity over time and yet are not locked into one physical form. She points to the paradox in living systems

15. Jim Collins, *Good to Great and the Social Sectors* (New York: Harper Business, 2005), 5.

as they adapt to change in their environment: "Each organism maintains a clear sense of its individual identity *within* a larger network of relationships that helps shape its identity. . . . If a living system can maintain its identity, it can self-organize to a higher level of complexity, a new form of itself that can deal better with the present."[16] For example, a stream of water adapts and changes configuration as it flows downhill and around rocks. The water creates new structures as it changes, but its purpose of answering to the pull of gravity or the call of the ocean remains consistent.

As living organisms in an ecclesial ecology, denominations that have a clear sense of their identity and yet are open and flexible to a changing environment are better positioned to deal with the opportunities and challenges of ministry. Denominations with a clear sense of identity are better able to respond in developing missional agencies that will remain consistent with their core identity and purpose. The clear sense of identity provides stability in the midst of uncertainty. Out of the denomination's sense of call to participate in God's mission flows the freedom it needs to form and reform in order to respond. A denomination's understanding of how it responds to the living Christ in its ecclesial ecology will determine its ecclesial narrative. Over time, this narrative shapes the expression of the denomination's identity.

A Hartford Institute for Religion Research study entitled "The Role of Judicatories in Interpreting Denominational Identity" has revealed clusters of vitality of denominational identity in local churches. It notes that signs of denominational loyalty and support include:

- self-identification with the denomination;
- adherence to core theological precepts and denominational policies; and
- resource support for national and regional mission priorities.[17]

16. Margaret J. Wheatley, *Leadership and the New Science: Discovering Order in a Chaotic World,* 2nd ed. (San Francisco: Berrett-Koehler Publishers, 1999), 17, 20-21.

17. Adair T. Lummis, *The Role of Judicatories in Interpreting Denominational Identity* (Hartford, CT: Hartford Institute for Religious Research, Hartford Seminary, 1999). The study included judicatory leaders from seven denominations: the Assemblies of God, the Association of Vineyard Churches, the Episcopal Church, the Lutheran Church–Missouri Synod, the Reformed Church in America, the United Church of Christ, and the United Methodist Church.

The study found the strongest sense of shared identity in the Assemblies of God and the Association of Vineyard Churches; it found mixed or moderate identity in the Episcopal Church and the Lutheran Church–Missouri Synod; and it found the weakest sense of shared identity in the Reformed Church in America, the United Church of Christ, and the United Methodist Church (p. 5). Overall, the respondents in this study perceived denominational identity to be a current problem for denominations. There was a strong correlation between the respondents' perceptions of denominational effectiveness in maintaining congregational commitment and keeping unity of purpose within the denomination.

> Unity of purpose may be viewed by many regional leaders as not only a potential outcome of denominational identity but almost part of its definition. (p. 3)

Another Hartford Institute study, which included congregations, denominational offices, and judicatories across eight denominations, reported, not surprisingly, that "a congregation's sense of identification with a particular denominational tradition is closely tied to how many of its members grew up in the tradition." It is also not surprising that the strongest denominational identities were found more in rural areas than in urban areas; more in the South and Midwest than the rest of the country; and more among Catholics and very sectarian groups (e.g., Jehovah's Witnesses) than in any sector of mainline Protestantism. The study further noted that "those for whom denomination is a salient identity seemed to be working rather consciously to make it so."[18] They do not expect their denominations to survive and thrive without attention to their identity. This study also revealed that particular connection with denominational identity seemed to flourish among ministries like global missions and relief agencies.

> There is an essential role for *organizational intent and identity*. Without a clear sense of who they are, and what they are trying to accomplish, organizations get tossed and turned by shifts in their environment. No person or organization can be an effective co-creator with its environment without clarity about who it is intending to become.[19]

18. "New Life for Denominationalism," Christian Century Foundation, 2000, available at http://hirr.harsem.edu/org/faith_denominations_articles.html.
19. Wheatley, *Leadership and the New Science*, 39.

As denominations continue to ground themselves in their God-given core identity of being created by God to participate in God's mission for the sake of the world — missional church — they are better able to renew and reform their particular theological, confessional, and political identities. Their particularity is revealed as they engage their purpose at any given time in any given context. They express this engagement throughout their ecclesial ecology, and they make it visible in their local and national structures.

Authority and Agency

In order to examine more closely the national expression of denominational structures and how they develop missional agencies, let us consider the function of authority and agency within denominational structures. In "Denominations as Dual Structures," Mark Chaves argues that national denominational structures have been misunderstood in a fundamental way. Rather than treating them as unitary organizations, he makes a case for parallel structures of authority and agency.[20] His primary objective is to reveal "a better analytical tool for the analysis of organizational developments within American religion, including developments of major importance such as internal conflict and schism" (p. 176). My inclusion of his point in this essay is for its insight into the relationship of authority and agency.

Chaves defines religious authority as "a social structure that attempts to enforce its order and reach its ends by controlling the access of individuals to some desired good, where the legitimation of that control includes some supernatural component, however weak" (p. 177). Therefore, "religious authority structures are distinguished by the fact that their claims are legitimated at least by a *language* of the supernatural" (p. 178). Chaves's definition is a sociological construct. At the most basic level, I understand religious authority in denominational structures to be an *expression* of the right granted to the church by Christ to proclaim, teach, baptize, witness, and serve. I accept Chaves's sociological construct for religious authority structures, but I would also emphasize here the *theological* nature of a denomination's authority. This is, of course, Chaves's point about supernatu-

20. Chaves, "Denominations as Dual Structures," 175.

ral legitimacy: the church's ultimate authority is given to it by Christ and is carried out under Christ's rule and authority.[21] The Evangelical Lutheran Church in America, which I will use as a case study later in this essay, shares this authority in three expressions: congregations, synods, and churchwide. The ELCA has found this mutuality preferable to a hierarchical system of authority.

As I noted above, denominational agencies are generally functionally organized to carry out the purposes of a church body on a national and/or regional scale. They vary in size and scope, and they may or may not have related formal boards or associations; but most have visible authority structures, such as assemblies, conventions, bishops, officers, pastors, and elected leaders for the oversight of the denomination's ministries. Authority is most often inherent in positions of governance and may be restricted to geographical area, as with bishops of dioceses or synods. Different religious traditions have differing authority structures: for example, Roman Catholics are more hierarchical and Southern Baptists are more dispersed. While denominations vary in authority structures, they are very similar in their agency structures.

Denominations use different language to describe their agency structures, for example, divisions, departments, boards, programs, units, and offices. Agency functions are quite isomorphic: Chaves reports similarities between the nine denominations he studied, with similar patterns occurring in those of 1916 and those of 1986 (p. 179). It becomes apparent that there is a fairly consistent pattern of denominational organizational agency structure over time in this country. This structure generally includes domestic and foreign missions, publications, Christian education, church planting or extensions, and higher education and seminaries. It is worth noting that while denominational structures are similar, the use of authority and delivery of ministry within those structures varies by particular denomination.

As denominations develop missional agencies, the following dynamics are at work. There is a shift in power between authority structures and agency structures. In some denominations during the twentieth century, the agencies became more autonomous, depending less on funding their national budgets from congregational giving. Chaves points out that, at

---

21. "Nature of the Church," chap. 3.01., Evangelical Lutheran Church in America, Constitution, 2005.

the beginning of the 1990s, an average of 79 percent of money that was contributed to (U.S.) congregations stayed in the congregation (p. 187). In the Evangelical Lutheran Church in America today, congregations keep 90 percent of their income for local ministry. It is interesting that 80 percent of the ELCA's national budget is built on contributions from congregations, and this is obviously a serious concern for this church body. At the beginning of the twenty-first century, local denominational judicatories have become more programmatic and less invested in national ministries. I will say more about this later. The internal changes I have just noted are deeply related to authority and agency and the challenge to denominations to develop missional agencies. These changes, along with the external contextual realities, are changing the overall mission environment.

Changing Context(s) of Mission

The environment for mission changed dramatically in the United States in the latter half of the twentieth century and the beginning of the twenty-first. Ideologically, postmodernity brought changes to how we understand authority and truth: that is, truth has become customized and subjectivized; local experience has usurped the idea of a metanarrative; authority must be earned more than granted. The emphasis is now on relationships rather than positions of authority. What was once legitimated by tradition or position must now be earned through trust. The question of *who makes the rules* is a critical one in a postmodern environment.

Technologically, the advent of the digital age has changed the way we communicate and process information; the speed at which things happen has shrunk our global village. In denominational agencies, decision-making and response time are challenged to keep pace. Sociologically, wide-ranging cultural shifts have ushered in changes in the mission environment. Increases in the population from newer immigrant communities have changed the complexion of North America. The validity of the experience and knowledge of people of color is demanding more recognition and inclusion within our churches as well as in the educational and political arenas.

Population changes in the United States are creating challenges to ecclesial ecologies that have historically developed in a racist, culturally divided nation. The reality of pluralism is felt not only in our large cities but also in our small towns and rural areas. As was noted in the 2004 Lutheran World Federation mission document, churches in the Northern Hemisphere are facing dramatic changes in their environment.

> A new challenge for the church in mission, especially in the North, is to address the religious and cultural plurality in its midst. Large-scale migration of people across regions and continents, seeking financial opportunities or fleeing from oppression and violence, has led to an ever-larger diversity of religion and cultures in the major cities of the world. Religious cultures are no longer isolated from each other. In such multicultural situations people feel that their self-understanding or identity is brought into question.[22]

Another new reality for churches in the United States is that missionaries are now being sent *to* this country. The churches planted around the world, but mainly in the Southern Hemisphere, by missionaries from the Northern Hemisphere during the nineteenth and twentieth centuries are now growing at a faster rate than their Northern counterparts. These young indigenous churches from the South are now sending missionaries to bring the Good News to the North.[23] At the same time, judicatories and some local congregations now have the resources and technology to reach out globally on their own. They are no longer totally dependent on national denominational agencies to connect them with global missions. This move toward more direct contact with global mission on the part of judicatories and congregations is very important in the denominational agency narrative. The reader will recall that the Hartford study reported that the strongest identities congregations felt with national agencies concerned global missions and relief efforts. These and other changes raise the question of the location of denominational ministry, which obviously has implications for resources and staffing for denominations.

22. *Mission in Context: Transformation, Reconciliation, Empowerment,* Lutheran World Federation, Department of Mission and Development (Switzerland: The Lutheran World Federation, 2004), 19.

23. Philip Jenkins, *The Next Christendom: The Coming of Global Christianity* (Oxford: Oxford University Press, 2002).

Case Study: Evangelical Lutheran Church in America

The Evangelical Lutheran Church in America (ELCA) was organized in May 1987. It brought together three strains of Lutheran church bodies: the Lutheran Church in America, the American Lutheran Church, and the Association of Evangelical Lutheran Churches. (When referring to the ELCA's denominational national office, I will use the term "churchwide expression" for what have been called agency structures.) When the ELCA began functioning in January 1988, it had a national churchwide structure that included the following (Plan 1):

> **Officers/Offices:** Bishop; Secretary; Ecumenical Affairs; Finance; Personnel; Research, Planning, and Evaluation
>
> **Divisions:** Congregational Life; Education; Global Mission; Ministry; Outreach; Social Ministry Organizations
>
> **Commissions:** Church in Society; Financial Support; Multicultural; Women; Communication
>
> **Others:** Board of Pensions; Church Periodical; ELCA Foundation; ELCA Loan Fund; Publishing House; Women of the ELCA

The ELCA began its operation with eleven thousand congregations, sixty-five synods, and nine regions. Regarding its formal authority structures, the ELCA organized initially with a church council and a conference of bishops. The highest legislative body in the ELCA is its Biennial Churchwide Assembly, which is composed of voting members from its 65 synods. Within the congregations, authority rests with congregational councils and rostered and elected lay leaders. Synodical authority is vested in synod councils and assemblies and with the bishop and the bishop's staff.

In addition to its elected or appointed authority structures, the denomination began with eight seminaries, twenty-nine colleges and universities, and hundreds of social ministry organizations and camps. The education and preparation of rostered leaders in the seminaries are also part of the network of authority in this denomination. Much of the denomination's tradition and culture is passed on in and through these institutions, and all these institutions continue today, except for one college.

In 1992 the ELCA national office reorganized itself to address changing mission needs and a reduction in resources (Plan 2):

Officers: Bishop; Secretary; Treasurer
Divisions: Church in Society; Congregational Ministries; Global Mission; Higher Education and Schools; Ministry Outreach
Departments: Communication; Ecumenical Affairs; Human Resources; Research and Evaluation; Synodical Relations
Commissions: Multicultural; Women
Others: Board of Pensions; Church Periodical; Foundation; Publishing House; Women of the ELCA; Loan Fund

The 1992 reorganization of administrative and service units was intended to bring greater clarity and focus to churchwide expression. However, the ministry and work of these newly formed units became more separated and compartmentalized than had been intended in the reorganization. Units focused on their particular area of assignment for efficiency, and they often did not make the necessary cross-functional connections that would have assisted in the health and vitality of the organization. Thus, while the reorganization did achieve some efficiency, it did not always strengthen overall coordination and shared mission.

Moving forward into the twenty-first century, in a liminal environment, the ELCA has reached twenty years of its life and faces increased complexity and a continuing decline in resources coming from the congregations to the synodical and churchwide expressions of the church. The churchwide agency was reorganized in 2005 in response to this complexity and resource decline; this was also an effort to bring even greater clarity and less compartmentalization to the denomination's churchwide expression. Work on this new design began in December 2001, and it involved participation from all expressions, institutions, and agencies.

The process of input and feedback was extensive, and it was intended to result in a clearer self-understanding and a structure that reflected what the denomination believed God was calling it to at this time in its life. Out of this process, the denomination's churchwide assembly adopted a Plan for Mission in August 2005. And the deeper work of articulating the denomination's identity is ongoing. The new churchwide structure emerged (Plan 3):

Officers: Presiding Bishop; Secretary; Treasurer
Program Units: Church in Society; Evangelical Outreach and Congregational Mission; Global Mission; Multicultural Ministry; Publishing House; Vocation and Education; Women of the ELCA

Service Units: Board of Pensions; Church Periodical; Communication; Development; Foundation; Mission Investment

Sections: Ecumenical and Interreligious; Human Resources; Information Technology; Management Services; Research and Evaluation; Synodical Relations; Worship and Liturgical Resources

Throughout its short history, the ELCA has had a national churchwide structure that reflects the historic pattern of denominations. For example, there has consistently been a domestic and global mission unit, funding for new congregations, a publishing house, and an emphasis on church in society. While the primary location for responsibilities of these ministries has been at the churchwide expression, the work has always been shared in partnership with synods and congregations.

There has also continued to be a unit to engage the area of multicultural ministries. Multicultural ministries, along with women's ministries, have been carried out in an interdependent system. However, given the tension in these two areas, the churchwide expression has played more of a challenging and urging role with its partners in the ELCA ecology.

It is also important to note the commitment to ecumenical relations that is evidenced by a continued agency for that work. This commitment has moved the denomination forward to form full communion agreements with the Reformed Church in America, the Presbyterian Church (USA), the United Church of Christ, the Moravian Church, and the Episcopal Church. The ELCA is also in dialogue with the African Methodist Episcopal, Disciples of Christ, Mennonite, Orthodox, Roman Catholic, and United Methodist church bodies. These efforts appreciate and support a rich ecology of Christian unity. As the ELCA engages the challenges of developing missional agencies in the twenty-first century, its leadership in ecumenical relations is one of the areas to be celebrated. At the same time, this ecumenical sharing begs for a clarity of theological and confessional identity so that the denomination does not lose whatever distinctive Lutheran contribution it can make to the wider ecosystem. As the new Plan for Mission began operation in 2006, the denomination was facing a continuing decline in membership and the number of congregations. At that time, there were 10,549 congregations and 4,850,776 members.[24] These fig-

---

24. Office of the Secretary, Report to the Conference of Bishops, Oct. 5-10, 2006, Exhibit B, Part 2, p. 1.

ures represent a steady decline since the denomination's inception and an accelerated rate of decline over the five-year period of 2001-2006. If this trend is to be slowed or reversed, there will need to be a balance between a strong identity and openness to new mission opportunities.

The Plan for Mission is designed to move the ELCA from a fairly modernist organizational approach (Plan 2) to a more relational, post-modern approach (Plan 3). While the designs appear similar on paper, the new design's network of authority is structured to reduce compartmental-ization and increase cooperation, coordination, and collaboration: the units are more integrated in their exercise of authority, and authority patterns have been flattened and cooperation across units increased. This integration is demonstrated throughout the organization in the networks, teams, and alliances being created for attending to mission.

In an effort to bring greater clarity to the denomination's identity and purpose, the ELCA adopted a new mission and vision statement, along with five strategic directions specifically intended to guide the denomination's churchwide expression. The mission statement orients the denomination to being sent for the sake of the world. This holds great promise that a deeper missional understanding may emerge.

Mission Statement of the ELCA

Marked with the cross of Christ forever, we are claimed,
gathered, and sent for the sake of the world.

Signature Phrase

Living in God's amazing grace

Vision Statement of the ELCA

Claimed by God's grace for the sake of the world, we are a new creation through God's living Word by the power of the Holy Spirit;

Gathered by God's grace for the sake of the world, we will live among God's faithful people, hear God's Word, and share Christ's supper;

Sent by God's grace for the sake of the world, we will proclaim the good news of God in Christ through word and deed, serve all people following the example of our Lord Jesus, and strive for justice and peace in all the world.

Strategic Directions for the Churchwide Organization

*Claimed, gathered, and sent by God's grace for the sake of the world,
the Evangelical Lutheran Church in America in and
through its churchwide expression will:*

- **Support congregations** in their call to be faithful, welcoming, and generous, sharing the mind of Christ;
- Assist members, congregations, synods, and institutions and agencies of this church to **grow in evangelical outreach**;
- **Step forward as a public church** that witnesses boldly to God's love for all that God has created;
- **Deepen and extend our global, ecumenical, and interfaith relationships** for the sake of God's mission; and
- Assist this church to **bring forth and support faithful, wise, and courageous leaders** whose vocations serve God's mission in a pluralistic world.

The Plan for Mission will be effective from the churchwide expression if there is clarity and agreement on the identity and purpose of the denomination. The image of an ecosystem may be helpful for the denomination to engage the complexity, diversity, unity, and interdependence of its identity and purpose. Relationships are the key to a healthy ecosystem. Within living systems there are critical connections. Understanding the leadership role of the churchwide expression as it relates to the other expressions (synod and congregations) and institutions in the ecology of the ELCA is extremely important. Some of the relationships are naturally visible, while others are not as obvious. Openness to the potential of new relationships and ways of being church will be needed if U.S. denominations are to be effective in this century. There are networks and fields of authority and agency in this new ecology that are yet to be discovered.

Within the new design of the ELCA, the areas of authority and agency are still unfolding. For example, the roles of synods (middle judicatories) and of churchwide agencies are changing. Synods, like congregations, are doing more mission locally. Congregations are more locally involved in serving as teaching congregations and starting new congregations. More of the resources that were formerly given by congregations to support the two other expressions of this church are being kept locally. The sharing of benevolence (mission support) dollars is a current urgent topic of conversation in the denomination, as discussions continue concerning the best location for primary responsibility for the denomination's ministries.

As the churchwide expression implements this new design, it is using networking as a key operational methodology and convening as a principal form of authority. The churchwide expression has the opportunity to convene networks and communities of practice from across the denomination, as well as ecumenically and globally.[25] This authority can bring together partners to frame issues, teach, consider action, and endorse and legitimate. The churchwide expression can call together wisdom from throughout this church and then widely disseminate it.[26]

A Missiological Vision: Accompaniment

One of the new units in the ecology of the new ELCA churchwide organization is also an old unit: Global Mission (GM; formerly the Division for Global Mission). At the beginning of the twenty-first century, the GM program unit set forth a mission-planning document called "Global Mission in the Twenty-first Century: A Vision of Evangelical Faithfulness in God's Mission." This vision reframed the ELCA's mission work and relationships around the world. The document names *accompaniment* as the missiological vision for the twenty-first century and identifies twelve "signposts" as criteria of accompaniment. These signposts are:

1. Witness in word and deed
   Everyone, everywhere has the right to hear the Good News of Jesus Christ.
2. Witness under the cross
   The church's witness is a cruciformed, compassionate witness.

---

25. Margaret Wheatley, *Finding Our Way: Leadership for an Uncertain Time* (San Francisco: Berrett-Koehler Publishers, 2005), 177. Wheatley describes communities of practice as different from networks in the following way: "[T]hey are different in significant ways. They are communities, which means that people make a commitment to be available to each other, to offer support, to share learning, to consciously develop new knowledge. They are not only for their own needs but for the needs of others. . . . Also in a community of practice, the focus extends beyond the work of the community. There is an intentional commitment to advance the field of practice and to share those discoveries with anyone engaged in such work."

26. This material derives from my conversations with the office of the presiding bishop and the Vocation and Education unit on church ecology.

3. Interfaith witness and dialogue
   Have respect for people of diverse faiths.
4. Ecumenical approach
   Stimulate conversation and cooperation with ecumenical partners.
5. Wholistic approach
   Consider the spiritual, social, physical, and communal implications.
6. Justice, peace, and integrity of creation
   Nurture an intentional concern for justice, peace, and care of creation.
7. South-South Program
   Receive the gifts of leaders and churches from the Southern Hemisphere.
8. Racial Diversity and Gender Equity
   Receive the gifts and energy of racial diversity and women leaders.
9. Transparency in communication and finance
   Make honesty and transparency a high value.
10. Shared decision-making
    Make decisions through consultation.
11. Diversity of Gifts
    Use an asset-gifts-based approach.
12. Contextualization
    Engage in discernment and contextual analysis.

The signposts articulated in the GM document are not merely applicable to mission in other lands; they are also valuable for living out the denomination's purpose in the United States. These signposts help us understand the *accompaniment* mission approach: it means walking together side by side. Its roots are found in the Emmaus road story in Luke 24:13-35. Walking together implies mutuality and interdependence: accompaniment implies companionship and mutual respect.[27] This approach is grounded in a cruciform witness to the gospel of Jesus Christ. It is respectful, dialogical, has a concern for justice, and shares the decision-making. This shared decision-making addresses questions of authority: "Who makes the rules?" The accompaniment approach holds the promise of a mission environment that is diverse, contextual, and part of a postmodern sociological framework. It offers a missiology for today's ecclesial ecology.

If a denomination uses this approach, what are the implications for

27. *Global Mission in the Twenty-first Century: A Vision of Evangelical Faithfulness in God's Mission,* Evangelical Lutheran Church in America, Division for Global Mission, 12.

leadership? What kind of leadership can denominations provide and produce that would be most effective? How might leaders in denominational agencies see themselves less as control centers in a competitive ecclesial environment, and more as stewards with and on behalf of the church?

Leadership for Today's Mission Agencies

Just as denominations need to be clear about their identity and purpose, they also need leaders who are clear. Leaders who are unsure about their understanding of identity in God bring great potential for destructive behavior into the ecclesial environment. The need for leaders to be able to change and lead communities through change and transformative processes is paramount. But if leaders are going to be able to be flexible and change, they need to be, first of all, grounded in their baptismal identity and vocation. Being able to handle change constructively requires being thus grounded in identity, and denominational leaders must find their identity first and foremost in Jesus Christ. In baptism, God claims and names us as God's people. Our call to leadership is a vocational call that is rooted in our baptism. I have experienced my own transformation as a leader over the past several years. My identity in Christ and my sense of leadership as baptismal vocation have made the difference for my health and effectiveness as a leader.

The recent reorganization at the ELCA churchwide office has meant huge changes for my leadership: the unit I had led for over a decade was dismantled and the work placed into three new units. When that happened, I considered my call completed and prepared to leave the organization. However, the Spirit guided me into a new call within the organization. I was reluctant. I was not looking forward to embracing the change that would be necessary for an effective move. In the final decision-making process, I came to terms with my leadership choices as part of a community. Rather than being isolated or individualistic, I had to remind myself that I am called to participate in God's mission, and that is larger than my personal preferences. At that time, I was called out of my comfort zone to become part of a new plan. The process changed me and my leadership in a positive way.

Serving as the executive for Leadership Development in the Evangelical Lutheran Church in America for the past year and a half, I have immersed myself in my denomination's leadership systems. I have had the privilege of coordinating the denomination's evangelism and ethnic ministry strategies' leadership development components. I continue to be impressed with the level of commitment that leaders bring to be the best they can be in their calling. I am convinced that leaders want to be effective; I am further convinced that they are seeking ways to thrive in this new ecology. A working group of diverse leaders at the churchwide expression of the ELCA has suggested the following profile for leaders.

> Leaders in the Evangelical Lutheran Church in America will assist its congregations, synods, institutions and churchwide organization in creating a vision for participating in God's mission. ELCA leaders embody Christ-centered servanthood and will empower others, thus multiplying leadership in this church. Leaders will assist this church to become a more multicultural church, to learn from diversity, share power and build a system that flourishes from diversity. ELCA leaders will identify gifts and assets in persons and communities. They will partner with others to transform communities to be in mission in a pluralistic world.

> The group also identified "Qualities of Leadership." The top seven are:

1. A person of faith with a personal commitment to Jesus Christ
2. A person of integrity, courage, and vision
3. One who is missional and has a clear sense of purpose ·
4. One who is able to mentor, equip, and inspire
5. One who is open to new ideas and is characterized by creativity and vitality
6. Ability to demonstrate one's faith and values
7. Ability to listen to and learn from others, work collaboratively, and clearly communicate a vision

Applying the above leadership profile to the accompaniment missiological vision offers an approach that denominations should consider using to develop leaders for missional agencies today. Missional agencies can emerge out of mutual conversation and discernment within the denomination. All of the parties affected by the ministry would be invited to discern the best location and authority for the execution of the denomination's purpose. After the question "What is God doing and calling us to do?" comes the question "What needs to be done, and who can do it best?"[28] This may seem a little messy, but it is grounded in a high value placed on relationships and mutuality: it honors the various roles and gifts within an ecology and allows for the change of primary responsibility and location of ministry based on God's activity in the world and in the church. It requires leaders who are open to change and willing to change.

An example of this kind of approach is the conversation now underway in the ELCA among its synods and its churchwide expression about the starting up of new congregations. Since its inception, the churchwide expression of the denomination has had a primary role in decision-making regarding new starts, including funding; gradually, it has opened up the process to congregations to share more directly in the development of new mission starts. Now synods and congregations are starting congregations locally and are using dollars formerly shared directly with the churchwide expression to accomplish this effort. This new way of doing congregational starts evokes the question of the denomination's purpose and what division of labor and funds serves it best. This begins to get at the deeper question of the denomination's self-understanding with respect to the starting of new congregations in today's mission environment.

Denominations must face these deeper questions and look at the brutal facts. In *Leadership Without Easy Answers,* Ron Heifetz argues for a leadership approach to today's organizations that he calls *adaptive:* adaptive leadership "mobilizes people to tackle tough problems."[29] Adaptive work addresses problems for which there are no clear-cut "technical" solutions. Adaptive situations call for leaders who are willing to work with those with whom they are called to lead to discern and define the problem or opportunity and learn ways to address it. Heifetz suggests that the role of authority in adaptive situations that need direction is to identify the adaptive challenges, provide a diagnosis of the situation, and produce definitions and solutions. This is a change from the role of "experts" in the past. In the area of conflict, authority either exposes conflict or allows it to emerge. Furthermore, authority is not afraid to challenge the norms. De-

28. H. George Anderson, *Ecclesiology, Mission, and Structure,* April 2004.

29. Ron Heifetz, *Leadership Without Easy Answers* (Cambridge, MA: Harvard University Press, 1994), 15.

nominations critically need leaders in their missional agencies who are willing to do adaptive work, leaders who are open to explore with their partners the possibilities for solving today's challenges for effective agency ministry.

One of the major twenty-first-century opportunities and challenges for Protestant denominations is how to be multicultural in an increasing multicultural environment. As I have observed earlier in this essay, the problems of racial divisions in the United States go back to the broken relationships with and oppression of American Indians and the enslavement of blacks. Denominations are still part of that divide. Welcoming people different from those already in our congregations and receiving their gifts is not one of our strengths. Denominations are called to go beyond benevolence in their relationships with people of color and people who are racially/ethnically different from the churches' majority population. Denominations must face the challenge of raising up leaders with cross-cultural skills to lead a multicultural church.

This kind of leadership will require people who are willing to enter into relationships with new people. The accompaniment missiological vision provides a way of entering into these relationships, and I suggest that the leadership engage the twelve signposts I have noted above by using four core practices for leadership: *listen, discern, speak,* and *act.* I also recommend these practices as interrelated functions for congregations to use to create an evangelizing culture.[30] I list an abbreviated version of the practices here because I believe they translate to the denominational missional agency setting, especially as these agencies engage communities of color. These practices are interactive and nonlinear.

- *Listen* — to God through Scripture, prayer, worship, and fellowship, and to the many voices in a given context.
- *Discern* — perceive, recognize, and differentiate; become aware and sensitive; see with the heart as well as with the eyes; do contextual analysis.
- *Speak* — speak the vision; name the opportunity; speak God's Word in the situation; speak the truth.
- *Act* — serve and equip; multiply leaders by teaching and sending.

30. Bullock, "Called Out of Our Comfort Zone," 76.

If denominational agency leaders do not open themselves to the gifts and leadership from communities of color, the denominations' membership will not increase in these communities. Articulating a vision for this growth in new communities requires listening to God and the community. It requires deep discernment to perceive beyond the barriers of race and socioeconomic issues to the real gifts of the other; it certainly requires saying what we believe and acting like we believe it; and it requires speaking the truth in love in difficult situations. Until leaders are willing to face the facts of our past and present, we will have great difficulty imagining a future together. Because this is difficult work, it calls for leaders who are willing to stay for the long journey and open themselves to dying to self.

Dying to self is not a new concept for Christian leaders. When Jesus called the first disciples, he explained that if they followed him they would lose their lives (Mark 8:34-38). Leaders are called to be transformed as they accompany Jesus into what God is doing in the world today. It is a journey of letting go of our many familiar ways of doing things and opening up to a range of new possibilities for ministry. For example, the way that denominations have identified, prepared, and assigned leaders in the past is not keeping pace with the need in many denominations. It is time to allow new models to emerge.

How we understand leadership education and preparation is slowly changing. We need to educate for leadership, for example, teaching leaders how to train other leaders and work in teams. It is very important to equip leaders for leadership in public life in the world, not just the life of the congregation. Denominations need leaders who have the capacity to bless what God is already doing in the world.

Conclusion

In *Chasing Down a Rumor*, Bacher and Inskeep say that denominations are here and will be around for a while to come.[31] I agree with them, for we have this treasure in earthen ecologies. Denominations will need to continue to wrestle with identity and purpose in light of God's mission and their call to participate in it. What shape denominations take in the years to come remains to be seen, but because God is faithful, the church will remain.

31. Bacher and Inskeep, *Chasing Down a Rumor*, 161.

A MISSIONAL REFRAMING OF ECCLESIOLOGY AND POLITY FOR SPECIFIC DENOMINATIONS

"So what does a missional church look like?" is a question that is often asked. Or we might put it this way: "What would a congregation look like if it had a missional identity?" Much of the missional church literature to date has offered hints regarding how to address such questions, but the specifics are still missing. The essays in this section seek to engage in an explicit effort to answer these questions. They do so by taking up the task of engaging a particular denomination's ecclesiology and polity, as this was developed historically, and then bringing it into conversation with a missional understanding. The following chapters address four denominations: the Episcopal Church (USA), the Evangelical Lutheran Church in America, the Evangelical Covenant Church, and the Baptist General Conference. The reader will want to be aware of three themes that are at work within each of these essays.

First, these essays note that it is critical to engage deeply in understanding and critiquing the specific historical development of the particular denominations. These chapters make it clear that one cannot bring a missional imagination to denominations in general and then hope to be able to help congregations develop a missional identity. We must take the particulars of each denomination's history and traditions seriously. These essays provide provocative insights into the particularities of each of these four designated denominations, and thoughts on how to engage these from a missional perspective.

Second, these chapters note that it is crucial to bring a missional imagination to bear on the rethinking, reframing, and reclaiming of a denomination's life and ministry for participation in God's mission in the world. They make it clear that such a missional imagination needs to be deeply informed by Trinitarian foundations, from both the Western tradition, which focuses more on the *sending* character of God, and the Eastern tradition, which focuses more on the *social reality* within the Godhead. All too often, denominations have developed their primary understanding of ecclesiology and polity by invoking primarily a high Christology. This approach tends to underplay the relational mutuality that is so essential for understanding the purpose of the church; it also overplays authority and hierarchy in developing organization and structures in the church. These essays refine these issues by bringing Trinitarian foundations into conversation with the distinct ecclesiologies and polities of these four different denominations.

Third, these chapters note that it is necessary to develop the specific implications that a missional identity has for both a denomination and its congregations with respect to organizational structures and leadership practices. Each chapter interacts critically and creatively in an attempt to reshape the polity of its particular denomination from a missional perspective. The insights that are offered provide a rich resource for people seeking to engage the polity of their own denomination.

The necessity of developing a polity is unavoidable because organizational structures and leadership practices are inherent in denominational and congregational life. The issue is not whether to have a polity; rather, it is to explore what kind of polity one will develop. All too often, however, denominations and congregations have drawn on secular organizational and leadership models without thinking them through from biblical and theological perspectives. The following chapters all demonstrate the truth of that point within each of the denominations being examined, but they also demonstrate how a missional identity can redemptively reframe the polity of each.

CHAPTER 5

A More True "Domestic and Foreign Missionary Society": Toward a Missional Polity for the Episcopal Church

Dwight Zscheile

> *There is no reason in the world wherefore we should esteem it as necessary always to do, as always to believe, the same things; seeing every man knoweth that the matter of faith is constant, the matter contrariwise of action daily changeable, especially the matter of action belonging unto church polity.*

> Richard Hooker, *Laws of Ecclesiastical Polity*, III.x.7[1]

Context, Polity, and the Episcopal Church

The polity of the Christian church is always contextual. From the early church's adaptation of leadership roles from the first-century synagogue, to the incorporation of Roman models of office into the Constantinian church, to Calvin's use of the assembly system in Reformed Geneva, Christians have always taken organizational and leadership structures from local cultures and transformed them for church use.[2] In that process they have sought to integrate these structures with biblical and theological norms. The contextual nature of polity reflects the incarnational nature of

1. Richard Hooker, *Ecclesiastical Polity*, ed. Arthur Pollard (Manchester, UK: Carcanet, 1990), 120. Hooker (1553/4-1600) is the classic early exponent of Anglican polity.
2. See James Tunstead Burtchaell, *From Synagogue to Church: Public Services and Offices in the Earliest Christian Communities* (New York: Cambridge University Press, 1992).

133

the gospel and the church's life: Christianity is always embodied in local cultures, embracing, calling into question, and transforming the norms and presuppositions of those cultures.[3] As the Richard Hooker quotation above suggests, polity is dynamic and must adapt to the church's changing contexts in order to serve, rather than constrain, God's mission.

The current polity of the Episcopal Church (USA) reflects three major contextual influences: (1) the established state church of the English Reformation and Colonial eras; (2) American representative democracy; and (3) modern corporate bureaucracy. However, the twenty-first-century American context of the Episcopal Church is shifting dramatically, calling for a critical appraisal of the assumptions and norms embedded in its polity. In this chapter I seek to explore the contextual influences — both theological and cultural — that underlie the organization of the Episcopal Church today in light of the realities now facing the church. Anglicanism has historically cherished a balance between continuity and discontinuity, universality and locality: that is, carrying forward core values and traditions from the past while still allowing flexibility for local adaptation and responsiveness in light of changing circumstances. It is in this spirit that I will offer a preliminary sketch of some principles for reconceiving Episcopal polity in an emerging missional era.

Establishment and the Legacy of Christendom: Sixteenth- to Eighteenth-Century Roots

The Episcopal Church began as the Church of England in colonial America, where it was the established state church in the southern colonies. As such, the basic underlying assumptions of sixteenth- and seventeenth-century England were transferred across the Atlantic. These include the integration of church and state, the division of territory into geographical domains (parishes and dioceses) ruled by monarchical rectors (derived from the Latin *regere*, "to rule") and bishops, with the assumption that everyone was at least nominally Christian. The church was at the center of

---

3. "[T]he gospel, which is from the beginning to the end embodied in culturally conditioned forms, calls into question all cultures, including the one in which it was originally embodied." Lesslie Newbigin, *Foolishness to the Greeks: The Gospel and Western Culture* (Grand Rapids: Eerdmans, 1986), 4.

society, which was reflected in the taxation that funded its activities and by the commissary, or deputy, who oversaw the church at the behest of the bishop of London, under whose charge the colonial English churches lay.[4]

The classic Anglican compromise of uniformity (the required use of the Book of Common Prayer, for instance) and flexibility (a diversity of pieties and theological commitments) came alive as Anglicanism began to take fresh forms on American soil. Since there were no Anglican bishops in America until Samuel Seabury was consecrated in 1784, a lay governance system evolved in the colonies that differed significantly from England. In Virginia and other Southern colonies, vestries comprised of prominent lay people (usually the landed gentry) exercised much greater control over local clergy and the affairs of the church than had been known in England.[5] This would lead to an important modification of the monarchical rule by clergy that was more typical of the church in England and New England. The roots for a more collaborative, lay-involved polity had been laid.

The parish system took root only tenuously in the United States.[6] Unlike in England, where residents of a particular parish were expected to attend church of that parish, the American preference for freedom of choice eventually led to looser practices of domain. This was particularly true in those colonies where the Anglican church was not established, for example, in New England. The trajectory of American religious life was headed increasingly in a voluntary direction, shaped in part by the settling of the continent by people who had resisted England's expectations of religious conformity. Nonetheless, the parish concept remains deeply influential in Episcopal polity to this day, even though it has never functioned very effectively.

The Late-Eighteenth-Century Democratic Synthesis

At the time of the American Revolution, the Church of England in the colonies faced a major crisis. Anglicanism was directly and symbolically

4. David Hein and Gardiner H. Shattuck, *The Episcopalians* (Westport, CT: Praeger Publishers, 2004), 16.

5. Robert W. Prichard, *A History of the Episcopal Church,* rev. ed. (Harrisburg, PA: Morehouse Pub., 1999), 10.

6. Sydney E. Ahlstrom, *A Religious History of the American People* (New Haven: Yale University Press, 1972), 191-92.

linked to the imperial power that the revolutionaries sought to overthrow (prayers for the king were included in the liturgy), and the distinguishing feature of its polity — bishops — represented exactly the kind of monarchy that Americans were rejecting in favor of democratic rule. Many Anglicans, especially in New England, openly sided with the Tories (including Samuel Seabury). Yet the Revolution also presented a dramatic opportunity to recontextualize Anglicanism in America.

The process for revising the polity of the colonial Church of England to serve a disestablished Anglican church in the new United States involved considerable negotiation between the low-church Southern Anglicans and high-church Northerners like Samuel Seabury. Its most notable feature was the integration of historic Anglican norms with the representative democracy so valued by the revolutionaries. It is probably no coincidence that the crafting of the original Constitution and Canons of the Protestant Episcopal Church in the United States took place parallel to the development of the United States Constitution in Philadelphia. William White, the rector of Christ Church in Philadelphia and chaplain of the Continental Congress, proposed this synthesis in *The Case of the Episcopal Churches in the United States Considered* (1782). White argued for retaining the historic orders of bishop, priest, and deacon alongside a democratic governance structure in which clergy and laity both participated in church councils at the local, regional, and national levels.[7]

Democracy has remained a defining feature of the Episcopal Church's polity. On the one hand, it represents a move toward contextualization that still resonates strongly with American cultural values today. The monarchical, autocratic hierarchy reflected in the Church of England at the time was modified in the direction of greater collaboration: it established greater local autonomy and checks and balances to authority. However, the synthesis of hierarchical conceptions of office and democratic conceptions of majority rule took place primarily along *cultural,* rather than theological, lines: that is, the rationale for this integration was primarily one of *fit* with the emerging democratic nation, rather than one of clear biblical or theological reasoning. White argued pragmatically and provisionally; occasionally he invoked historical authorities such as Hooker and Cranmer, but he made no attempt to develop a sustained bib-

7. William White, *The Case of the Episcopal Churches in the United States Considered* (Philadelphia: Church Historical Society, 1954).

lical or theological argument for the polity innovations he introduced. Anglican theology since Hooker has made a theological case for flexibility in response to changing circumstances for the church. However, the changes introduced were not always proposed on theological grounds.

This has led to a somewhat contradictory tendency deep within Episcopal polity today: the affirmation of the authority and legitimacy of hierarchical offices alongside an abiding cultural mistrust of hierarchy and authority. On the one hand, Episcopal polity suggests a hierarchical succession of orders (from laypeople to deacons to priests to bishops) in its conceptions of ordination; on the other hand, all four orders are expected to govern the church collaboratively.

Another legacy of democracy is its tendency to foster factionalism and coalition politics. Since the Elizabethan settlement, Anglicanism has wrestled with how to reconcile the varying theological sensibilities present in its midst. The great conflicts with the Puritans and Roman Catholics during the sixteenth and seventeenth centuries, the Evangelical/Anglo-Catholic battles of the nineteenth century, and today's culture wars over sexuality all speak to a repeated pattern of internecine conflict. Democracy tends to lead to political maneuvering in order to attain the victory of majority rule. But the minority party that loses can be disenfranchised in the process. Discernment of the Spirit and consensus-building, while not prohibited by democracy, are also not necessarily encouraged by it.

Underlying modern American democracy are Enlightenment ideas of personhood that are being questioned by theologians today.[8] As reflected in the Declaration of Independence and the United States Constitution, these ideas of personhood tend to be highly individualistic: they conceive of freedom as freedom *from* constraint by others rather than freedom *for* one another, or, as Jürgen Moltmann has put it, the freedom of lordship rather than love.[9] Individuals in modern democracy tend to focus more on individual rights than on obligations to others or on the good of the whole. There has been a tendency in recent years within the church to frame debates in terms of civil rights rather than theological categories.[10]

8. See, e.g., John D. Zizioulas, *Being as Communion: Studies in Personhood and the Church* (Crestwood, NY: St. Vladimir's, 1985).

9. See Jürgen Moltmann, *The Trinity and the Kingdom: The Doctrine of God* (Minneapolis: Fortress, 1993), 215.

10. For example, in 2003, V. Gene Robinson, the openly gay bishop of New Hampshire, told the media that his ordination to the episcopate was a matter of civil rights.

While it has been argued that modern democracy's roots lie in covenant ideals from the Hebrew Bible, American democracy has tended to eclipse the key actor in that covenant process — God.[11]

Modern Corporate Bureaucracy: The Twentieth Century

The Episcopal Church grew in numbers and influence as it gradually recovered from the aftermath of the Revolution and reasserted its place in nineteenth-century American life. The church in the early twentieth century increasingly began to adopt the organizational forms and assumptions of the modern bureaucracies that were in ascendance in corporate America at that time. This trend occurred across mainline American denominations, as churches embraced the new "scientific" management principles espoused by Frederick Taylor, Henri Fayol, Max Weber, and others as a way of organizing an increasingly complex world along rational lines.[12] During this period the Episcopal Church developed a centralized administrative and program bureaucracy in New York City. This bureaucracy grew large enough that it needed to acquire a new denominational headquarters at 815 Second Avenue in New York City in 1960, with triple the space of the previous offices. It was also at this time that the office of presiding bishop became a full-time job.[13]

Modernist bureaucracy as an organizational form was developed in the late nineteenth and early twentieth centuries as a means to organize the complexity of mass industrial production. It was based on a number of assumptions characteristic of Enlightenment modernity and a Newtonian cosmology, including predictability and linearity, command-and-control, hierarchy, and interchangeable parts. In the church this came to be expressed in a new emphasis on running the church "like a business," as denominational, diocesan, and congregational boards and committees multiplied, centralized planning came into vogue, and organizational charts with clear lines of control proliferated across the American religious landscape.

11. Daniel Judah Elazar, *Covenant and Polity in Biblical Israel: Biblical Foundations and Jewish Expressions* (New Brunswick, NJ: Transaction Publishers, 1995).

12. Craig Van Gelder, "From Corporate Church to Missional Church: The Challenge Facing Congregations Today," *Review & Expositor* 101, no. 3 (2004).

13. Prichard, *History of the Episcopal Church*, 234.

One of the major features of the modern corporate understanding of church is the professional paradigm for clergy. The roots of this idea lie in Friedrich Schleiermacher's designs for the new University of Berlin in 1810, in which he asserted a place for theology in the Enlightenment-era university by treating it as a profession, such as medicine or law.[14] While the idea that Anglican clergy should be well educated (university and/or seminary trained) and devoted full-time to their pastoral work had long been held, there emerged in the nineteenth century a more clearly *professional* understanding of the priest's vocation.[15] The professional ideal was strengthened and reiterated in the mid-twentieth century in America by writers such as H. Richard Niebuhr.[16] In the second half of the twentieth century, this professional paradigm developed three expressions: (1) the counselor/therapist (1970s); (2) the manager (1980s and 1990s); and (3) the technician (1990s).[17] In each case, the priest or pastor is understood as a professional (like doctors, lawyers, psychologists and other specialists) with unique training and skills, to whom one goes for expertise in spiritual matters, or who is charged with managing a nonprofit corporation that provides services to its members and the community.

The legacy of the modern corporate bureaucracy and its accompanying professional view of clergy is deeply reflected in the current polity of the Episcopal Church. The process for the selection, screening, training, and ordination of clergy has become a bureaucratic labyrinth requiring many years, much paperwork, and a major investment of resources to navigate. The layers of screening (medical, psychological, marital, and background examinations) reflect corporate liability concerns on the part of the church and its associated bodies (e.g., the Church Pension Group). It is common to hear talk today, not only from the Pension Group but also from local bishops, about *clergy wellness* that sounds very similar to secular corporate wellness programs.

Moreover, the mechanistic concept of interchangeable parts shapes

14. Friedrich Schleiermacher, *Brief Outline on the Study of Theology*, trans. Terrence N. Tice (Richmond, VA: John Knox Press, 1966).

15. R. David Cox, *Priesthood in a New Millennium: Toward an Understanding of Anglican Presbyterate in the Twenty-First Century* (New York: Church Publishing, 2004), 4.

16. H. Richard Niebuhr, *The Purpose of the Church and Its Ministry: Reflections on the Aims of Theological Education* (New York: Harper, 1956).

17. See Darrell L. Guder et al., *Missional Church: A Vision for the Sending of the Church in North America* (Grand Rapids: Eerdmans, 1998), 196-98.

the deployment of clergy, who are understood to be capable of functioning in virtually any context in the church. When candidates for the priesthood and diaconate begin the training process and are deployed subsequent to ordination, most dioceses prohibit them from returning to the congregation in which their call to leadership was first discerned. Like employees of modern corporations, clergy are expected to relocate at the will of the corporate system. While Anglicanism's understanding of ordination as being for the whole church, not just a local congregation or diocese, seeks to avoid provincialism and affirm the church's catholicity, it also severs leaders from the indigenous missionary and relational contexts out of which they emerged.

The denomination, dioceses, and even congregations have multiple boards, commissions, and committees around which they organize their activities. These are reflected in the current canons. Denominational offices across the United States have come under increasing stress in recent years, and it is not clear how long the corporate, bureaucratic paradigm of organizational life can persist. I should note that in recent years the corporations on which U.S. denominations modeled themselves in the early part of the century have streamlined their bureaucracies, eliminated layers of hierarchy, and adopted more flexible organizational models, such as networks, in order to adapt to today's dynamic global context.[18] As is typical, the church lags a generation or two behind in making such organizational changes.

When the Episcopal Church, like other mainline denominations, began a period of steep decline in the mid-1960s, the denominational and diocesan corporate bodies sought to reassert legitimacy by shifting into a regulatory mode.[19] This last phase of the modern corporate paradigm is alive and well in the Episcopal Church today. It is significant to note that Title IV, the disciplinary canons, constitutes the largest of any of the sections of the Constitution and Canons of 2003. Proposals to expand the disciplinary canons to encompass the work of laypeople in addition to just clergy came under consideration at the 2006 General Convention. While the impulse behind this expansion was a legitimate one — protecting the vulnerable from abuse by church officials, both lay and ordained — it also

18. See, e.g., Ronald N. Ashkenas, *The Boundaryless Organization: Breaking the Chains of Organizational Structure,* 2nd ed. (San Francisco: Jossey-Bass, 2002).

19. Van Gelder, "From Corporate Church to Missional Church," 436-37.

reflects the current recourse to regulation and control. Many bishops today find their schedules and budgets consumed more and more by lawyers, liability concerns, battles about control over dissident congregations (and their property), and the licensing and credentialing of laity and clergy. Embedded in this activity and these polity provisions are lingering hierarchical conceptions of ministry from the Church of England, alongside modern corporate bureaucratic notions of command-and-control.

Lawrence Miller's work on organizational lifecycles offers a provocative lens through which to view these dimensions of the church's life. Miller charts six leadership roles that characterize the phases of an organization's life, from founding to death: the prophet, the barbarian, the builder, the administrator, the bureaucrat, and the aristocrat.[20] When an organization reaches the administrator phase, decline begins: the tighter the emphasis on control and regulation that follows, the deeper into the death cycle an organization has progressed. The fact that many Episcopal churches and dioceses are living off endowments as their membership dwindles may be interpreted as an ominous sign of the aristocrat phase.

Today's Changed Context

The context for the Episcopal Church in the United States bears little resemblance to the Christendom world that shaped Episcopal polity from the English Reformation to the 1950s. The Episcopal Church has consistently viewed itself through the lens of establishment even after it ceased to be established, priding itself in being the church of America's socioeconomic elite.[21] Some scholars argue that establishment was the hallmark feature of Anglican identity through its early history, and when this began to dissolve, Anglicanism found itself in an identity crisis that pervades the church today.[22] This conception of an ecclesiastical identity at the center of society simply no longer accords with reality. The Episcopal Church ac-

20. Lawrence M. Miller, *Barbarians to Bureaucrats: Corporate Life Cycle Strategies: Lessons from the Rise and Fall of Civilizations* (New York: C. N. Potter, 1989).

21. See, e.g., Kit Konolige and Frederica Konolige, *The Power of Their Glory: America's Ruling Class: The Episcopalians* (New York: Wyden Books, 1978).

22. William L. Sachs, *The Transformation of Anglicanism: From State Church to Global Communion* (New York: Cambridge University Press, 1993); see also Stephen Sykes, *The Integrity of Anglicanism* (New York: Seabury Press, 1978).

counts for a very small and shrinking percentage of the U.S. population.[23] And its influence is diminishing along with its membership. Where it once spoke to the centers of power and expected to be heard, its voice today is generally disregarded.

Since the Revolution, society in America has progressed through several stages of disestablishment, from the initial separation of church and state, to the increasing presence of Roman Catholics and Jews alongside Protestants, to today's individualistic and highly pluralist society.[24] Basic acquaintance with the Christian story can no longer be assumed on any level. This is particularly true with emerging postmodern generations. Moreover, the Christendom division of geography is being challenged on several fronts. The parish (or neighborhood church) system around which Episcopal dioceses are typically organized in the United States is increasingly irrelevant. The U.S. experiment in reorganizing church as a voluntary association has led to people making choices about where to go to church, even if they cross from one side of a city to another and pass multiple congregations of their own denomination on the way. The ideas of domain that have long been hallmarks of Anglican conceptions of the episcopate are also under attack: international and missionary bishops (e.g., from Africa or the Anglican Mission in the United States) have asserted oversight over disaffected conservative congregations in liberal dioceses.

Mission Assumptions of Current Polity

While the church's missionary context is changing beyond recognition, the current polity of the Episcopal Church reflects mission-theory assumptions from the Christendom era. The underlying mission paradigm in Episcopal polity is a Christendom expansion or colonial model. That is, mission is primarily understood as extending the church's geographical domain into foreign lands. Historically, this has meant extending European culture and political rule alongside the gospel, whether across the U.S. frontier in the nineteenth century or overseas through foreign mis-

---

23. In 2004, average Sunday attendance for the whole Episcopal Church (including nondomestic dioceses), was 801,652, out of a total U.S. population of over 298,000,000 (sources: www.episcopalchurch.org and www.census.gov [accessed May 17, 2006]).

24. Guder, *Missional Church,* 48-53.

sions. Episcopal polity since 1835 has provided for a parallel classification of *missionary bishops* and *missionary dioceses* alongside ordinary bishops and dioceses.[25] One such missionary bishop was Jackson Kemper, the missionary bishop of the Northwest who sought to establish the church across a huge territory in the Midwest in the middle of the nineteenth century. The assumption was that missionary bishops function in that capacity only so long as it takes to set up a proper diocese. When the missionary function ceased, the bishop and diocese graduated to regular status. A similar distinction pertains between *mission congregations* and full-fledged *parishes.*

The role of missionary bishops has also historically reflected a high Christology more than a Trinitarian conception of mission. Mission efforts, particularly among evangelical Anglicans even to this day, have generally proceeded from obedience to the Great Commission.[26] Just as Christ commands his followers to make disciples, so too does the monarchical bishop charge the church to go forth into the mission field for the same purpose. While obedience to the Great Commission is a biblically valid understanding of mission, it represents only a narrow dimension of the biblical narrative's treatment of mission. Perhaps most significantly, it does not take into consideration the major developments in ecumenical mission thinking since the 1950s.

The Copernican Revolution in Mission and Ecclesiology

In the mid-twentieth century, a paradigm shift began to take place in missiological circles regarding the relationship between the church, mission, and God. Drawing from the biblical theology movement, the influence of Karl Barth, and fresh attentiveness to the doctrine of the Trinity — combined with a growing awareness of the problematic legacy of the colonial approach to mission — leading mission theologians sought to reground mission in the doctrine of God, and specifically in the Trinity. Subsequent to the 1952 International Missionary Council meeting in

25. Hein, *The Episcopalians,* 70.
26. For a recent example, see Claude E. Payne and Hamilton Beazley, *Reclaiming the Great Commission: A Practical Model for Transforming Denominations and Congregations* (San Francisco: Jossey-Bass, 2000).

Willingen, Germany, this was expressed as *missio Dei* — the idea that God is a missionary God.[27] The Father sends the Son, the Father and Son send the Spirit, and the Father, Son, and Spirit send the church into the world in mission. Thus mission is not a church-centered activity but rather a God-centered activity, the essential nature of the church itself.[28] Mission is *God's* initiative, in which the church participates. This missional ecclesiology was affirmed by Vatican II in *Ad Gentes:* "The church on earth is by its very nature missionary since, according to the plan of the Father, it has its origin in the mission of the Son and the Holy Spirit."[29] This is the global Christian consensus today, reflected in documents of the World Council of Churches, the Roman Catholic Church, and the evangelical Lausanne Committee for World Evangelization.

The polity of the Episcopal Church generally reflects the colonial, or Christendom-era, expansion paradigm of mission; but there is one interesting exception. While other American denominations were creating ancillary mission societies in the nineteenth century as parachurch organizations, in accordance with the view that mission was an activity done by specialists within the church and on behalf of the church, the Episcopal Church chose to go another route. Bishop Charles McIlvaine of Ohio anticipated the twentieth-century revolution in missional ecclesiology when he argued: "The Church is a Missionary Society, in its grand design, in the spirit and object of its Divine Founder."[30] The Domestic and Foreign Missionary Society, created in 1820 to support evangelism in the United States, became the official legal name of the denomination itself in 1835, so that "the Episcopal Church was itself a missionary society to which every Episcopalian by virtue of his or her baptism belonged."[31] To this day, the Domestic and Foreign Missionary Society remains the Episcopal Church's legal corporate name, registered in the state of New York.

A missional ecclesiology calls for rethinking many basic underlying assumptions about the church and its participation in God's mission. For

---

27. David Jacobus Bosch, *Transforming Mission: Paradigm Shifts in Theology of Mission* (Maryknoll, NY: Orbis Books, 1991), 390.

28. See Craig Van Gelder, *The Essence of the Church: A Community Created by the Spirit* (Grand Rapids: Baker, 2000).

29. Austin P. Flannery, ed., *Documents of Vatican II* (Grand Rapids: Eerdmans, 1975), 814.

30. Hein, *The Episcopalians,* 69.

31. Hein, 69.

one, the Christendom idea of domain, in which the church controls certain areas in order to provide sacramental service and pastoral care to settled Christian populations, collapses under the much more expansive horizon of God's mission to bring restoration to all creation. The church is turned inside out: instead of focusing inward and on tending to its members' needs, its purpose and primary activities are out in the world as it participates in God's redeeming work as a sign, foretaste, and instrument of the reign of God.[32] "Missionary" and nonmissionary territories, organizations, and roles can no longer be distinguished. *Everything* the church is and does must be missionary in character. In this light, North America is a mission field, just as the rest of the world is. It is a mission field not just in the sense that Christianity has lost its dominant influence and the gospel needs to be reintroduced, but also because all of God's creation is the field of God's redeeming activity, and the church is called to share in it. We can no longer portion off mission as a subordinate activity or program of the church. Mission is the very reason for the church's being and its lifeblood.

Episcopal Polity in Our Context: Foundations

In order to begin reframing the Episcopal Church's organization and governance in the twenty-first century to be in line with a missional ecclesiology, we must first delve more deeply into theological foundations. Modern Anglicanism in the West has been dominated by two primary theological strands. The first (and more influential in America) is liberal Catholicism, a marriage of broad and high-church concerns that emerged in the late nineteenth century. As articulated in such seminal texts as *Lux Mundi* (1889), a collection of essays edited by Charles Gore, liberal Catholicism asserts the underlying unity of the Catholic faith and modern experience, and it emphasizes the doctrine of the Incarnation.[33] R. David Cox has traced how the incarnational emphasis of liberal Catholicism led to a *representative* understanding of ordained office.[34]

A competing strand is Evangelicalism: its roots lie more in Reformed

32. See Guder, *Missional Church*, 102.
33. Sachs, *Transformation of Anglicanism*, 153.
34. Cox, *Priesthood in a New Millennium*, 32-34.

theology, and it tends to emphasize the doctrine of the atonement.[35] Evangelicalism tends to be far less sanguine about human nature and modernity than is liberal Catholicism. These two strands can at times make such differing assumptions about human nature and the church that it can be difficult to reconcile them. That difficulty accounts for much of the partisanship and conflict that have been part of Anglicanism over the past century.

Recently, however, a *koinonia* ecclesiology rooted in the doctrine of the Trinity has gained prominence in ecumenical circles and has entered Anglican theology.[36] It is reflected in the *Virginia Report* (1997) and the *Windsor Report* (2004), both produced by international Anglican Communion commissions.[37] Behind this ecclesiology lies the seminal influence of the Orthodox theologian John D. Zizioulas, an active participant in ecumenical dialogue over the past decades. His book *Being as Communion: Studies in Personhood and the Church* reconceptualizes human personhood and the nature and organization of the church through the doctrine of the Trinity, particularly as developed by the Cappadocians, emphasizing the social, perichoretic character of the Trinity as opposed to the economic emphasis typical in the West.

A *koinonia* ecclesiology is particularly fruitful today for several reasons. The first is that it encourages us to move beyond the individualistic conceptions of personhood that have so problematically shaped modernity in the West. A more relational, interdependent sense of the self, based in the social Trinity, better reflects the worldview and assumptions of the biblical and patristic sources that are so cherished by Anglican theology. It also invites us into a fresh imagination about human interdependence and communion across racial, tribal, socioeconomic, geographical, and cultural boundaries in an increasingly complex world. As the *Windsor Report* suggests, understanding the church and its diversity through the lens of *koinonia,* or communion, offers a rich theological framework for reconciled diversity in mission.

35. See Paul F. M. Zahl, *The Protestant Face of Anglicanism* (Grand Rapids: Eerdmans, 1998).

36. See World Council of Churches Commission on Faith and Order, *The Nature and Purpose of the Church: A Stage on the Way to a Common Statement,* Faith and Order Paper, No. 181 (Geneva: WCC/Faith and Order, 1998).

37. Inter-Anglican Theological and Doctrinal Commission, *The Virginia Report* (London: Anglican Consultative Council, 1997); Lambeth Commission on Communion, *The Windsor Report* (Harrisburg, PA: Morehouse, 2004).

Today these emergent *koinonia* and *missio Dei* ecclesiologies have generally been treated separately in theological discussions. Yet linking them provides a rich Trinitarian fabric for holistically reconceiving how the church's purpose is rooted in God's character as both a social and a sending God. It also presents an opportunity to reframe and enrich the theological debate within Anglicanism beyond the current polarities. An ecclesiology that emphasizes both communion and God's mission begins with the proposition that God creates the world out of the generative love of the Trinity for communion with Godself; it is through communion that God seeks to reconcile the world. The missionary character of God is evident through creation, the ministry of Christ, and the sending of the Spirit to lead the church in continued embodiment and proclamation of the reign of God. The content of salvation history cannot be understood apart from the communion that is constitutive of the divine life and thus of the church's essence and ministry. A missional *koinonia* ecclesiology sees communion as the destiny of creation toward which God is actively working.

Koinonia also presents a paradigm for understanding how the church's diverse structures, bodies, and offices can collaboratively serve God's mission, reflecting reconciled diversity aligned in service to the reign of God. As an overarching metaphor, *koinonia* offers a theological framework for integrating leadership and participation, unity and difference, catholicity and autonomy. Attending more explicitly to the theological foundations of Episcopal polity will strengthen the church's participation in God's mission and serve perhaps in some small way to correct the historic Anglican tendency to make organizational decisions based first on politics and then, if at all, on theology.

From Mission to Ministry to Organization to Office

Episcopal polity, as it has adapted itself to changing circumstances, has affirmed both continuities and discontinuities. So far in this essay I have emphasized the discontinuities, elements of Episcopal polity that date from contexts highly dissimilar to our own and thus warrant critical reflection. Yet there are also significant continuities, aspects of the current polity that remain pertinent and vital. It is my assumption, for instance, that democracy remains a relevant principle for our context and will continue to shape Episcopal polity significantly, just as it continues to shape American life today. Likewise, the historic Anglican balance between connectional unity and local autonomy, expressed in a variety of ways in the current governance of the Episcopal Church, is crucial to faithfulness to biblical and theological sources and to effectiveness in mission. I also assume the continuing historical validity and usefulness for mission of the fourfold understanding of office in the church — layperson, bishop, priest, and deacon — though I will offer a reenvisioning of those roles in light of a missional ecclesiology and fresh attention to the doctrine of the Trinity.

Given these assumptions, we must nonetheless begin with mission before proceeding to ministry, organization, and office; otherwise, we run the risk of limiting and inhibiting the church's participation in God's mission by the structures and roles we design or have inherited. *Mission-Shaped Church*, a recent document from the Church of England, puts it this way: "It is not the church of God that has a mission in the world, but the God of mission that has a church in the world. . . . God is on the move and the church is always catching up with him. We join his mission. We should not ask him to join ours."[38]

What, then, is the church's mission? A missional ecclesiology suggests that the mission of the church is fundamentally the *missio Dei*, the triune God's mission to reconcile and renew all creation. The Prayer Book says, "The mission of the church is to restore all people to unity with God and one another in Christ."[39] The church is created and called to continue Christ's ministry of announcing and embodying the reign of God in the power of the Holy Spirit, inviting and drawing all peoples and all things into communion with the Father.

This challenges us to attend to the role of the Holy Spirit, which has been significantly underemphasized in the modern era, just as the doctrine of the Trinity has been. The book of Acts and the New Testament Epistles repeatedly emphasize that the Holy Spirit, not human power, is the animating force in the life of the church. Modernity has tended to place its confidence in the latter, neglecting the Spirit's central role. When we consider the implications of this for polity, it is striking to observe that the Holy Spirit is structurally extraneous to current Episcopal polity: that is,

38. Church of England, *Mission-Shaped Church* (London: Church House Publishing, 2004), 85-86.

39. Episcopal Church, *The Book of Common Prayer* (New York: Church Hymnal Corporation and Seabury Press, 1979), 855.

the current polity makes no explicit recognition of the Spirit's governance of the church or provision for discerning the Spirit's leading. This is not to say that the polity prohibits the Spirit from acting; that would give our structures more power than they actually have. Rather, the Spirit is ancillary, optional, an add-on that may or may not play a role.

If the mission of the church is the mission of God and thus a given, how can we understand the *ministry* of the church? From the perspective of a missional ecclesiology, the ministry of the church is the service by which the church participates in God's mission in the world through practices that bear witness to the reign of God. Ministry takes place through four primary expressions of the church: the ministry of the laity in their daily vocations in the world, the ministry of congregations, the ministry of dioceses, and the ministry of the denomination. These four levels cannot be understood apart from one another; rather, they are interdependent and collaborative, mutually enriching, supporting, and enabling one another to fulfill the larger purpose of mission.

While the metaphor of the Trinity should not be pushed too far with respect to the church,[40] it is nonetheless possible to construe the cooperative participation of these four expressions of church as a kind of communion, or *koinonia*, in which distinct, interdependent entities in a common life characterized by generative love and service reach out for the sake of renewing the world. The church as the laity dispersed into the world on a daily basis is unified on the local level in the congregation, on the regional level by the diocese, and on the national level by the denomination. Symbolically, this logic can be applied to the Anglican Communion at the global level as well.

Liturgically, the dispersed members of the "Domestic and Foreign Missionary Society," or the assembly of called-out people *(ekklesia),* are gathered into an eschatological sign of unity in the weekly congregational Eucharist, where the local priest serves as an icon of unity in the liturgical narrative. This occurs on the regional level when the bishop, as representative of the catholicity of the universal church, celebrates the Eucharist, particularly at confirmations, ordinations, and diocesan convocations; and it occurs at the General Convention, similarly in the Eucharist, with the presiding bishop as icon of the unity of the denomination. Given the central-

---

40. On the limits of Trinitarian correlation, see Miroslav Volf, *After Our Likeness: The Church as the Image of the Trinity* (Grand Rapids: Eerdmans, 1998), 198-200.

ity of liturgy in shaping Anglican theology, it is vital to note that the *centripetal* movement of the liturgy, which culminates in the Eucharist, always shifts in the dismissal toward a corresponding *centrifugal* movement into the world.[41]

The Ministry of the Laity in the World

Historically, due to the legacy of Christendom, the ministry of the laity in the world has been accorded the least attention relative to the ministry of the clergy. In part, this is because of the Reformation tendency to define the church not according to the four marks of the Nicene Creed (one, holy, catholic, and apostolic), but rather as a *place* where certain things happen, generally performed by clergy (i.e., preaching, administration of sacraments, and, for the Reformed tradition, church discipline).[42] The Thirty-Nine Articles reflects this Reformation view when it defines the church as "a congregation of faithful men, in which the pure Word of God is preached, and the Sacraments . . . duly administered according to Christ's ordinance, in all those things that of necessity are requisite to the same."[43] As long as the focus remains on the *gathering* to the exclusion of the *sending*, the church will lose sight of its missionary character: it will lose sight of the fact that the frontline missionaries are not intended to be specialists sent overseas but rather ordinary Christians in their daily spheres of influence.

What would it mean for Episcopal polity to assert a priority on the ministry of the laity in the world as the *primary* expression of the ministry of the church? To begin with, the other expressions of ministry (congregations, dioceses, and denominations) would be invited to rediscover their purpose in supporting and equipping the laity for such service. Ephesians 4 speaks to this: "The gifts he gave were that some would be apostles, some prophets, some evangelists, some pastors and teachers, to equip the saints for the work of ministry." It is crucial to note in this Ephesians passage that such equipping is not merely a technical matter (done by professional church experts) but rather has a larger eschatological purpose: "[U]ntil all of us come to unity of the faith and knowledge of the Son of God, to matu-

---

41. See Bosch, *Transforming Mission*, 207.
42. Van Gelder, *Essence of the Church*, 54-56.
43. *Book of Common Prayer*, 871.

rity, to the measure of the full stature of Christ" (Eph. 4:11-13). The church is to grow into a fully mature likeness of Christ in its capacity to announce and embody the reign of God; no member can be omitted from this maturation process if the church is to be the church and represent faithfully the *koinonia* of the Trinity. Moreover, that process is mutual rather than one-directional: all members share in building one another up.

The Ministry of the Congregation

What is the ministry of congregations? Congregations are local expressions of the gathered church organized around core missional practices that enable all of their members to reach maturity in mission while at the same time serving as signs, foretastes, and instruments of the reign of God in their own right. These core missional practices include the classical activities of worship *(leiturgia)*, witness *(martyria)*, fellowship *(koinonia)*, service *(diakonia)*, and proclamation *(kerygma)*. One might also include stewardship. The congregation is a local manifestation of the reconciled diversity of the reign of God. It is rooted in and reflects the matrix of relationships, geography, local cultures, and other particularities of a place as a force for the transformation and renewal of those localities.

Unfortunately, Anglican ecclesiology has tended to downplay the centrality of congregations in favor of dioceses (and bishops). Yet one of the well-documented realities of the Episcopal Church today is a turn toward congregations: "At its grass roots level, Episcopal life has moved from preoccupation with the intricacies of denominational life toward a practical focus on local community and mission."[44] While it may be threatening to diocesan and denominational structures, this may actually be a helpful development.

The Ministry of the Diocese

Congregations are connected together into the *koinonia* of a diocese, itself a regional representation of reconciled diversity. Dioceses might more ap-

---

44. William L. Sachs, Thomas P. Holland, and Episcopal Church Foundation, *Restoring the Ties That Bind: The Grassroots Transformation of the Episcopal Church* (New York: Church Publishing, 2003), 8.

propriately be recast today, from the Christendom domains of hierarchical authority and regulation to apostolic *networks* that serve to support, equip, and unify local mission outposts. As an organizational paradigm, networks have increasing cultural relevance in our North American context. To begin with, the governing cultural metaphor for emerging postmodern generations is the internet, a highly decentralized network in which resources, information, and relationships are shared spontaneously and mutually around the world.

Networks have arisen in response to the dramatic increase in the pace of change in the global organizational environment in the twenty-first century. Networks facilitate rapid and continuous adaptation through multiple and dispersed information processing. As organizational scholar Mary Jo Hatch notes, "Relative independence of decision making allows experimentation and learning, and the product of this learning can be rapidly diffused through the network."[45] This fosters the creation and diffusion of innovations. There are two challenges inherent in network organizations that must be attended to. The first is that networks depend on teamwork and relationships that must be led, managed, and facilitated. The second is that the diversity fostered by networks requires the intentional cultivation and maintenance of a unifying identity.[46]

Just as beginning with the ministry of laity in the world as the primary expression of church shifts the emphasis from the hierarchy to the grass roots, so too does recasting dioceses as networks. The ministry of the diocese is to support, equip, and empower local congregations and their members for mission through missional practices. For dioceses, these missional practices include leadership recruitment and development, resource sharing, partnership facilitation, teaching/interpretive leadership, oversight and accountability, and the sacramental expressions of unity traditionally reserved for the episcopate (confirmation, ordination, the consecration of churches, and so on).

45. Mary Jo Hatch, *Organization Theory: Modern, Symbolic, and Postmodern Perspectives* (New York: Oxford University Press, 1997), 192.
46. Hatch, *Organization Theory*, 192.

The Ministry of the Denomination

Building on the overarching ecclesiological and organizational concepts of
koinonia and network, the denomination links dioceses, congregations,
and church members on the national level for mission. Currently, the
denominational-level structures in the Episcopal Church are facing an
even greater crisis of legitimacy than are diocesan structures.[47] The corporate emphasis that made so much sense fifty years ago seems increasingly
disconnected from the local realities of congregations and their members.
General Conventions since the 1960s have been occasions for bitter parti-
san battles, and this is a trend that shows no sign of diminishing.

Missiologists such as Lesslie Newbigin have argued vigorously
against the concept of denominationalism as a modern Western cultural
form that should be abandoned in a missional era.[48] Another stream of
scholarship has declared the continued relevance of denominations
through their role in identity development and cultivation.[49] Within a
missional ecclesiology in the U.S. context, it seems to me that there remains a valid, though reconfigured, role for the denomination. As a network organized around missional practices that support the ministries of
laypeople, congregations, and dioceses in the world, the denomination is
uniquely positioned to build theological identity, facilitate resource sharing, and link mission partners on a national and international scale. The
core practices of the denomination lie in identity development, resource
development and sharing, ecumenical relations for mission, global advocacy, and relief work. These activities are best organized not within one
massive central bureaucracy but rather through a network of linked organizations. This is currently the case with the Church Pension Group and
Episcopal Relief and Development, for instance, which are organizationally independent of the Domestic and Foreign Missionary Society, yet retain a strong denominational identity and purpose.

As in other denominations, identity development and clarification is
crucial for the Episcopal Church's survival today; and given worldwide An-

47. See Sachs and Holland, *Restoring the Ties That Bind.*

48. Newbigin, *Foolishness to the Greeks,* 144-45.

49. See Jackson W. Carroll and Wade Clark Roof, *Beyond Establishment: Protestant
Identity in a Post-Protestant Age* (Louisville: Westminster/John Knox Press, 1993); see also
David A. Roozen and James R. Nieman, *Church, Identity, and Change: Theology and Denom-
inational Structures in Unsettled Times* (Grand Rapids: Eerdmans, 2005).

glicanism's current identity crisis, this is particularly important. Within the Christendom context of England or colonial America, unity was sustained via establishment, the Book of Common Prayer, and the episcopate in a largely homogeneous cultural context. Within a plurality of cultures and languages, with an episcopate weakened by its own legitimacy crisis, and reflecting the divisive culture wars of American society, the Episcopal Church today must tend to theology. The lingering class elitism that would construe Episcopal identity around establishmentarianism is not only contradictory to the gospel and sinful; it is also less and less functional as the church ages.

This denomination, reconceptualized as a network of linked resources and institutions (including seminaries), has the potential to contribute significantly to mission in our context. But it must tend directly to the theological identity work the church has been so slow to embrace. Its purpose must derive directly from serving the mission of God through serving the ministries of the other expressions of church, rather than expecting congregations and dioceses to serve *its* purposes. Genuine responsiveness to the mission needs of the laity, congregations and dioceses would help the denomination deal with its legitimacy crisis and become relevant once more.

Recasting the Episcopal Church's various expressions as a Trinitarian *koinonia* of interdependent, mission-focused bodies who share resources and a common life would resolve the Christendom and bureaucratic legacy of conceiving the church's expressions as hierarchically ordered. As long as the church seeks to maintain the conception of the laity serving congregations, congregations serving dioceses, and dioceses serving the national church (in ascending levels of hierarchical importance and authority), the grass-roots revolt will only grow stronger and diocesan and denominational structures weaker. Reenvisioned in the image of the Trinity and networked in mission, these expressions of church could discover a fresh sense of unity and purpose in God rather than unraveling in internal conflict.

In this proposal of a paradigm shift from corporate hierarchy to Trinitarian network, there remains the question of accountability and power. On the one hand, corporate hierarchies carry risks of domination, privilege, and the concentration of power that flatter structures characterized by greater mutuality might avoid. On the other hand, Anglicanism has always cherished the principle of *good order* in its polity, worship, and life,

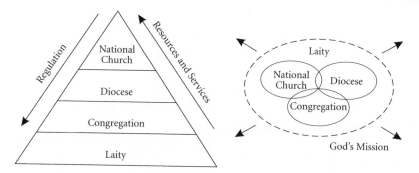

Christendom Bureaucratic Paradigm   Missional Koinonia Paradigm

and the reality of human sin (both personal and corporate) must be reckoned with. To use Avery Dulles's typologies, the Episcopal Church has tended to emphasize "church as institution" above other models of the church.[50] By suggesting a Trinitarian paradigm, I do not intend simply to swing to the opposite pole of "church as mystical communion" and reject the church's institutional character. Rethinking Episcopal polity along these lines involves a careful integration of spiritual and structural accountability with greater flexibility and freedom that would empower all members of the church (particularly those on the margins of the church's institutional life today) to participate and flourish in mission. The question is how the church's institutional life can best embody the character and life of God.

The Leadership of the Laity

A recent Episcopal Church Foundation study of leadership in the church discovered widespread "confusion about leadership roles" among laity and clergy.[51] The Catechism in the 1979 Book of Common Prayer lists the laity first among the ministers of the church; yet the laity too often seem to be at the sidelines, rather than the center, of the Episcopal Church's life and

---

50. Avery Dulles, S.J., *Models of the Church*, exp. ed. (New York: Image/Doubleday, 2002).

51. L. Ann Hallisey et al., "The Search for Coherence: Soundings on the State of Leadership among Episcopalians," available at http://www.episcopalfoundation.org/library/search%20%for%20%coherence (accessed July 31, 2008).

ministry. A missional ecclesiology calls for a rethinking of the leadership of the laity from complementing the rule of monarchical clergy to developing mission and ministry teams in the world. In Romans 12:8, *leadership* is listed among the spiritual gifts given by God to the members of the body of Christ. Throughout Anglican history, leadership has tended to be equated with office, primarily with respect to clergy, but also for the laity (i.e, "lay leaders" in the congregation are understood to be the vestry and perhaps some committee chairs). Understanding lay leadership as restricted to membership on the governing board or overseeing an internal committee fails to recognize the missionary nature of the church.

A missional polity encourages and equips those laypeople in the congregation who have the spiritual gift of leadership to lead teams in mission in the world. This might take a wide variety of forms, from short-term mission trips and partnerships to different kinds of entrepreneurial initiatives that seek to meet needs in the community. These mission teams are understood not to be extraordinary and occasional experiences in the life of the church and its members (as is the case presently), but rather to be ongoing, central dimensions of the church's life. The multiplication and growth of the church and its impact in the world require the multiplication and growth of lay leaders.

Presently, most laypeople in the Episcopal Church who have the spiritual gift of leadership exercise that gift to great effect in their daily jobs or through other community roles without necessarily being equipped to reflect on and align their leadership with the gospel and the reign of God. It is the church's responsibility to help them do so. Lay leadership must be understood not only as pertaining to explicit congregation- or diocesan-based mission initiatives, but also to the exercise of Christian leadership in whatever vocation and sphere of influence a leader may be placed. In this sense, the Catechism is more missional than the Canons when it says: "The ministry of lay persons is to represent Christ and his Church; to bear witness to him wherever they may be; and, according to the gifts given to them, to carry on Christ's work of reconciliation in the world. . . ."[52]

Laypeople have a crucial role to play in the governance of congregations, dioceses, and the denomination, but their leadership must be understood holistically and collaboratively. They are partners on an equal basis with clergy, and their sphere of influence must not be restricted to mere fi-

52. *Book of Common Prayer*, 855.

duciary oversight over the institution and its property. Like other leaders in the church, they have fiduciary responsibility for the *gospel* and the church's mission. Laypeople, whether serving on a congregational, diocesan, or denomination staff, or as elected representatives, must be equipped to exercise the spiritual leadership the church so desperately needs.

The Leadership of Bishops

The centrality of bishops to Anglican ecclesiology, while a given on one level, is also somewhat disputed. Historically, there has been a tendency among low-church, evangelical Anglicans to assert that bishops are of the *bene esse* (well-being) of the church.[53] On the other hand, high-church Anglicans have more typically emphasized that bishops are necessary *(esse)* for the church to be the church. In mission history, this first position played out in the practice of the Church Missionary Society, under the influence of Henry Venn, to see the raising up of indigenous bishops as one of the final stages of the missionary endeavor. However, Anglo-Catholics tended to begin with bishops in mission, as in the practice of sending missionary bishops across the American frontier.[54]

The three primary functions of bishops historically may be described as teaching, sending/developing leaders, and governance/oversight. While these are reflected in the Catechism's description of the ministry of a bishop, current realities are heavily weighted toward the governance/oversight function. While bishops in the Roman Catholic Church, for instance, have issued a series of significant teaching statements in the past decades that address various aspects of life in our context (social, ethical, economic, and so on), it has been argued that the House of Bishops, like the General Convention, generally does not speak coherently on matters of theology, ethics, and discipleship.[55]

53. See, for instance, Paul F. M. Zahl, "The Bishop-Led Church: The Episcopal or Anglican Polity Weighed, Affirmed and Defended," in Chad Brand and R. Stanton Norman, eds., *Perspectives on Church Government: Five Views of Church Polity* (Nashville: Broadman and Holman, 2004).

54. Titus Leonard Presler, *Horizons of Mission* (Cambridge, MA: Cowley Publications, 2001), 99.

55. See Timothy F. Sedgwick and Philip Turner, *The Crisis in Moral Teaching in the Episcopal Church* (Harrisburg, PA: Morehouse Publishing, 1992).

The role of bishops within a missional polity is crucial. Bishops in the Episcopal Church have the authority to lead system-wide change, creating what organizational scholar Ronald Heifetz calls a "holding environment" to facilitate adaptation on the part of members of the system to a changed context.[56] Within a missional polity, the episcopate must be shed of its regulatory, bureaucratic weight and freed up for a focus on mission. This means that dioceses should stop trying to safeguard or maintain institutional identity through regulation and control and instead focus on cultivating it through *interpretive leadership.*

Interpretive (or sense-making) leadership has its roots in the work of Philip Selznick in the 1950s: Selznick understood leadership as the definition and articulation of organizational identity and mission.[57] It has recently come into sharper focus within the field of organizational studies through such writers as Karl Weick.[58] The paradigm shift from a Newtonian cosmology, with its corresponding modernist bureaucracy, to a quantum cosmology has led organizational scholars to question the premises of command-and-control. Instead, attention has shifted to the leader's capacity to help others make meaning and define identity in a changing, adaptive environment.[59] Bishops would do well to reclaim their apostolic teaching role as interpretive leaders who help the church make sense out of its place in a postmodern world by linking the biblical narrative to the lives of church members today.

Bishops also should shift from seeing themselves as providers of pastoral care to the clergy *(pastor to the pastors)* to instead reclaiming more directly an apostolic leadership development role. The bishop can cultivate relational communities of leadership formation, creating a dialogue and learning space in which established and budding leaders can reflect together theologically and biblically on what God is doing in the world and how the church can align with it. There will always be a certain amount of

---

56. Ronald A. Heifetz, *Leadership without Easy Answers* (Cambridge, MA: Belknap Press of Harvard University Press, 1994), 104.

57. Philip Selznick, *Leadership in Administration: A Sociological Interpretation* (Evanston, IL: Row, 1957).

58. See Karl E. Weick, *Sensemaking in Organizations* (Thousand Oaks, CA: Sage Publications, 1995). For a recent exploration of the interpretive dimension of church leadership, see Scott Cormode, *Making Spiritual Sense* (Nashville: Abingdon, 2006).

59. See Margaret J. Wheatley, *Leadership and the New Science: Discovering Order in a Chaotic World,* 2nd ed. (San Francisco: Berrett-Koehler Publishers, 1999), 147-50.

administration that dioceses must engage in; however, bishops should to a great extent delegate this to competent administrators and focus instead on leading teams of missionary leaders.

This is where the complementary understandings of the social and sending Trinity offer a fruitful framework for reimagining the episcopate. On the one hand, the bishop's identity is defined relationally by her or his participation in the community *(koinonia)* that is the church, and particularly by collaboration with a team of leaders for mission in a particular area. On the other hand, the bishop's role is one of "sending" *(apostollein)* in mission. This Trinitarian conception provides for both leadership (teaching and sending) and partnership (sharing the work). It is a way of reconceptualizing the monarchical episcopate that moves the participation of others from mere democracy or counterbalancing authority to interdependent, collaborative partnership.

The Leadership of Priests

Currently, priests are still predominantly trained to be professional chaplains who cater to private spiritual needs. When they get into the parish, they find that they are also expected to be institutional managers, a role for which they are generally ill equipped. Both of these understandings of the presbyterate reflect deep Christendom assumptions: that the ministry of priests takes place largely in settled congregations whose greatest need is pastoral care, and that the church is primarily an institutional, nonprofit voluntary society that provides religious goods and services to its members and the community.

R. David Cox has described the prevailing view of the priesthood in Anglicanism as a *ministerial representative* model, tracing it back to the liberal Catholic Victorian theologian R. C. Moberly (1845-1903).[60] Working from an incarnational ecclesiology, Moberly understood the priest to represent the collective priesthood of all believers in a concentrated way: "to Godward for man, to manward for God."[61] Added to this is the ideal of service (ministry). It is noteworthy that the "representative" language appears in the Catechism of the 1979 *Book of Common Prayer* as the first function

60. Cox, *Priesthood in a New Millennium,* 33-70.
61. Cox, *Priesthood,* 60.

listed for *all orders of ministry.*[62] It is not restricted to priests. Moreover, service is characteristic of all disciples of Christ, who are encouraged to follow his kenotic (self-emptying) example by washing one another's feet (John 13). The concepts of representation and service fail to distinguish the presbyterate from the other orders of ministers in the church.

We might begin to reconceptualize the office of the presbyterate within a missional polity by focusing on the following three elements: *cultivating missional communities, interpretive leadership,* and *leadership multiplication/sending.* Rather than the presbyter merely sharing with the bishop in the governance of the church, she or he should also share in the bishop's apostolic function: teaching and sending leaders. One striking thing about the ministry of Jesus is the extent to which he focused on replicating his own leadership in a team of followers, whom he empowered with the Holy Spirit and sent to continue the announcement and embodiment of the reign of God that he began. The first apostles developed and multiplied subsequent generations of leaders in turn. In the case of priests in a missional twenty-first-century Episcopal Church, that leadership multiplication process is primarily focused on lay leaders to lead the mission and ministry teams, through which most of the congregation's service in the world is done.

The priest's particular role is to cultivate the gathered and dispersed community through teaching and interpretive leadership that opens up the biblical narrative to engagement by the missional imagination of all of God's people.[63] This narrative leadership role has three intersecting dimensions: a *modeling* role, in which the priest articulates the gospel story enfleshed in the particularity of her or his own life; a *pedagogical* role, in which the priest teaches and interprets the gospel story through Scripture and theology; and a *liturgical* role, in which the priest convenes and serves as the icon of unity within the sacramental telling of the story, and in which the various orders of ministry collaborate to enact together the Eucharist and other celebrations as eschatological signs of the reign of God.

Cultivating missional communities requires developing the capacity

62. *Book of Common Prayer,* 855-56.
63. See Mark Lau Branson, "Ecclesiology and Leadership for the Missional Church," in Craig Van Gelder, ed., *The Missional Church in Context: Helping Congregations Develop Contextual Ministry* (Grand Rapids: Eerdmans, 2007); see also Alan J. Roxburgh and Fred Romanuk, *The Missional Leader: Equipping Your Church to Reach a Changing World* (San Francisco: Jossey-Bass, 2006).

of God's people to discern vocation on the personal and corporate (congregational or mission-team) levels. This means facilitating dialogue spaces so that it places attentiveness to the Holy Spirit and the biblical Word at the forefront as people learn to listen to God and one another. A missional ecclesiology is by definition a *contextual* ecclesiology, and church members must be equipped to read their context. Local priests have important roles to play in convening such spaces and fostering such attentiveness.

The Leadership of Deacons

The Anglican Catechism describes the ministry of deacons as "to represent Christ and his Church, particularly as a servant of those in need; and to assist bishops and priests in the proclamation of the Gospel and the administration of the sacraments."[64] As in the "representative ministerial" conception of priesthood I referred to above, what is to distinguish the service of deacons from the missionary service of all of the church's members toward the needy? Even as it continues to be revived in the Episcopal Church today, the diaconate is ambiguous and calls for redefinition.

For most of Anglican history, the diaconate was a transition period immediately preceding ordination to the priesthood, a kind of apprentice priest role. This concept, retained from medieval Catholicism, is still part of current polity, as those called to the presbyterate must first be ordained deacons (and solemnly swear that they are called to the diaconate!) for at least six months before ordination to the priesthood. Deep behind this idea is the progressive concept of orders, which reflects the Roman imperial career track.[65] In the twentieth century, the diaconate has seen a revival as a permanent order within Roman Catholicism, Anglicanism, Lutheranism, and Methodism. In the Episcopal Church it has been construed primarily as an order dedicated to serving the needy in the community, typically in a nonstipendiary capacity under the oversight of the bishop.

Recent scholarship has called this concept of the diaconate deeply into question.[66] Within a missional polity, the diaconate takes on a differ-

---

64. *Book of Common Prayer*, 856.
65. Cox, *Priesthood*, 314.
66. See John N. Collins, *Diakonia: Re-Interpreting the Ancient Sources* (New York: Ox-

ent role from this prevalent (mis)conception of care-giving service. Indeed, serving the needy in the community is a ministry of the whole church, not just deacons; setting apart some congregants by way of ordination for the diaconate only feeds the distorted view that mission is an activity done by specialists. As John N. Collins has pointed out, the biblical and apostolic understanding of the diaconate was much more missionary in character than today's prevailing conceptions of it. The *diakonos* role was one of significance in that such men and women were entrusted with important communications and executive authority. In the New Testament context, this included the proclamation of the gospel. Later in the early church, deacons worked closely with bishops as administrators of ministry in large areas. In the third century, for instance, there were seven deacons responsible for overseeing the church's ministry in various parts of Rome, including the treasury.[67]

Within a twenty-first century missional polity, deacons in the Episcopal Church may be fruitfully understood as mobile leaders who initiate, lead, and facilitate the church's missionary witness in the world across congregational boundaries. As such, it is a highly entrepreneurial, connectional office that links ministry teams, congregations, community leaders, resources, and partners to participate in mission.

The ordination liturgy for deacons speaks to the interpretive character of diaconal leadership: "As a deacon in the Church . . . [y]ou are to make Christ and his redemptive love known, by your word and example, to those among whom you live, and work, and worship. You are to interpret to the Church the needs, concerns and hopes of the world."[68] Just as the bishop and priest exercise interpretive leadership overseeing the diocese and congregation, respectively, the deacon also assists members of congregations and the diocese to interpret the mission of God in their context. As emissaries of the bishop, deacons bear the sacred commission of the gospel across boundaries within the larger diocesan mission field,

---

ford University Press, 1990). Through an extensive word study, Collins demonstrates that the term *diakonos* referred in the New Testament context to an attendant, delegate, or emissary sent on a sacred commission. In contrast, the service of which *diakonia* is commonly understood to consist is more appropriate to a *doulos* (servant or slave). It was nineteenth-century German Pietism, not the New Testament, that defined *diakonia* as care-giving service.

67. John N. Collins, *Deacons and the Church: Making Connections between Old and New* (Harrisburg, PA: Morehouse Publishing, 2002), 116.

68. *Book of Common Prayer*, 543.

facilitating the development of mission and ministry initiatives that might involve members of multiple congregations. Theirs is primarily a *regional* (or cross-congregational) ministry, while the priest's is primarily a *local* (congregation-specific) ministry.

Rethinking Diocesan Conventions and General Convention

Outside of those who relish church politics, most Episcopalians approach diocesan conventions and General Convention with apprehension, for these gatherings are typically characterized by coalition politics, parliamentary maneuvering, and divisiveness. Within the structure of these gatherings, Bible study and theological reflection are typically subordinated to the central content — the legislative process. This approach to church assemblies reflects not only the downside of democratic rule, but also the assumptions of Christendom that legislative governance is the primary reason for the church's representatives to assemble on regional and national levels. Governance must take place, and policy must be made; yet the spirit with which it is undertaken should reflect a larger missionary purpose.

To begin with, we might reconceptualize such conventions as convocations of missionaries who gather first and foremost to cast vision, share best practices, and build one another up in ministry. In such a model, prayer, Bible study, and theological reflection would take center stage as the main event — with legislation relegated to the sidelines. This would begin to reshape the way the Holy Spirit is attended to in the councils of the church by placing discernment at the heart of things. Conferees could share stories of mission experiences that would spark the imagination of those present. Collaborative networking for mission partnerships would be a key feature of such events.

Conclusion: A True Domestic and Foreign Missionary Society

At its worst, Anglicanism's *via media* approach to ecclesiology leads to an undigested assortment of contradictory theological impulses that lacks clarity and cohesion. At its best, however, Anglicanism represents an integration of the richness of the wider Christian tradition: Protestant, Catholic, and Orthodox, as well as high, low, and broad church. A missional ecclesiology and polity would leverage that richness as a living sign of reconciled diversity, an expression of *koinonia* whose identity is grounded first and foremost in the triune God's mission to renew all creation. The ecumenical movement in the twentieth century petered out when it sought to discover its unity in shared doctrine and polity. Lowest-common-denominator statements such as *Baptism, Eucharist and Ministry* failed to do justice to the riches of any one tradition.[69] Perhaps the future of ecumenical cooperation lies not in doctrine or polity but rather in mission. The Episcopal Church, set within one of the most diverse and dynamic mission contexts in the world today, could contribute significantly to an emerging missional church in North America if it were to live more truly into the comprehensiveness it has historically claimed.

69. World Council of Churches, *Baptism, Eucharist and Ministry* (Geneva: World Council of Churches, 1982).

Appendix: Episcopal Church Membership Trends, 1930-2004

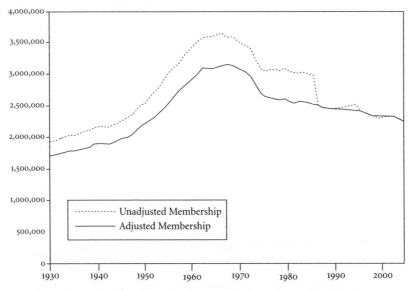

Episcopal Church Membership: 1930-2004

Unadjusted membership falls into line with adjusted membership in 1985, when non-domestic dioceses were removed and the definition of membership changed to include active members only.

CHAPTER 6

Missional DNA of the Evangelical
Lutheran Church in America

Daniel R. Anderson

Luther's Rose

Luther's Rose is an icon of Martin Luther's theology. He referred to it as his *compendium theologiae* ("summary of theology"), and it is a symbol of Lutheranism.[1] The Evangelical Lutheran Church in America (ELCA) is a hybrid rose formed from the DNA of earlier strands of Lutheranism but resulting in a new creation. The birth of the ELCA in 1988 was the result of a merger process that had begun in the mid-1970s. The hope and expectation throughout the process was that a *new* Lutheran church was being formed.[2]

The DNA of the ELCA can be traced directly to the work of Martin Luther and the sixteenth-century Reformation, which gave birth to the movement and its confessions. The reformers sought to reform the medieval Roman Catholic Church, but they were unable to alter the mutant DNA of practices and theology that they perceived to be errant. They soon found themselves to be part of new branches growing from the roots of Catholicism; those branches spread throughout northern Europe and by

1. See the appendix at the end of this chapter for Luther's explanation of the Rose.

2. Commission for a New Lutheran Church — CNLC, "Report and Recommendations of the Commission for a New Lutheran Church" (Evangelical Lutheran Church in America, 1986), viii. In 1982 the three predecessor bodies of the ELCA formed a "Commission for a New Lutheran Church for the purpose of planning, developing, and recommending to these churches and to the constituting convention of a church to be established all actions necessary for the formation of a *new Lutheran church* . . ." (italics added).

1620 had been transplanted to the New World. After being nourished in the soil of the European Renaissance, the Lutheran movement was further shaped by the rise of democracy and the formation of a new country, which would become the United States of America. Waves of immigration and a century of mergers eventually led to the formation in 1988 of the *new* Evangelical Lutheran Church in America, shaped most immediately by the DNA of the three predecessor denominations.

What sources of DNA produced this hybrid rose? What additional strands of DNA are necessary for the ELCA to be a *missional* church? This essay will explore the emerging DNA of a missional church movement, the DNA of the ELCA, and how they might be brought together to form a missional ELCA.[3]

Missional DNA

In all its expressions, the church is created and called to be *missional*. A missiological and ecclesiological shift occurred in the middle of the twentieth century: from "church with mission to missional church."[4] Missional church embodies a God-centered understanding of mission: mission is first of all the *missio Dei,* the mission of God. The missions of the church — *missiones ecclesiae* — are directly related to and dependent on the mission of God. The church is called to join God in God's mission in the world; therefore, the *missiones ecclesiae* can take on many contextual forms in service of God's mission.

The theological DNA of the missional church movement is Trinitarian. Classic Trinitarian views of God as a *sending* God (Western tradition)[5]

---

3. Ancient methods of hybridization, such as grafting, are biblical images. Genetic mapping and genetic engineering are twenty-first-century processes that elicit ethical questions and emotional responses. The language of DNA is being used in this paper as a metaphor for the level, kinds, and processes of change that are involved in becoming a missional church. The possibility of combining particular strands of DNA to achieve particular purposes raises ethical questions in bioengineering, but it is a helpful metaphor for our consideration of the introduction of missional DNA into existing church bodies.

4. Darrell L. Guder et al., *Missional Church: A Vision for the Sending of the Church in North America* (Grand Rapids: Eerdmans, 1998), 6.

5. David Jacobus Bosch, *Transforming Mission: Paradigm Shifts in Theology of Mission* (Maryknoll, NY: Orbis Books, 1991), 390. Bosch explains clearly the connection between the "sending" understanding of the Trinity and the sending of the church into the world.

and as a *relational* God (Eastern tradition of *perichoresis*)[6] have received renewed attention in recent decades. These views serve as the DNA of a missiological understanding of the Trinity and thus of a missiological understanding of the church, which is created by the Spirit — *imago Trinitatis* ("in the image of the Trinity").[7] The classic Western understanding of the Trinity is that God the Father sends the Son, and God the Father and the Son send the Spirit. The missiological move for the church is that God the Father, Son, and Holy Spirit send the church into the world. This sending of the church in mission is a necessary part of the DNA of a missional understanding of church.

The sending of the church in mission is biblically grounded. The Great Commission text of Matthew 28, where Jesus tells his disciples to "Go!" is clearly a *sending* text (Matt. 28:19-20). Jesus spoke of sending his disciples into the world of mission in his farewell prayer in the Gospel of John: "As you have sent me into the world, so I have sent them into the world" (John 17:18, NRSV). The biblical sending of the disciples is our sending as well. God's story of redemption and the doxological reconciliation of all creation in the already-not-yet reign of God are further biblical grounding in the nature and *telos* of God's mission.[8]

While the Western understanding of Trinity provides DNA for the sending of the church in mission, the Eastern understanding of Trinity provides DNA for the nature of that sending. The Eastern Orthodox understanding of Trinity focuses on the relational, perichoretic intersubjectivity of the Father, Son, and Holy Spirit. "*Perichoresis,* or interpenetration, among the persons of the Trinity reveals that 'the nature of God is communion.'"[9] The nature of that communion is *intersubjective*. The persons of the Trinity relate to one another "subject to subject." The intersubjectivity

6. Miroslav Volf, *After Our Likeness: The Church as the Image of the Trinity* (Grand Rapids: Eerdmans, 1998). John Zizioulas, *Being as Communion: Studies in Personhood and the Church* (Crestwood, NY: St. Vladimir's, 1985). Both Volf and Zizioulas deal with the relationship of the church and the perichoretic understanding of Trinity from perspectives of missiology and ecclesiology.

7. Leonardo Boff, *Trinity and Society* (Maryknoll, NY: Orbis Books, 1988), 11-13. Boff argues that not only the church but all of society should be created or modeled in the image of the Trinity.

8. Craig Van Gelder, *The Essence of the Church: A Community Created by the Spirit* (Grand Rapids: Baker, 2000), 73-74. Van Gelder develops this biblical, theological framework in his chapter "The Church and the Redemptive Reign of God."

9. Guder, *Missional Church,* 82.

of the perichoretic Trinity offers a model for the sending of the church in mission. The church is sent subject-to-subject rather than subject-to-object. Subject-to-object is an "I to it" relationship; subject-to-subject is an "I to I" relationship; perichoretic intersubjectivity is an "I to I within a we" relationship.

The proposition that the church is created *imago Trinitatis* includes both Trinitarian images: as sent and as perichoretic relationship with God and the world. *Perichoresis* tempers and qualifies the sending of the church. For example, missionary colonialism of the modern era imposed a cultural Christianity that reflected a view of those to whom the church was sent as "objects" of the church's missionary and evangelistic endeavors. Current understandings of intercultural missions speak of "partnering" with the other and recognizing the inherent translatability of the gospel into the context of receiving cultures. The DNA of being sent is subject-to-subject.

The procession of Father sends the Son sends the Spirit sends the church implies a hierarchy, or monarchy, of the Father that has been translated historically into a hierarchy of church structures and leadership.[10] The perichoretic understanding of Trinity counters that hierarchical view with a view of the persons of the Trinity in a differentiated, intersubjective relationship that is free from domination. Nonhierarchical models of leadership that are free from domination are a part of what it means for the church to be an icon of the Trinity in the world and have implications for the DNA of missional models of leadership.[11]

In summary, missional DNA is built on God's mission and the church's partnership in God's mission; missional DNA is Trinitarian and has to do with being sent into the world in perichoretic relationship with God, one another, and the world for the sake of the coming of God's reign. Missional DNA leads to action, and the horizon of such action is God's world.[12]

---

10. This phrasing of the processional formula is intentionally ambiguous. The Western tradition argues that Father and Son send the Spirit; the Eastern tradition argues that Father sends Son and Spirit. Biblically speaking, there are several permutations.

11. Jürgen Moltmann, "The Triune God: Rich in Relationships," *Living Pulpit* 8, no. 2 (1999): 5. Moltmann deals with the church as an icon of the Trinity and its implications for the church regarding hierarchy and domination in leadership.

12. Craig Van Gelder, "The Hermeneutics of Leading in Mission," *Journal of Religious Leadership* (2004): 15. Van Gelder proposes "biblically/theologically framed, theoretically informed, communally discerned strategic action" as a hermeneutic for engaging God's mission.

Historical DNA of the ELCA

With the nailing of Ninety-five Theses to the door of the church in Wittenberg on October 31, 1517, Martin Luther called into question the theology and practice of the Roman Catholic Church, particularly as it related to indulgences. Luther was declared guilty of high treason by the Catholic Church at the Diet of Worms in 1521 for refusing to recant his writings. Conflict and debate over the issues raised by the Reformers continued, ultimately culminating in a hearing called by Emperor Charles V at the Diet of Augsburg in 1530.

A Confessional Movement

The Augsburg Confession, written by lay theologian Philipp Melanchthon, summarized the theological and ecclesiological positions of the Lutheran reformers.[13] An initially conciliatory response to the Confession, as well as amiable dialogue, were unable to overcome the pressure from both sides to not make concessions. The Diet of Augsburg ultimately rejected the Augsburg Confession and called for the enforcement of the Edict of Worms of 1521, which had condemned Luther.[14] Decades of conflict and bloodshed ensued, until the schism between the Catholic Church and the Lutheran reformers was crystallized in the Peace of Augsburg in 1555. Lutheran and Catholic territorial rulers were recognized as heads of church and state: the understanding was that "whoever rules the region determines its religion" — *cuius regio, eius religio*.[15] Part of the early DNA of Lutheranism is found in this medieval concept of Christendom, the fusion of church and state.

Lutheranism took hold particularly in the northern and eastern parts of Germany, in the Scandinavian countries, and in pockets of northern and eastern Europe. Over the course of the next twenty-five years (1555-1580), the Lutheran confessions developed, partly as a response to the Catholic Church's Council of Trent (1545-1563) and partly in response to

13. The Augsburg Confession continues to be the basis of the confession of Lutheran churches. In many places around the world the Lutheran churches are called churches of the Augsburg Confession.

14. Eric W. Gritsch, *A History of Lutheranism* (Minneapolis: Fortress, 2002), 45-48.

15. Gritsch, 67.

intra-Lutheran controversies that emerged. The publication in 1580 of the Book of Concord (later subtitled "The Confessions of the Evangelical Lutheran Church") sought to create harmony among Lutheran churches through a common biblical/theological confession. Part of the original DNA of the Lutheran movement is that it is a *confessional* movement.

Orthodoxy and Pietism

Over the course of the next century (1580-1675) Lutheran confession evolved into orthodoxy, which emphasized right praise and right belief — that is, pure doctrine. German universities trained theologians and pastors in doctrine, and they, in turn, wrote systematic theologies. They made arguments for the truth of the Bible on the basis of *authenticity, sufficiency, efficacy,* and *inerrancy.*[16] The Bible came to be viewed as the book of divinely inspired truth, and Lutheranism became almost exclusively a religion of the mind. Lutheran orthodoxy became an enforced custom by 1700, and there was little or no emphasis on a spiritual life. The Lutheran church was in need of reform, and that reform came in the form of Pietism (1675-1817).

Pietism emphasized a religion of the heart over a religion of the mind. In the place of a legally enforced adherence to dogma, liturgy, and polity, Pietism called for a true commitment of the heart to the Word of God. And Pietism called for certain reforms: (a) a richer presence of the Word of God; (b) a revival of the common priesthood of all believers; (c) Christianity that consists more of practice than knowledge; (d) no unnecessary theological controversies; (e) a thorough reform of theological education; (f) simple and edifying preaching; and (g) gathering the pious into *ecclesiolae in ecclesia* ("little churches in the church").[17]

Pietism had its roots in the work of John Arndt (1555-1621), the author of *True Christianity,* Philip Jakob Spener (1635-1705), the author of *Pia Desideria* ("pious desires"), and August Herman Francke (1663-1727), founder of the Halle Foundation. Halle became a center for missionary

---

16. Gritsch, 140. Biblical inerrancy reemerged in the modern era as a response to empirical claims to truth made by science. Biblical truth was either substantiated from rational, critical processes of interpretation or claimed to be an inerrant foundation of truth. Conflicting understandings of the authority of Scripture continue to exist and are sources of doctrinal and ecclesial division within the church.

17. Gritsch, 144-45. Gritsch summarizes from Spener's *Pia Desideria.*

training, with a focus on foreign mission. One of Halle's graduates, Henry Melchior Muhlenberg, was sent to America in 1742 to "pacify and organize the quarreling Lutherans." He became the "church father" of Lutheranism in the United States.[18]

Lutheran orthodoxy (expressed as "confessional purity") and Pietism are both significant strands of Lutheran DNA, and their conflicting values continue to have a polarizing effect within the ELCA today. The managing of the tension in this polarity of orthodox confession and piety is a challenge for the identity and future of the ELCA.

Migration to the Colonies

Immigrants from the Netherlands and Sweden were the first Lutherans to settle in the New World by 1620. Then waves of immigrants came from predominantly Lutheran European strongholds, such as Germany and the Scandinavian countries. They moved from places of dominance as established state churches to the New World, where the separation of church and state was beginning to be practiced and where it would later be legally recognized in the First Amendment to the Constitution of the United States.

Lutherans were ethnic and religious minority groups in the New World. They continued to speak and worship in their native languages, they formed congregations, and they collectively formed ethnic/language-based synods.[19] Initially, worship resources and pastors were supplied from the Lutheran homelands in Europe. The need for English-language resources, catechisms, hymnals, and theological training emerged as second- and third-generation Lutherans in America made the transition to English as their primary language. Lutheran synods began working together to develop such resources. The *Common Service*, published in 1888, united many of the Lutheran synods in a common service of worship in English, and that liturgy became a source of cultural identity for Lutheran churches.[20]

---

18. Gritsch, 173.

19. The word *synod* means "the way together" or "on the road together." It is the term used to name the gathering of Lutheran congregations in relationship with one another. The term "synod" continues to be used in the polity of the ELCA.

20. The Lutheran Churches, *Service Book and Hymnal* (Minneapolis: Augsburg, 1958), vii. The move to a Common Service was a much-debated move away from diverse, indigenous-language, and culture-based forms of worship. The need for worship in English

Between 1840 and 1875, fifty-eight different Lutheran synods were formed in the United States.[21] The Lutheran church in this context was an immigrant church, as heavy immigration from traditionally Lutheran European nations continued through the first two decades of the twentieth century. Until the 1930s, a major focus of the mission of the Lutheran church in the United States was to "missionize and care for" the massive numbers of northern European immigrants.[22] These roots in ethnic immigrations are a part of the DNA of U.S. Lutheranism, and they have strongly influenced congregational traditions and practices.

The Development of Lutheranism in the United States

Two key figures in American Lutheranism were Henry M. Muhlenberg and Samuel S. Schmucker. Muhlenberg came as a missionary to Pennsylvania from Halle for the purpose of helping to organize the Lutherans. By 1748, Muhlenberg had organized the Ministerium of North America, which was the beginning of the organized church among the Lutherans. He spent much of his time in New York and Pennsylvania trying to establish peace between the "orthodoxists" and the Pietists.[23] Muhlenberg reported to Halle that accommodations to "American liberty" had been made in church governance.[24] Some parties in the churches insisted on selecting their own pastors, and members also insisted on the right to vote or have a hand in voting. This democratic influence continues to be a part of the DNA of the ELCA.

Samuel Schmucker (1799-1873) served as professor and founding president of the first Lutheran seminary in the United States, in Gettys-

---

and the desire for a shared Lutheran identity and witness eventually triumphed. In our time, diversity is returning to the worship life of the church, which reflects the Reformation principles of ceremonial freedom and putting worship in the language of the people.

21. ELCA, *Roots of the Evangelical Lutheran Church in America* (website of the Evangelical Lutheran Church in America, 2006. Available at http://www.elca.org/communications/roots.html (accessed Feb. 20, 2006).

22. Robert Benne, *The Paradoxical Vision: A Public Theology for the Twenty-First Century* (Minneapolis: Fortress, 1995), 105.

23. Eric W. Gritsch, *Fortress Introduction to Lutheranism* (Minneapolis: Fortress, 1994), 57.

24. Richard P. Cimino, *Lutherans Today: American Lutheran Identity in the Twenty-First Century* (Grand Rapids: Eerdmans, 2003), 6.

burg, Pennsylvania. Schmucker attempted to further Americanize — one might say "contextualize" — Lutheranism by teaching what he entitled "Popular Theology."[25] He offered a revised version of the Augsburg Confession, a version written from an American perspective. His proposal influenced pastors whom he educated at Gettysburg Seminary, but it was ultimately rejected.[26] American Lutheranism was embroiled in controversies and polarized by issues such as the American context and immigrant cultures, orthodoxy and Pietism, democracy and European models of church organization. Such polarities, along with their inherent tensions, continue to be a part of the DNA of the ELCA.

The Modern Influence

The nineteenth century saw the explosion of technological and scientific advances, industrialization, social and economic development including capitalism and free-market economies, and movements for civil and human rights. God was declared dead by Friedrich Nietzsche (1844-1900), the pope was declared infallible by the First Vatican Council (1870), and slaves were declared free by Abraham Lincoln's Emancipation Proclamation on January 1, 1863.

The nineteenth century was an era of diversification in global Lutheranism, which developed uniquely in different contexts. For example, Lutheranism was closely connected with the state in Scandinavian countries and Germany, but was separated from the state in America. A "neo-Lutheran" theology emerged in Germany, calling for a renewed commitment to Luther and the Lutheran Confessions. Alongside this confessional movement emerged a more pietistic "inner mission" movement, which focused on home mission: to love the neighbor and deal with social issues such as poverty and prison reform.[27] And Lutheranism spread around the world via foreign mission efforts.[28]

25. Gritsch, *Fortress Introduction*, 59.

26. Schmucker's proposal was too confessionally focused for the Pietists and too unorthodox a confession for the orthodoxists.

27. Such social issues are also biblical issues, and thus missional issues.

28. Gritsch, *History of Lutheranism*, 204-11. Foreign missions expanded to include the following countries: India, Indonesia, Australia, New Zealand, New Guinea, China, Hong Kong, Japan, Korea, Ethiopia, South Africa, Eritrea, Kenya, Madagascar, Tanzania, the Gold

Concerns for social welfare in the United States, with its fast-growing immigrant population and challenges of assimilation, brought about an *inner mission* movement that was modeled after the movement in Germany that was led by William A. Passavant. In 1849 it founded the first Protestant hospital in Pittsburgh, and it supported the institution of a deaconess movement sponsored by German Pietists.[29] Addressing these health and social service needs became another focus of mission for the Lutheran church in the United States,[30] and that DNA continues to thrive in the present-day Lutheran Services in America.[31]

Twentieth-Century Ecumenism, Theological Conversation, and Mergers

A longing for world peace and human unity arose after World War I, which was reflected in a desire for Christian unity. A growing ecumenical movement emerged, with organizations such as the World Alliance of Churches for Promoting International Friendship and events such as the Universal Conference of the Church of Christ on Life and Work (Stockholm, 1925) and the World Conference on Faith and Order (Lausanne, 1927; Edinburgh, 1937) seeking communion among church bodies. Nathan Söderblom, the Lutheran Bishop of Sweden, was a driving force behind these ecumenical efforts, and his work for ecumenism and world peace earned him the Nobel Prize for Peace in 1930.[32]

The Lutheran World Convention met in Eisenach in 1923, and that raised hopes for Lutheran unity. Put on hold by World War II, ecumenical efforts resumed following the war with the organization of the Lutheran World Federation (Lund, Sweden, 1947) and the World Council of

---

Coast, Israel, Jordan, Lebanon, Egypt, Iran, Syria, Turkey, Brazil, Puerto Rico, Virgin Islands, Guyana, Suriname, Peru, Argentina, Chile, Paraguay, and Uruguay.

29. Gritsch, *Fortress Introduction*, 61.

30. Benne, *The Paradoxical Vision*, 105.

31. Lutheran Services in America is jointly sponsored by the ELCA and the Lutheran Church–Missouri Synod. It is one of the largest social service organizations in America, with more than 300 organizations serving over six million people in the past year. Services range from healthcare, elder care, and hospice, to adoption services and refugee services, to care for mental health and counseling. Lutheran Services in America: www.lutheranservices.org.

32. Gritsch, *History of Lutheranism*, 221.

Churches (1948). In the second half of the twentieth century, the Lutheran World Federation engaged in bilateral ecumenical dialogues with the Roman Catholic, Reformed, Anglican, Orthodox, Baptist, Methodist, and other church bodies. This ecumenical impulse continues as part of the DNA of the ELCA, which has been a leader and catalyst of ecumenical dialogue from its inception.[33]

Significant theological and hermeneutical developments occurred in the twentieth century. Lutheran theologians such as Rudolf Bultmann (1884-1976), Gerhard Ebeling (1912-2001), Wolfhart Pannenberg (1928-), and others joined in rich theological dialogue and debate with scholars of all churches. Lutheran theology has been shaped and challenged by the resurgence of Trinitarian theology, along with the emergence of liberation, feminist, global, and contextual theologies. From the beginning, the Lutheran Reformation was an academic movement that was instigated by a professor at the University of Wittenberg. As a confessional church, it is part of the DNA of the Lutheran church to bring its theological and confessional voice to global conversations.

Numerous ethnic- and language-based Lutheran synods merged during the twentieth century. World War I instigated the formation of the National Lutheran Commission, as synods joined together out of concern for the spiritual well-being of U.S. military personnel being sent into combat. In 1918 the National Lutheran Council was formed as a coalition of Lutheran synods, partly for the benefit of military personnel but also to answer a growing need for domestic and international missionaries. Such inter-synodical cooperation contributed to mergers among Lutheran synods.

In 1960, the American Lutheran Church (German), United Evangelical Lutheran Church (Danish), and the Evangelical Lutheran Church (Norwegian) merged to form the American Lutheran Church (ALC); the Lutheran Free Church (Norwegian) joined them in 1963. In 1962, the

---

33. ELCA, "About the ELCA," Evangelical Lutheran Church in America, www.elca .org/about.html. The ELCA is in full communion with Lutheran World Federation, The Episcopal Church USA, The Moravian Church in America, Presbyterian Church (USA), Reformed Church in America, and the United Church of Christ. The ELCA is currently in ecumenical dialogues with the African Methodist Episcopal, Christian Church (Disciples of Christ), Mennonite, Orthodox, Roman Catholic, and United Methodist Churches. The Lutheran doctrine of "satis est" (Augsburg Confession, Article VII) makes such dialogues possible; the conviction of the Augsburg Confession that "one holy church is to continue forever" makes it necessary.

United Lutheran Church in America (German, Slovak, and Icelandic), the Augustana Evangelical Lutheran Church (Swedish), the Finnish Evangelical Lutheran Church, and the American Evangelical Lutheran Church (Danish) merged to form the Lutheran Church in America (LCA). An additional synod was formed in 1976 by moderate Lutherans who left the conservative Lutheran Church–Missouri Synod (LCMS) to form the Association of Evangelical Lutheran Churches (AELC). Those three synods (ALC, LCA, and AELC) began merger talks in the late 1970s that continued into the 1980s, with the formation of the Commission for a New Lutheran Church in 1982. This work was consummated in the formation of the Evangelical Lutheran Church in America (ELCA), effective January 1, 1988.

Biblical, creedal, confessional, and constitutional warrants drive the Lutheran desire for Christian unity expressed in mergers, full-communion relationships, ecumenical dialogues, and partnerships in mission.[34] There is "one flock, one shepherd" (John 10:16) and "one body" (Col. 3:15); there is "one holy, catholic and apostolic Church" (Nicene Creed). That "one holy Church is to continue for ever" (Augsburg Confession, Article VII). The ELCA is a part of "the one holy Church," and it uses those distinct designations throughout its constitution. The desire for the unity of the church is part of the DNA of the ELCA.

DNA of the AELC, ALC, and LCA

The ELCA is most directly formed from the combined DNA of the AELC, ALC, and LCA. The DNA of a hybrid will be unique and unlike any of its predecessors, yet it will bear recognizable strands of each. The merging church bodies held strands of DNA in common from their shared Lutheran history and heritage: each was a Lutheran rose, yet with its own unique characteristics and genetic map. These hybrid roses merged into a *new* Lutheran church, which drew its DNA — both weaknesses and strengths — from the roses that formed it.[35]

Soon after it had formed in 1976, after having split off from the Lu-

---

34. William G. Rusch and Evangelical Lutheran Church in America, *A Commentary On "Ecumenism: The Vision of the ELCA"* (Minneapolis: Augsburg, 1990), 17, 27.

35. Todd W. Nichol, *All These Lutherans: Three Paths toward a New Lutheran Church* (Minneapolis: Augsburg, 1986). Nichol is helpful in identifying the characteristics and unique identities of each of the predecessor bodies.

theran Church–Missouri Synod, the AELC, in its efforts to survive, invited the ALC and LCA to consider merger. The leadership of the ALC initially preferred cooperative ministry to merger; the LCA, on the other hand, was excited to consider merger for the sake of Christian unity and witness. Necessity, reticence, and excitement all influenced the merger process. While the church bodies shared a common confessional tradition, the issues of ecclesiology and polity emerged as differing strands of DNA that needed to be resolved.

The AELC had left the more conservative LCMS over three primary concerns: (1) the interpretation of Scripture; (2) the roles of women in church leadership; and (3) openness to ecumenical relationships. Regarding the interpretation of Scripture, the AELC rejected the position of inerrancy held by LCMS; it was open to the use of historical critical methods in biblical scholarship, which was also the position of the LCA. The inerrancy of Scripture was held as an official position of the ALC in its constitution; but not many of its clergy adhered to it, and many were willing and even eager to move beyond a position of inerrancy.[36] Regarding the roles of women in the church, all three merging bodies accepted women in leadership in the church, including their ordination as clergy. Regarding openness to ecumenism, the AELC rejected the sectarianism and closed communion of the LCMS as part of their reason for departure from that body; the ALC appreciated ecumenism but did not hold it as a focus of its mission; and the LCA valued ecumenism highly, and emphasized the universal church as part of its worldview.

Regarding their views of the nature of the church, the AELC, reflecting its heritage in the LCMS, had a congregationalist priority in its polity, as did the ALC. The ALC, centered in the upper Midwest, described its membership as "low church populists" with a high regard for lay leadership and a national church office that exercised only the power ceded to it by congregations.[37] Members of the ALC clergy were only allowed to be delegates to their annual synod assemblies if selected by their congregation as representatives. On the other hand, the LCA, centered in the eastern United States, understood congregations, synods, and the national church

36. Edgar R. Trexler, *Anatomy of a Merger: People, Dynamics, and Decisions That Shaped the ELCA* (Minneapolis: Augsburg, 1991). Trexler chronicled the merger as a journalist and editor of *The Lutheran* magazine throughout the merger process.
37. Trexler, *Anatomy*, 53.

to be interrelated; thus they held a high regard for the role of clergy. All clergy were automatically delegates to annual synod assemblies. Differing views of the nature of the church were resolved when the merging parties adopted the language of the LCA constitution concerning the interrelated nature of church as congregations, synods, and national body into the new constitution of the emerging ELCA, and by admitting all *active* clergy as voting delegates at synod assemblies.[38]

The Commission for a New Lutheran Church (CNLC) was finally able to reach consensus regarding issues of ecclesiology and polity, and this consensus agreement was approved by the three merging bodies in their constitutional conventions in 1987.[39] The ecclesiological differences that each church brought to the new church were celebrated as gifts: an emphasis on *congregations* from the ALC; an emphasis on the *universal church* and its worldview from the LCA; and an emphasis on *lay leadership* from the AELC.[40]

A churchwide organization and sixty-five newly formed synods immediately began to function under the new constitutions of the ELCA. But congregations were allowed to enter into the new church under their existing congregational constitutions. This process eased the transition of congregations into the new church, but it delayed the development of a new culture within the ELCA, because congregations continued to function within familiar patterns of DNA.

The ELCA at a Glance

As of 2006, the Evangelical Lutheran Church in America (ELCA) consisted of 4,930,429 baptized members, who were gathered in 10,585 congregations located in the United States, including Puerto Rico and the Virgin Islands. These congregations were organized into sixty-five synods clustered within nine geographic regions. Rostered leaders in the ELCA included 17,694 ordained clergy (3,140 female, 570 people of color), 1,249 Associates

38. Retired clergy and other clergy, such as those on leave from a call, have a voice but no vote in synod assemblies.

39. The CNLC was a seventy-member commission formed in 1982 to negotiate the merger of the three church bodies. The proportionate number of commission members was determined by quotas proportional to the membership of each church body.

40. Trexler, *Anatomy*, 245-46.

in Ministry (AIM), 98 diaconal ministers, and 65 deaconesses. Approximately 97 percent of the membership of the ELCA reflected its northern European immigrant ethnic heritage, though the denomination counted 146,785 "members of color."[41]

The population of the ELCA is heavily concentrated in the upper Midwest and the Northeast, but there are pockets of concentration in the Pacific Northwest, western California, and the gulf region of Texas and Florida.[42] Thirty-six languages other than English are used for worship in the ELCA. English is the primary language for worship in over 10,000 ELCA congregations.[43]

Forty-seven congregations of the ELCA have more than a thousand people in worship each week. Fewer than 500 people worship in 97 percent of ELCA congregations; fewer than 200 people worship in 80 percent of ELCA congregations; and fewer than 100 people worship on any given Sunday in 51.8 percent of ELCA congregations. More than 50 percent of ELCA congregations are in rural areas or small towns.[44]

DNA of the New Lutheran Church

The structural DNA of the ELCA, while rooted in the confessions, traditions, and structures of predecessor Lutheran bodies, reflects its late-twentieth-century context of formation. It is a young denomination: in 2008 it is just twenty years old as a new church. While there are inconsistencies between the intended formal structures of the ELCA and the actual practices of leadership and organization within the ELCA, the incongru-

41. ELCA, "ELCA Quick Facts," Evangelical Lutheran Church in America: http://www.elca.org/communication/quick.html. Statistics regarding the ELCA are from the ELCA website (accessed Oct. 14, 2006). Members of color include African-American/Black (54,241), Latino/Hispanic (38,255), Asian/Pacific Islander (22,395), Multiethnic (11,036), American Indian/Alaska Native (6,780), Arab/Middle Eastern (1,638), and other (12,440). The ELCA began with over five million members in 1988.

42. Department of Research and Evaluation ELCA, "ELCA Congregations in the United States" (2002). Areas of concentration beyond the upper Midwest and Northeast are popular retirement destinations for Lutherans from colder climates.

43. Research and Evaluation Unit ELCA, "Worship Languages of the ELCA" (ELCA, 2005).

44. Research and Evaluation Unit ELCA, "How Large Is Your Congregation Compared with All ELCA Congregations?" (ELCA, 2003).

ence is not because formal structures are out of date.[45] The ELCA lives the Reformation principle that "the church is always reforming" *(semper reformanda est ecclesiae)*. The initial formal structures of the ELCA were revised in churchwide assembly as soon as 1991, and then they were revised again by the 2005 churchwide assembly. Those formal structures offer DNA that is conducive to the formation of a missional church.

Confessional Unity/Identity

The common elements of a shared Confession of Faith and Statement of Purpose are intended to create unity and provide identity within the ELCA.[46] Those elements are required sections in the constitutions of congregations, synods, and the churchwide expression of the ELCA. "Beyond these common elements, congregations and synods shall be free to organize in such manners as each deems appropriate for its jurisdiction."[47] ELCA unity and identity are not found in its structure; rather, they are expressed in its flexibility of structure. H. George Anderson, former presiding bishop of the ELCA, notes that "we do have extraordinary fluidity because the ELCA is not riveted to one single form of governance."[48] This fluidity of structure is grounded confessionally in the concepts of *satis est* and *adiaphora*. Article VII of the Augsburg Confession says that "it is enough *(satis est)* for the true unity of the Christian church that there the Gospel is preached . . . and the sacraments are administered in conformity with the divine Word."[49] Everything else is *adiaphora* — "indifferent mat-

---

45. Executive Committee of the Church Council — ELCA, "Report for the Church Council on Governance" (Evangelical Lutheran Church in America, 2004), 2. A 2004 report from the executive committee of the ELCA Church Council stated that the ELCA "has not realized fully its potential for interdependent ministry . . . that was envisioned for it by the framers of this church." The areas of unrealized potential are significant for the future of the ELCA as a missional church.

46. ELCA, "Constitutions, Bylaws, and Continuing Resolutions of the Evangelical Lutheran Church in America" (Philadelphia: Augsburg Fortress, 1987), chaps. 2-4.

47. Ibid., 5.01.d. From a missional hermeneutic, the word "mission" would be more appropriate than "jurisdiction."

48. H. George Anderson, "Ecclesiology, Mission, and Structure," available at http://archives.ELCA.org/planning/ECCLESIOLOGY.pdf (accessed July 31, 2008).

49. Robert Kolb, Timothy J. Wengert, and Charles P. Arand, *The Book of Concord: The Confessions of the Evangelical Lutheran Church* (Minneapolis: Fortress, 2000), 42.

ters neither commanded nor forbidden by God . . . established only for good order and decorum."[50] Structure serves the gospel.[51] It is part of the immaturity of the ELCA that many of its congregations do not yet understand the flexibility of organization that is open to them to structure themselves for the sake of mission. A missional church needs to structure itself for mission, and ELCA churches are free to do so.

Interdependence: One Church in Three Expressions

The church is the people of God who gather in congregations that are a part of synods and unite in a churchwide organization for the sake of God's mission in the world. It is important to understand the ELCA as one church in three expressions: *congregations, synods,* and *churchwide.*[52]

Congregations and synods have great independence within a context of interdependence. Congregations and synods establish their own constitutions and select their own leadership within confessional parameters, which establish basic unity and identity. Expressions of church — congregation, synod, and churchwide — function as distinct yet interdependent partners within the ELCA that share in God's mission.

The tendency and common error is to see the congregation-synod-churchwide organizational structure as a hierarchy or form of bureaucracy. In such an institutional view, synod and churchwide offices exist to provide resources to congregations or to impose denominational control. Bishops and pastors serve as administrators and custodians.

There is an element of truth in that image because there is a constitutional differentiation of roles among the three expressions of church. Each is responsible for mission within its purview. Churchwide is responsible for

50. Kolb et al., *Book of Concord,* 515. From the Epitome, Article X: Ecclesiastical Practices. From a missional hermeneutic, *adiaphora* would be established for good order and decorum for the sake of God's mission.

51. E. Clifford Nelson, *The Lutherans in North America,* rev. ed. (Philadelphia: Fortress, 1980), 540. Nelson says that "central to Lutheran ecclesiology is the conviction that structure must always assume the form of a servant; any other form would be inappropriate to the gospel."

52. ELCA, "Constitutions, Bylaws, etc.," 1.01.01, 5.01.c available at http://archives .ELCA.org/secretary/constitutions/ConstitutionBylawsandContinuingResolutionsAugust 2007.pdf (accessed July31, 2008).

global ecumenical relationships, training and credentialing of clergy, seminaries, colleges, and universities, publishing, pensions, and other matters that are for the sake of the whole. Synods provide opportunities for congregational cooperation and networking in geographical areas. Bishops' offices of synods provide support to congregations and clergy. Through their benevolence congregations provide the financial resources that support the ministries of synods and the churchwide organization, while they are also on the frontlines of mission in their local communities. This differentiation of roles allows for the independence and interdependence of all three church expressions; yet each expression is conceived of as a church in mission.

Congregations are local expressions of the universal community of the church.[53] Synods are the people of God on the road together in mission as church in their larger community. The churchwide ELCA is nearly 5 million people of God united for the sake of God's mission in the world. Pastors and bishops are called to lead the church in mission. Each person who is a part of the ELCA is a part of each expression of church and shares in its mission. This as yet unrealized DNA of an interdependent church in three expressions holds great promise for the possibility of a missional ELCA.

Expanded Interdependence

The interdependence among congregations, synods, and churchwide was expanded to include global and ecumenical partners, institutions, and agencies in the 2005 restructuring of the churchwide organization of the ELCA. This expanded interdependence is to reflect "cooperation, coordination, and collaboration."[54] The ELCA is a part of the universal church. In restructuring, the ELCA expressed its interdependence with global expressions of church. Ecumenism is one example of this interdependence that is both a part of the historical DNA of the ELCA and has a constitutional mandate. This is essentially a commitment of congregations, synods, and churchwide to interdependent relationships with the larger church for the sake of Christian unity and mission.

53. Ibid., 3.02.
54. Mark Hanson, "*Faithful yet Changing:* Design for Mission through the Churchwide Organization of the Evangelical Lutheran Church in America" (Evangelical Lutheran Church in America, 2005), 4.

Quotas

The constitution of the ELCA reflects the political context of its formation in the late twentieth century. The civil rights movement and affirmative action initiatives were a part of the U.S. cultural and political landscape. Affirmative action in the form of quotas is a part of the ELCA constitutional polity. Synod assemblies and the churchwide assembly are the highest authority of governance in ELCA synods and the churchwide expression. "Assemblies, councils, committees, boards, and other organizational units" have three constitutional quotas to meet: 50 percent male, 50 percent female, at least 60 percent laypeople, and at least 10 percent people of color or those with a primary language other than English.[55]

These quotas, while cumbersome to fulfill and limited in their effectiveness as criteria for forming organizational units, reflect the values of the ELCA that are significant, and they have missional significance. The mandate for equal representation of males and females reflects the ELCA's confession of the equality of women and men as leaders in the church. The mandate that organizational units be at least 60 percent laity reflects a commitment to the priesthood of all believers and an attempt to limit the power of clericalism in the church. The mandate that at least 10 percent of organizational unit members be persons of color or with a primary language other than English reflects the goal of the ELCA to be inclusive and diverse.[56] Gender equality, prominence of the laity, inclusiveness, and diversity are important commitments on the part of the ELCA, and quotas are an attempt to alter the DNA of the ELCA in those directions.

55. ELCA, "Constitutions, Bylaws, etc.," 5.01f.
56. One might challenge the limitation of quotas to gender, clergy-laity, and racial-ethnic concerns and wonder about the representation of people with disabilities, GLBT, and other minority voices. Of course, one might also challenge the effectiveness of quotas and affirmative action to accomplish goals of inclusiveness and diversity. While 10 percent diversity does not reflect the demographics of the diversity of the nation, it is a significant stretch from the current ELCA demographic of a higher than 97 percent Anglo-American membership.

The ELCA as a Missional Church

> The Church is a people created by God in Christ, empowered by the Holy Spirit, called and sent to bear witness to God's creative, redeeming, and sanctifying activity in the world.[57]

Those are the opening words of the Statement of Purpose, which is included in all ELCA constitutions. The statement continues with these words: "To participate in God's mission, this church shall. . . ."[58] This is missional language that acknowledges God's activity in the world and acknowledges the church as a people of God called and sent to participate in God's mission.One might presume from this understanding of purpose that the ELCA and its congregations and synods could be offered as models of the missional church. Unfortunately, that is not the typical view of the Lutheran church (including the ELCA).

One explanation already offered for this difference between possibility and perception is that the ELCA has not yet grown into its potential. The budding rose of a new church has not yet fully bloomed. As a young church, perhaps it has not grown out of its familiar practices and into the missional potential of its intended constitutional form and confessions. While that explanation is most certainly true, it is not enough.

The ELCA Sidetracked

The immigrant history of the Lutheran Church in America, with the role of the church as a place of safety to gather with other familiar and similar faces, is still reflected in the ethnic and cultural traditions of Lutheranism in the United States. Furthermore, the experience of Christendom and the heritage of Lutheranism as an established state church set up the church primarily as a place for rites of passage (baptism, confirmation, weddings, and funerals), with little expectation of evangelistic outreach. This DNA of the Lutheran church from its ethnic/immigrant heritage and the era of Christendom tended to create a culture of inward focus. Many churches exist for the sake of their members — with the pastor serving as chaplain.

---

57. ELCA, "Constitutions, Bylaws, etc.," 4.01.
58. Ibid., 4.02. A list of six purposes follows this opening phrase, related to proclamation, evangelism, service, worship, nurture, and unity.

The "mission" in such cases is often to get, keep, or pay a pastor, maintain congregational culture and traditions, and survive as aging and declining congregations.[59] This inward focus and the struggle to survive have sidetracked many ELCA congregations from their missional potential.

Other ELCA congregations are sidetracked by alternative sources of DNA that displace the DNA of their own tradition. The rich theological, confessional, and ecclesial resources of Lutheran DNA that could be offered to the missional church conversation are notably absent or underdeveloped in many Lutheran congregations.[60] The lament that most people in the United States are biblically illiterate is common; however, it is also lamentable that most Lutherans are *confessionally* illiterate and are shaped by religious influences counter to their own confession and tradition.[61] Many Lutherans are unaware of the rich gifts their own tradition has to offer their journeys of faith — and those of their neighbors.

The concern that is raised is a daunting one for the ELCA. Mark Noll has articulated the issue in this way:

> Whether Lutherans are in a position to offer such gifts from their own tradition to Americans more generally would seem to depend on two matters: on how much genuine Lutheranism is left in American Lutheranism, and on whether Lutherans can bring this Lutheranism to bear.[62]

59. This is a form of Lutheranism that is well known in the mythical Lake Wobegon of Garrison Keillor. It is a Lutheranism of green Jell-O, tater-tot hotdish, potluck suppers, and lutefisk dinners. Ole and Lena have been faithful members since birth, cradle-to-grave Lutherans. "How many Lutherans does it take to change a light bulb? Change?" "WNDITWB — We've never done it that way before!" Stereotypes have power because they are caricatures of the truth. This is a caricature of Lutheranism that sells tickets in the theaters of the upper Midwest, but it sidetracks some congregations of the ELCA from fulfilling their missional potential.

60. Richard H. Bliese and Craig Van Gelder, *The Evangelizing Church: A Lutheran Contribution* (Minneapolis: Augsburg Fortress, 2005). Lutheran contributions with regard to evangelizing relate closely to Lutheran contributions to a missional hermeneutic and are the subject of *The Evangelizing Church.*

61. Kenneth Inskeep, "Religious Commitment in the Evangelical Lutheran Church in America: Findings from the *Faith Practices Survey,* 2001," 11, available at http://archive.ELCA.org/Research/reports/faithprac.pdf (accessed July 31, 2008). Diversity in Christian belief is *the* pattern of doctrine in the ELCA, which seems unfortunate for a church whose identity is confessionally based.

62. Quoted in Cimino, *Lutherans Today,* 21.

How much genuine Lutheranism is left in American Lutheranism? Lutheran churches have grafted in strands of DNA that are in competition with the DNA of genuine Lutheranism. Certain influences of U.S. religious movements have reshaped Lutheranism in their own images: evangelicalism, the church-growth movements of the late twentieth century, and programmatic approaches to ministry promulgated by megachurch teaching congregations with annual national conferences.[63] The best practices promoted by and gleaned from business and leadership literatures have been put to use in running, building, and *marketing* the church.[64] Churches have bought into the modern consumer-oriented missiology that seeks to meet the felt needs of people and that views them as "objects" rather than as active "subjects" of the church's mission. The church gets sidetracked by offering programmatic answers to missional questions. In the end, missional answers will be necessary to get the church on track.

Genuine Lutheranism in Mission

The initial mission of the Lutheran church was reform. Confession grew out of the process of reformation: confessions became formulated statements of faith, and confessing was the living proclamation of faith. *Reform* and *confession* are aspects of genuine Lutheranism.

Orthodoxy and orthopraxis have historically been at odds in the Lutheran tradition. But confession and piety — though they are polarities — are also elements of genuine Lutheranism's DNA, and it must hold them in creative tension and balance. There is an alternative to these conflicting polarities: they can be drawn together in mission as *confessional piety*.[65]

---

63. Music resources, programs such as *Purpose-Driven Life* and *Alpha,* and seeker-targeted models of ministry are often uncritically appropriated without a consideration of the theologies, ecclesiologies, and missiologies behind them.

64. Actually, this is true in only a small percentage of churches. Most congregations are far behind in the fields of organizational structure and leadership and could benefit from the exploration of current organizational theory and practice for the sake of mission. Congregations must think outside the boxes of model constitutions and bureaucracy. There is also a danger in taking these literatures uncritically. The church is not a business or for-profit organization. The Holy Spirit is not the driving force of corporate America or its organizational theory.

65. Patrick Keifert shared this concept as a "higher order of pietism," in which confes-

The content and practice of faith need not be at odds; they can support each other as critical aspects of a missional church.

The initial mission of the Lutheran church in the United States was to address the religious, cultural, and assimilation needs of Lutheran immigrants who gathered in ethnic- and language-based congregations and synods. The mission of welcoming immigrants to this land and into the community of God remains just as vital today, as new waves of immigrants continue to come from the far corners of the world. Because immigration has shifted from northern European Lutherans to peoples of diverse nations and faiths (primarily Asian, African, and Latin American), immigrant mission now means welcoming the stranger. Part of the *newness* intended in the formation of a "new" Lutheran church was the movement from a church of northern European ethnic identity to one of intentional diversity. Genuine Lutheranism will be culturally and ethnically *diverse.*[66]

The second thrust of the initial mission of the Lutheran church in the United States dealt with the social concerns that emerged in a developing nation. The foci of mission became social ministries and concerns of compassion and justice. *Compassion* and *justice* are concerns of genuine Lutheranism and are constitutional priorities of the ELCA.

A third thrust of the Lutheran mission in the United States is reflected in the twentieth-century emphasis on ecumenism. Unity of the church for the sake of the gospel continues to be a focus of the ELCA. Mergers and ecumenical dialogues, along with ongoing work in social ministries, has consumed much of the focus of the Lutheran church in the twentieth century. The Lutheran church has always been a church with mission — reform, confession, assimilation of immigrants, social concerns, and ecumenism. Those missions have revealed some of the DNA of genuine Lutheranism: reform, confession, piety, diversity, compassion, justice, and desire for the unity of the church. The mission of the ELCA in the twenty-first century is to make the move from a church with mission to a missional church.

---

sion is an act of piety: "You shall love the Lord your God with all your heart, and with all your soul, and with all your strength, and with all your mind" (Luke 10:27, NRSV). (The Congregation, Luther Seminary, October 10, 2006.)

66. Notice that genuine Lutheranism is not only about what Lutheranism was; it is also about what Lutheranism could be.

Genuine Lutheranism Meets Missional Church

A missional ELCA is a hybrid rose that has yet to be created. To combine the DNA of genuine Lutheranism and the DNA of missional church could create a rose worthy of a place in God's garden. Such an act of creation requires a *missional imagination.* The church-effectiveness movement invites congregations to look deeply and honestly into what is, to imagine what could be, and to do what is necessary to bring it about.[67] The missional church movement challenges churches to look deeply and honestly into what God is up to, to imagine how we might bring the best of our gifts to that mission, and to offer our lives and our church as a living sacrifice in that mission.[68] A missional imagination shifts the focus from building, maintaining, and strengthening the church to wondering how we can possibly keep up with God. In the Bible, disciples in mission were expected to travel light.[69]

A Missional Evangelical Lutheran Church in America

A missional ELCA is a missional people of God who gather in missional congregations that are a part of missional synods and unite in a missional churchwide organization for the sake of God's mission in the world.[70] Each is an expression of the church; each is related to the others in interdependent relationships.

Missional People of God

The church is composed of the people of God gathered in Word and sacrament and sent in mission. From a Lutheran theological and confessional

67. There are some excellent resources to help with this process, including Kennon Callahan's *Twelve Keys to an Effective Church* (New York: Harper & Row, 1983), and Christian A. Schwarz, *Natural Church Development* (St. Charles, IL: Churchsmart Resources, 1996). These are primarily resources for church improvement and technical change.

68. Romans 12:1-2 would suggest that God asks no less of us.

69. See Mark 6:6b-13 (the sending of the 12 disciples in mission) and Luke 10:1-12 (the sending of the 70 in mission).

70. *Missional church* is an ecclesiology (a way of understanding church) rather than a *polity* (a way of structuring church). This is a view of missional church from the perspective of a Lutheran ecclesiology of one church in three expressions.

perspective, people are created in the image of God (Gen. 1:31), and thus they are simultaneously saint and sinner — *simul justus et peccator*. Together with a theology of the cross, this combination helps keep humanity, sin, and the world in perspective. In baptism the people of God are called, ordained, and gifted for ministry in God's church and world. The people of God are part of the priesthood of all believers in doxological relationship with God. The people of God are members of the body of Christ, disciples of Jesus Christ, and apostles called by the Spirit and sent by the church in mission. Missional people of God live faithfully and missionally in the vocations to which they are called (family, work, community, church, and world), and they discern what God is up to and act accordingly.

The movement in recent decades has been to define the church from a congregational perspective. Many congregations have functioned as nonprofit corporations designed to offer religious goods and services to consumers and seekers who come to receive what they have to offer. In such churches, people are the objects of the church's ministry. On the other hand, missional people of God are the subjects of the church's mission: it is their responsibility and call to be the church, and it is the church's responsibility to equip and support them for their calling.[71] In the understanding of the ELCA, missional people of God are united in mission through congregations, synods, and as a churchwide organization; it is thus one church in three expressions formed by one missional people of God.

Missional Congregations

Congregations are an expression of the church.[72] Each congregation is a community of missional people of God gathered doxologically: that is, they are in communion with God and with one another, and are united in wor-

---

71. ELCA, "Constitutions, Bylaws, etc.," 7.11. "This church affirms the universal priesthood of all its baptized members. In its function and its structure this church commits itself to the equipping and supporting of all its members for their ministries in the world and in this church."

72. Ibid., 9.11. "A congregation is a community of baptized persons whose existence depends on the proclamation of the Gospel and the administration of the sacraments and whose purpose is to worship God, to nurture its members, and to reach out in witness and service to the world."

ship and mission. Worship expresses their relationship with God and one another; mission expresses their relationship with God and the world.[73]

Theologically — from a missional perspective — the church is created in the image of the Trinity *(imago Trinitatis)*. Missional churches understand themselves to be sent by the Spirit in mission as perichoretic communities of God's people. Confessionally — from a Lutheran perspective — the church is defined as the "assembly of all believers among whom the Gospel is purely preached and the holy sacraments are administered according to the Gospel."[74] Assembly. Word. Sacrament. One could note that mission is not explicit in this definition of church; yet the people who assemble are called and engaged in mission. The Word that is proclaimed, if it is the gospel purely preached, speaks God's story of redemptive mission and proclaims the coming of God's reign. The sacraments baptize into mission and give a foretaste of a feast to come, which is the eternal *telos* of God's mission.

The Lutheran confessional understanding of *satis est* defines the church from a perspective of Word and Sacrament and leaves all else to the discretion of the church for the sake of God's mission.[75] One of the most profound, yet unrealized, missional aspects of the polity of the ELCA is the opportunity for each congregation and synod to structure itself for mission in its context. Unfortunately, many congregations have functioned as 5.01.c.3 nonprofit organizations and as corporate institutions. Pastors and lay leaders have functioned as administrators and conservators of church budgets and property. Pastoral care has become the mission of the church rather than a way of serving the church in mission. Congregations have adopted an attitude of *congregationalism* rather than living in interdependent relationships with other expressions of the church.

One of Luther's definitions of sin is being turned in on oneself *(incurvatus in se)*. A missional imagination can move congregations beyond themselves and into God's mission. Missional congregations seek to know what God is up to in their context and join God in that mission. Pastoral care and equipping the saints for mission happen en route.[76]

---

73. Romans 12:1-2; Amos 5:21-24. From a biblical perspective, worship and mission seem to be interdependent: both are doxological (give glory to God).

74. Kolb, Wengert, and Arand, *The Book of Concord: The Confessions of the Evangelical Lutheran Church*, 42.

75. Augsburg Confession, Article VII. "It is enough. . . ."

76. Eph. 4:11-13 reminds us of the church's role in equipping the saints for ministry. Public school teacher in-service training or military boot camp may be metaphors or mod-

Missional Synods

Missional people of God gather in missional congregations that are a part
of missional synods. Synods are an expression of the church, and they draw
missional congregations into God's mission together. Defining synods as
church and not primarily as judicatories is unique to Lutheran polity: the
synod is a church, and the bishop is the pastor and the missional leader of a
synodical church. There are certainly administrative and support aspects of
establishing and structuring a synod. But the more important work from a
missional perspective would be for the synod to discern God's common
mission for its congregations. The synod unites congregations in mission
for purposes greater than what can be accomplished by individual congregations.[77] Missional synods function as church and not primarily as governing bodies, and the effectiveness of the synod as an expression of church
depends on its ability to involve and unite congregations in mission. Synods
in the ELCA have no authority to force such involvement.

A missional imagination is necessary. Just as missional people are responsible to gather and be church together, missional congregations are
responsible to unite and be church together as synods. It is the role of synodical leaders to inspire such a missional imagination within their congregations. Constitutionally, the roles assigned to synods are a mixture of
oversight and mission.[78] It is the role of the synod to provide congregations with resources that are beyond the scope of any one congregation.
Synods engage in ecumenical conversations with other churches, assist in
developing new ministries, provide discipline for congregations and leaders as required, and put congregations into network with each other for
the purpose of mission. It is all done for the sake of mission.

However, it is not uncommon for synod staff members to get bogged
down in administration or to become burned out in their attempts to put

els for equipping the saints and Christian education or discipleship. They serve a greater
purpose and are not ends in themselves.

77. St. Paul Area Synod ELCA, "Three-Fold Vision," www.spas-elca.org/aboutsynod/
threefoldvision.htm. The threefold vision of the St. Paul Area Synod is an example of a
synod reaching out in mission. The vision includes training 10,000 leaders for mission, inviting every person within the synod to hear the story of Jesus, and ensuring that no one
within the synod will be forced to live in poverty. The synod is structured around this vision.

78. ELCA, "Constitutions, Bylaws, etc.," 10.21. The constitution gives each synod "primary responsibility for the oversight of the life and mission of the church in its territory."

out the fires of congregational conflict. It can also be tempting to define the ministry of a synod by the work of its staff rather than by the common efforts of congregations who form it and the people who form them. A synod could function as a collaborative of congregations together discerning what God is up to in their synod and together joining God in mission.

Connecting congregations in mission is a constitutional expectation of synods. Current ELCA polity encourages clusters of local congregations to gather — either geographically or around mission objectives. Non-geographic synods also exist within the ELCA and serve as another model of congregational collaboration. Synods are organized into nine regions for the sake of synodical collaboration in mission. It is exciting to imagine missional people of God and their congregations collaborating in mission in their larger area of ministry. Synodical staffs can function as missional leaders to facilitate that collaboration. And the Lutheran polity of one church in three expressions encourages that possibility.

Missional Churchwide Expression of Church

Missional people of God also unite in a missional churchwide expression of church for the sake of God's mission in the world. The ELCA is one church of nearly 5 million people of God united in God's mission.[79] The churchwide organization of the ELCA engages the world in mission on a scale that is not possible for congregations or synods to accomplish. While there is certainly a significant need for administration and coordination of an organization that includes 65 synods, over 10,000 congregations, and nearly 5 million members, the purpose of the churchwide organization is to lead and support this church in mission. The missional power of a churchwide organization comes from engaging and leading millions of people in mission.[80] The ELCA unites its regions, synods, and congrega-

79. Ibid., 11.11. "The churchwide organization shall serve on behalf of and in support of this church's members, congregations, and synods in proclaiming the Gospel, reaching out in witness and service both globally and throughout the territory of this church, nurturing the members of this church in the daily life of faith, and manifesting the unity of this church with the whole Church of Jesus Christ."

80. Prior to the U.S. invasion of Iraq after 9/11, the presiding bishop of the ELCA joined other denominational leaders in a statement that decried the proposed invasion as an unjust act of war. Their voices were not heeded by the U.S. administration. Unfortunately,

tions of missional people of God in mission, in dialogical communion with the global church, and in missional imagination.

Missional Leadership

A missional church in all of its expressions must have missional leadership, and missional leaders must have a missional imagination. There is no missional church without a missional imagination, which discerns what God is up to in the world, imagines possible ways to be involved in that mission, and invites people to take action. Missional leaders invite, encourage, equip, guide, and partner with others in discerning God's mission. People with missional imagination are called, ordained, gifted, and sent as leaders in service to God's mission.[81] Pastors and church staffs with missional imagination lead and equip God's missional people to discern and engage God's mission in the world. Bishops and synod staffs with missional imagination facilitate the collaboration of God's missional people and congregations in discerning God's mission in the world and their collective engagement with that mission. Churchwide staff with missional imagination lead God's missional people to join God in mission as a collective voice for the gospel in the world. The ELCA is one church in three expressions; missional leadership filled with missional imagination inspired by the Holy Spirit will be necessary to bring the church to life as a missional Evangelical Lutheran Church in America.

Luther's Rose

Martin Luther exhibited missional impulses. He had strong convictions about what God was up to in the world and committed his life to serving that mission. He imagined a church of people gathered in the presence of

the "official" position of the ELCA was not communicated well to its membership, and the collective political and prophetic voices of 5 million people were not heard. Missional leadership not only speaks for a people but leads them in speaking in the face of difficult political circumstances. Power is not found in speaking for others but in giving others voice to speak.

81. Such missional leadership may be expressed in the home, at work, through church, and in the community or in the world.

God's Word and the sacraments. He imagined a baptized people of God, a priesthood of believers rooted in day-to-day vocations, and a people serving God through their gifts. He imagined families and friends gathered in homes to study God's Word and to share in the sacraments.[82] He imagined the people of God reading the Bible and gathered to worship God in their own languages.

Luther's missional imagination discerned the mission of God in his context, and that inspired him and others to action. It is because of the implicitly missional character of Luther's theology and ecclesiology that his legacy lives on today. However, Luther could never have imagined the twenty-first-century world that the church bearing his name would inhabit. Yet there is much in the DNA of genuine Lutheranism that speaks to this twenty-first-century context. There are rich theological, confessional, and ecclesiological resources to draw on as the ELCA finds its way in this new century. It is the challenge and responsibility of the missional ELCA people of God who are to engage genuine Lutheran DNA with the emerging DNA of the missional church conversation for the sake of God's mission in the world, and to invite the church into that mission. It is a missional imagination that creates the possibility of a *new* Lutheran church that is truly missional and thus genuinely Lutheran.

---

82. Ulrich S. Leupold and Helmut T. Lehmann, eds., *Luther's Works: Liturgy and Hymns*, vol. 53 (Philadelphia: Fortress, 1965), 63-64.

Appendix: Luther's Explanation of the Rose

"Grace and peace from the Lord. As you desire to know whether my
painted seal, which you sent to me, has hit the mark, I shall answer most
amiably and tell you my original thoughts and reason about why my seal
is a symbol of my theology. The first should be a black cross in a heart,
which retains its natural color, so that I myself would be reminded that
faith in the Crucified saves us. 'For one who believes from the heart will
be justified' (Rom. 10:10). Although it is indeed a black cross, which mor-
tifies and which should also cause pain, it leaves the heart in its natural
color. It does not corrupt nature, that is, it does not kill but keeps alive.
'The just shall live by faith' (Rom. 1:17), but by faith in the crucified. Such
a heart should stand in the middle of a white rose, to show that faith
gives joy, comfort, and peace. In other words, it places the believer into a
white, joyous rose, for this faith does not give peace and joy like the
world gives (John 14:27). That is why the rose should be white and not
red, for white is the color of the spirits and the angels (cf. Matt. 28:3;
John 20:12). Such a rose should stand in a sky-blue field, symbolizing
that such joy in spirit and faith is a beginning of the heavenly future joy,
which begins already, but is grasped in hope, not yet revealed. And
around this field is a golden ring, symbolizing that such blessedness in
Heaven lasts forever and has no end. Such blessedness is exquisite, beyond all joy and goods, just as gold is the most valuable, most precious
and best metal. This is my *compendium theologiae* [summary of theol-
ogy]. I have wanted to show it to you in good friendship, hoping for your

appreciation. May Christ, our beloved Lord, be with your spirit until the life hereafter. Amen."[83]

---

83. Martin Luther, *Letter to Lazarus Spengler*, July 8, 1530, in Amy Marga, trans., "Luthers Siegel: Eine elementare Deutung seiner Theologie," *Luther* 67 (1996): 66-87. Translation printed in *Lutheran Quarterly* 14, no. 4 (Winter 2000): 409-10.

CHAPTER 7

Missional Ordered Ministry in the Evangelical Covenant Church: Moving Toward Apostolic Imagination

Kyle J. A. Small

Introduction

Three ministry staff members from the congregation where I serve were registered into the Evangelical Covenant Church's ministerial system, known as the Board of Ordered Ministry.[1] As an associate pastor, I was ordained to Word and Sacrament; at the same time, our youth pastor was licensed for pastoral office; and our children's minister had been commissioned some time before. A gracious member of our church asked our youth pastor what the difference between these titles meant and how they relate to the nature and mission of the church. These questions sent our youth pastor and me on a journey looking for answers to the distinctions. We spoke with other church leaders, our denominational headquarters, and friends in our respective seminaries. We did not receive a substantive explanation for the legitimation of the complex ministerial registration system.

Alan Roxburgh discusses the role of legitimation emerging from a narrative that involves "an explanatory framework" that connects with the group's understanding of community life.[2] We did not have an overarching narrative to explain the credentialing process, and the aforementioned

---

1. From here on I will refer to the Evangelical Covenant Church as "the Covenant" or "the ECC."

2. See Alan Roxburgh's essay, chap. 3 above.

questioner did not have a sense that the process lent itself to the group's basic understanding of life.

I write as a missiologist concerned with the life of a local congregation as sign, instrument, and foretaste of the kingdom of God to a watching and spiritually interested world. I seek to engage the identity of Covenant leadership through its historical, theological, and structural influences. Since the Covenant rests between several levels of polarity, categorizing everything to the satisfaction of everyone is impossible, as has been demonstrated throughout Covenant history. Nonetheless, in this essay I seek to take seriously the more free-church identity of the mission society history of the Covenant and its laity beginnings. I will also seek to address its structural development and focus on local congregations in order to reframe an understanding of the polity of Ordered Ministry through a missional imagination. My intention is to uphold both the free-church ideals and the Lutheran theological tradition that have formed and shaped the Covenant.[3]

In this chapter I want to revisit a conversation on the polity of Ordered Ministry in the Evangelical Covenant Church with a view toward considering the life of leadership as necessary for the theological identity of the church. The engagement within this chapter is between the 2002 revision of the Rules for Ordered Ministry and the missional church conversation.[4] In 2002, the Rules for Ordered Ministry were revised to update the polity in light of the denomination's constitutional revisions of 2000. The Rules sought to connect theological commitments with an organizational structure. Call and gift, education, inclusivity, the changing needs of the church, and a desire to be flexible guided the revisions.[5] The missional

3. Without rehearsing a detailed historical relationship, this tension is best illustrated between two Covenant fathers, Karl Johann Nyvall and Paul Peter Waldenstrom. See David Nyvall, *My Father's Testament: A Biography of the Preacher and Free Church Man, Karl Johann Nyvall* (Chicago: Covenant Publications, 1974).

4. Two documents are at work here: the first is the denomination's Constitution, and the second is the Rules for Ordered Ministry. Hereafter, I will refer to these documents as "the Constitution" and "the Rules," respectively. When I refer to "the Preambles," I will be specific about the document in which a specific preamble belongs.

5. David Kersten and Carol Lawson, *Looking Ahead with Promise: A New and Improved Version of the Rules for the Ordered Ministry* (Power Point Presentation [Chicago: Department of Ordered Ministry, 2002]). The purpose for revising the rules was as follows: "We are called to prepare the church for a new generation of gifted and Godly leaders. These new rules seek to open the door widely to empower them to serve while maintaining the high standards that have always been a part of the Evangelical Covenant Church."

church conversation argues that theology should drive the structural realities of denominations and local congregations, and that, considering the realities of North American culture, flexibility, reflection, and innovation are essential. This conversation does not begin at ground zero. Rather, it seeks to take the revision's intentions, as well as the Covenant's historical and theological commitments, into account as it reviews the Rules through a missional lens.

The Birth of the Evangelical Covenant Church in America

The Covenant is a vibrant and growing denomination of over 765 churches and 165,977 attendees, of whom over half are new to the church in the last ten years.[6] The denominational hub is located on the north side of Chicago.[7] Historically, the Evangelical Covenant Church began in 1885 and emerged out of Swedish Pietism, European immigration, and the mission-society and free-church movements in the United States. Theologically, the Covenant does not share a confession or creed: Scripture alone is its common concern. However, the Covenant does nurture an identity with respect to six affirmations.[8]

The roots of the Covenant Church go back to a gathering of Swedish immigrant leaders and delegates from both American Free and Lutheran churches in Chicago in 1885, where the following question was under discussion: Is it right that Christian congregations join together in work for the Kingdom of God, and on what basis can such a union oc-

6. The Covenant has been planting thirteen churches per year, seeing an increase in attendance (over 60 percent between 1995-2006), celebrating new life in Christ (conversion), and experiencing a surge of multiethnic congregations (currently more than 20 percent of the membership is non-Anglo). Most of the growth is occurring in new church starts, and the Covenant shares with other denominations in grieving the closing of historic, established congregations (21 congregations in the last two years).

7. The hub includes the denominational offices, Swedish Covenant Hospital, Covenant Retirement Communities headquarters, North Park University, and North Park Theological Seminary (the Covenant's only seminary).

8. The six affirmations are: the centrality of the Word of God; the necessity of the new birth; a commitment to the whole mission of the church; the church as a fellowship of believers; a conscious dependence on the Holy Spirit; and the reality of freedom in Christ. Philip Anderson et al., *Covenant Affirmations* available at: http://www.covchurch.org/cov/resources/affirmation.pdf (accessed Dec. 13, 2005).

cur?[9] The answer was a resounding "yes," and the Swedish Evangelical Mission Covenant in America was born in a joyful and pietistic spirit.[10] Within the first days of the gathering, pietistic emotion infused the minutes of the church, and the Mission Friends' identity emerged collectively with heartfelt appreciation. Those at that meeting fervently discussed whether it was right to join in union, and the Covenant was born as a voluntary association of local congregations based on free-church ecclesiology and the work of mission societies.[11]

Covenant became the essential term for understanding the life of the church: it was not construed in a Reformed, Calvinistic, or Puritan sense,[12] but was thought of as "a binding together of those who shared one common experience of regeneration and new life through faith in the crucified and risen Jesus."[13] "Covenant" was not a denominational name; rather, "it was intended in some sense to mean its opposite — that is fellowship, gathering, a joining of hands . . . something relational, functional, and dynamic."[14] Hospitality and embrace continually guide the Covenant's fellowship and mission.

9. Glenn P. Anderson, ed., *Covenant Roots: Sources and Affirmations,* 2nd ed. (Chicago: Covenant Press, 1999), 7.

10. G. Anderson, *Covenant Roots,* 11. The minutes read: "It was a blessed time. The faces of all those present shone with joy and satisfaction. The chairman of the afternoon's meeting led in prayer to God and with his whole heart called down his blessing on this action. In the eye of one and another a tear appeared to glimmer, but it was not sorrow's or melancholy's tear, but a tear of joy."

11. *Covenant Roots,* 10. The rationale was biblical, relational, and emotional: first, God's Word encourages it; second, union and harmony are the nature of the Christian life, both individually and collectively; and third, experience conveys its benefit. Anderson, *Covenant Roots,* 9. Acts 15, 2 Cor. 8, Eph. 4:1-16, and Rom. 12:4-5 served as clarifying texts for unity.

12. See Sydney E. Ahlstrom, *A Religious History of the American People,* 2nd ed. (New Haven: Yale University Press, 2004), 130-32.

13. Karl A. Olsson, *A Family of Faith; 90 Years of Covenant History,* Ninetieth Anniversary Heritage Series (Chicago: Covenant Press, 1975), 3.

14. Karl A. Olsson, *By One Spirit* (Chicago: Covenant Press, 1962). The opening sermon for the new church was from Psalm 90: "I am a companion of all who fear thee."

Ardor and Order in Tension: The Constitution of the Evangelical Covenant Church

Covenant order was originally constructed out of the ardor of the church. The zeal for home missions determined union, and the mission-society model formed communities of spiritual ardor that determined the early structure of the church.[15] Initially, the structures were minimal in order to "not be constitutive."[16] This ability to encourage order with freedom (ardor) is the Covenant's defense against dissolution.[17] Philip J. Anderson, historian of the Covenant, has noted elsewhere that the balance between ardor and order is necessary for the continuation of a relational Covenant polity.[18] Considering the missional possibilities, that polity may serve as the fulcrum for balancing ardor and order.

Dealing with polity can be precarious. Issues of Covenant polity have been hotly contested throughout the church's history, which, as Philip Anderson notes, "shows the inner identity of the Covenant as a group of believers united for the purpose of mission, which is manifest in an ongoing tension between spirit and structure, ardor and order."[19] The minimal structure of the Covenant allows that this tension not be forced onto the church, but allows the freedom to be debated, discerned, and acted on. The expectation is that the continuance of a minimal structure will allow the Covenant's ethos to succeed with future generations. In this chapter I will attempt to continue this debate and indicate the need for continuous discernment.

The most recent revision of the Rules for Ordered Ministry sought to clarify and simplify the former fragmented structure. It has potentially

15. G. Anderson, *Covenant Roots*, 171-72. "It is only the great zeal for world and home missions, so characteristic of our people, which has brought local congregations to feel the need for union. Thus the Covenant is not a churchly organization in the ordinary sense of the word but a voluntary union for common and general missionary purposes too great and extensive for the local congregations. Thus, from that viewpoint, the Covenant is simply a missionary society, but a missionary society with the uniqueness that it does not consist of individual members but of congregations and societies."

16. Olsson, *By One Spirit*, 323.

17. *By One Spirit*, 325.

18. Philip Anderson, "The Community of Friends in Christ: Order and the Evangelical Covenant Church," in James R. Hawkinson and Robert K. Johnston, eds., *Servant Leadership: Authority and Governance in the Evangelical Church*, vol. 1 (Chicago: Covenant Press, 1993).

19. Hawkinson and Johnston, *Servant Leadership*, vol. 1, 107.

created a more linear, hierarchical structure that, in fact, limits the very flexibility that it sought to construct; and it may complicate the historic principle of balancing ardor and order. The initial pages of the Official Documents of the Covenant convey the richness of the history, commitments, and mission of this immigrant mission-society-turned-denomination. However, this ardor seems to diminish in the Rules: centralized hierarchy and bureaucratic structures govern credentialed church leadership. For example, the Rules state: "The ECC recognizes its responsibility . . . to exercise support of and discipline *over* [ministers]."[20]

That document, when it uses "over," not "for" or "with," expresses a greater sense of hierarchy and command-and-control, which tends to assume discipline as a mark of ministry. The Covenant's relational, functional, and dynamic ardor of *with* and *for* one another begins to weaken when the Rules take jurisdiction *over* the local congregation.[21] American values, Christendom and Reformation structures, former models of organizational management, as well as bureaucratic (and traditional) authority, have co-opted many denominational polities, largely because of unnamed contextual forces. The Covenant's rules are not immune to these influences.

The Evangelical Covenant has always celebrated its history, and it has used the church's capacity to organize its government around its theological heritage. This calls for a polity that is relational (Incarnation and Trinity) and dynamic (pneumatology). Methodologically, the Covenant has faithfully engaged its freedom in biblical interpretation to question its polity.[22] Practically, the Covenant has celebrated a flexible identity to match

20. "Rules for Ordered Ministry," in Covenant External Orientation Program, *Reader: The Ordered Ministry of the Evangelical Covenant Church* (Chicago: Covenant Press, 2004), 44-45. Elsewhere in the polity, the document states that the Board of Ordered Ministry has the function of "general *supervision* over all ordained ministers, commissioned ministers, licensed ministers, and consecrated missionaries of the ECC, including . . . standing, *discipline, and the maintenance of high standards* in their ministry" (italics added).

21. One contextual reality is that the rules were revised during a time when pastors within the denomination were engaged in moral and ethical cases of discipline. I have often wondered how much the number of discipline cases during this time influenced the revision of the rules.

22. "What kind of church government we would want might be something upon which we are far from unanimous. . . . The need for order is not native. It is a need not inherited but acquired. . . . Without government no congregation of people can exist for any length of time. And further, in selecting a form of government, consideration must be given

the order of the church to the ardor of its theology. However, its theological identity has often been developed separate from the organizational identity of the church. Until the unnamed contextual forces are unmasked, the theological identity of the Covenant will continue to be largely absent from the structural documents of the denomination.

Framing Unity: Historical, Theological, and Structural Influences on the Polity of the Evangelical Covenant Church

Unity is so essential to the Mission Friends that preserving it will be its greatest gift as well as its greatest task. Therefore, being a free association of churches committed to freedom, common mission, and fellowship requires a form of government that promises unity for existence. This framework of unity and free association has emerged out of four major historical streams of influence, six theological commitments, and a dialectical view toward structure.

Historical

The four historical influences that the Covenant sought in order to establish unity were American democracy, the mission-society model, Swedish Pietism, and immigrant identity. Adopting democracy, first of all, with its emphasis on personal choice and free association, was necessary for legitimation in nineteenth-century America. Democracy also served as a natural partner for the Mission Friends through its connection with Pietism.[23] What emerged was a uniquely structured free-church government that located authority in the democratic Annual Meeting.[24] The Annual Meeting is the voice of delegates from local congregations: here there is majority rule with minority voice. The church grants authority to the Executive Board when the Annual Meeting is not in session. Democratic in ideals,

---

not only to what is best, but also to what is possible. . . ." Scott E. Erickson, *David Nyvall and the Shape of an Immigrant Church: Ethnic, Denominational, and Educational Priorities among Swedes in America* (Uppsala: Uppsala University, 1996), 228.

23. Dale W. Brown, *Understanding Pietism* (Grand Rapids: Eerdmans, 1978), 58-60.
24. Olsson, *By One Spirit,* 366ff., 60.

this body elects leaders; those leaders, in turn, garner power by centralizing authority and maintaining loyalty.[25]

Second, the Mission Friends in Sweden were Lutheran by birth yet Pietist by influence. As Pietism migrated north from Germany to Sweden, Lutherans were influenced by the Pietist principles explained in Spener's *Pia Desideria,* the social activism of Francke, and a healthy dose of joyful personal conversion as found in Zinzendorf.[26] The Lutherans outside the movement called the Pietists *läsare,* or "the Readers"; however, those participating in the Pietist movement referred to themselves as "Mission Friends."[27]

The Mission Friends were a lay movement that sought to reform the Lutheran church from the inside.[28] However, due to the Lutheran maltreatment, the Mission Friends slowly erected Mission Houses for Christian fellowship and edification. Similar to Luther's vision of a third devotional service,[29] Mission Friends gathered for prayer, song, and lay preaching, and within this emphasis was a commitment to both relational evangelism and social action.[30]

Historical Pietism, in its positive sense, contributed to a missional Ordered Ministry with its transference of spiritual authority from the clergy to the laity.[31] As Pietism emerged out of the German Lutheran Church, the authority embedded in Word and Sacrament was transferred to the laity. One can readily see how Pietism was a threat to establishment, order, and a formalized clergy. In rejecting the earlier clerical tradition, Pietism apparently also had a creative strain that did not simply reject structures of clerical leadership but reconfigured an authority for Ordered

25. Erickson, *David Nyvall,* 173.

26. Olsson, *By One Spirit,* 7-34; Brown, *Understanding Pietism,* 9-34.

27. G. Anderson, ed., *Covenant Roots,* 64. Others leading the work in Sweden included Methodist George Scott and Lutheran Carl Olaf Rosenius. Later, Paul Peter Waldenstrom, a biblical scholar, would lead the Mission Friends.

28. Erickson, *David Nyvall,* 140.

29. Ulrich S. Leupold and Helmut T. Lehmann, eds., *Liturgy and Hymns,* vol. 53, *Luther's Works* (Philadelphia: Fortress, 1965), 63-64.

30. Burton F. Nelson, "Pietist Heritage and Social Concerns," *Covenant Quarterly* 28, no. 1 (1970). The issue of social concern in Pietism emerges out of an eschatological hope for the world. Though some of the particular strains of eschatology need critique, the view toward the world is a helpful understanding in engaging Pietism and missional ecclesiology. See Brown, *Understanding Pietism,* 28.

31. Olsson, *By One Spirit,* 13.

Ministry, albeit for similar means (persons in leadership) and different ends (the gospel in the world).[32]

Third, the Covenant borrowed extensively from the mission-society model.[33] Prior to its formal organization, participation in local mission societies emerged alongside attendance at local Lutheran churches. Early mission meetings captured the mission-society spirit of relational and ethnic bonds for missionary endeavors, to reach both fellow immigrants and "the heathen."[34] These mission meetings consisted of lay preaching, discussion, and fellowship.[35]

The significant activity of the early mission meeting, with its pietistic spirit, was the service of the Lord's Table. Here, the Mission Friends broke with traditional church practice: laymen, on behalf of the society, served communion to all who walked in faith with Christ.[36] The passion of the Mission Friends emerged under the Mission Society, which was led by laypeople. Here is where the history of mission societies can be reclaimed in order to push the church to consider new narratives and metaphors for

32. In addition, the potential reading of a marriage between mission societies and Pietism, even with its quirks and connection to modernity, offers much to the identity of pastoral leadership and Ordered Ministry. It potentially transforms the work of leadership from pious isolation within the congregation to seeing the larger vision of God's reconciling relationship with the world.

33. Mission societies made a significant dent in traditional church order: unlike clergy-centered Protestant churches, "the voluntary associations were not restricted to ecclesiastics. . . . The voluntary society subverted the old Church structures: it altered their power base." Andrew F. Walls, *The Missionary Movement in Christian History: Studies in the Transmission of Faith* (Maryknoll, NY: Orbis Books, 1996), 249. Episcopal, Presbyterian, and Congregational polities were attacked by this anti-institutional, anticlerical movement. Walls notes that a new form of polity emerged that would alter all other polities from then on (p. 2). Mission societies were a lay movement: the Spirit of God had touched the uneducated, the young, and women, as well as the professional classes. This has significant theological implications that have the potential to reshape ordination and leadership understandings in churches that can borrow historically from Pietism and mission societies (Walls, 250).

34. Olsson, *By One Spirit*, 215. The mission meetings were "a meeting for the purpose of seeking to achieve a closer bond of union and a more intimate association for the promotion of missionary endeavor among our countrymen in America as well as among the heathen who do not know God. We like to believe that many share our conviction that such an association is needed."

35. Walls, *Missionary Movement*, 221-23. Discussion was of a practical and devotional nature; fellowship was friendship for the wayward traveler.

36. *Missionary Movement*, 226.

the Ordered Ministry. This has been pushed to some degree in the development of the Lay Minister's License.[37] The influence of nontraditional structures within the traditions of Christian practice lends itself to reclaiming the identity of the priesthood, and it lends itself to innovative models of formal leadership.

The history of the Mission Society offers much to the identity of pastoral leadership and Ordered Ministry. The deep passion of mission societies to transform the world, both at home and abroad, cannot be relinquished, though they do need to be critiqued. Constructively reclaiming the Mission Society model has the possibility of transforming the work of leadership from pious and professional isolation within the congregation to seeing the larger vision of God's reconciling relationship with the world to which congregations serve as a sign, instrument, and foretaste of God's good news.

Fourth, the Swedish immigrant status has been and continues to be a defining characteristic of the Covenant Church. Through nineteenth-century waves of immigration, the need for cultural preservation, and the valuing of ethnic bonds, the Covenant has enjoyed a long history of Swedish connection.[38] On the other hand, the Covenant's *immigrant* identity is now in transition due to its growth among new (i.e., non-Swedish) immigrant groups. The Covenant currently plants thirteen new churches every year, and when the leaders of these new churches attend the Annual Meeting, they bear little resemblance to the Swedish Covenant forebears. But they do share a connection to the immigrant story and the deep pietistic spirit of evangelism and social justice necessary for missional congregations today. This immigrant identity has superceded the specifically Swedish identity of an earlier time. Self-identifying as an immigrant is enough for relating to one another. In this way the Covenant has embraced not only the Swedish immigrant story but also the biblical immigrant story: "My father was a wandering Aramean . . ." (Deut. 26:5-9). Embracing identity without boundaries is the power of the biblical sojourner, or what Andrew Walls calls the "pilgrim principle."[39] Relating to this pilgrim principle calls forth leadership identity that questions indigenous influences,

---

37. "Rules for Ordered Ministry," 56; see Section 9.6.

38. Some churches, especially in the Midwest, continue to celebrate such Swedish events as Smorgasbord and Santa Lucia.

39. Walls, *Missionary Movement*, 9.

including those influences that limit the empowerment of calling and gifts. The immigrant identity should challenge current models as well as initiate new models for leadership and Ordered Ministry.

Congregational Identity: Free-Church Mind vs. State-Church Mind

What Craig Van Gelder describes as churches on the left and right,[40] the Covenant has described in state-church/free-church categories.[41] Unlike its Evangelical Free brothers and sisters, the Covenant made room for both the free-church mind and the state-church mind. The Mission Friends organized with a *congregational* identity locally and a more *presbyterian* identity nationally. However, "free church" does not necessarily mean apart from or opposed to the "state church." Instead, the Covenant has defined "free church" to mean "conversion, new life, experience, and freedom. The State Church mind tends to stress the confirmation of faith, the rational, and conformity."[42] The free-church mind was more or less a stream that emphasized revival, whereas the state-church mind was more like a stream that emphasized tradition.[43] Embracing both the free-church and state-church mindsets helps locate the Covenant as being both local in ministry and universal in history.[44] The categories of Ordered Ministry can be robust enough to continue to cultivate credentialed leaders who are able to live into the inherited faith of the church as well as lead local congregations into new territories of conversion[45] and ministry.[46]

---

40. See Craig Van Gelder's essay, chap. 1 above.

41. G. Anderson, *Covenant Roots*, 148-67; see also Erickson, *David Nyvall*, 223-33.

42. *Covenant Roots*, 178.

43. Erickson, *David Nyvall*, 228-29.

44. David Nyvall proposed the image of a sail and anchor. When the sail begins to blow too radically in one direction, the alternative voice can serve as an anchor. If the wind shifts, then the others drop the anchor. Though helpful to combat both fundamentalist and liberal movements, what does this image say about the Spirit blowing where it wills?

45. Darrell L. Guder, *The Continuing Conversion of the Church* (Grand Rapids: Eerdmans, 2000).

46. Stephen B. Bevans and Roger Schroeder, *Constants in Context: A Theology of Mission for Today* (Maryknoll, NY: Orbis Books, 2004). Bevans and Schroeder's conception of prophetic dialogue serves as a helpful tool in identifying the ministry of the church.

Theological Commitments

The theological unity of the Covenant Church rests in its inaugural meeting, where there was a calling from God that the church strands join together for purposes of worship, education, fellowship, and mission. As the denomination's Preamble notes, the Covenant church is a "communion of congregations."[47] The purpose of this union is obedience to the Great Commandment and Great Commission. For the Covenant, collaboration between local congregations is the means through which the church fulfills its purpose.

State vs. free church, Pietism vs. Reformation, infant baptism vs. believer baptism — these are the strains that exemplify the Covenant's paradoxical theological roots. On one hand, the Covenant has emerged Lutheran in its theology by upholding a thick commitment to the priesthood of all believers and to a doctrine of grace most notable in the affirmation and practice of infant baptism. On the other hand, the Covenant has celebrated its identity as a free, believers' church, congregational polity, and personal salvation, most notable in affirming the practice of believer's baptism.[48] This two-sided understanding is not wishy-washy; rather, it is necessary for the unity that is central to Covenant identity. Theologically, the Covenant has decided that minor issues will not divide the common mission of the church.

Second, the Covenant Church does not hold to a common creed; instead, it holds Scripture as primary, yet without being Biblicist.[49] The Covenant is continually committed to pious devotional reading and to critical

47. P. Anderson, *Covenant Affirmations.*

48. In the pursuit of unity, Covenant pastors are required to sign a statement agreeing to the practice of both infant and believer baptism. In signing, one agrees to the following: (1) While Covenant pastors may, and must, hold their own convictions concerning baptism, they must guard against presenting their own view in such a way as to disparage the other. (2) A Covenant pastor must be willing to administer both infant baptism and believer baptism. (3) A Covenant pastor must protect the right of the minority or majority (whatever its persuasion) to full participation and expression within the life of the church, always within the limits set by Holy Scripture and the principle of Christian freedom. (4) A Covenant pastor has the responsibility to exercise pastoral discernment in individual cases. The full policy can be found at: http://www.covchurch.org/cov/resources/ordered-ministry/baptism-in-the-evangelical-covenant-church.

49. The catechetical statement for the Covenant is that "the Holy Scriptures, both the Old and New Testament, is the Word of God, and the only perfect rule for faith, doctrine and conduct."

examination of Scripture. Taking the Bible seriously requires that encountering it will shape the head, the heart, and the hands.[50] The Covenant Church's six affirmations serve as guiding theological principles for the denomination.[51] Being nonconfessional, the Covenant does not exact a vow regarding these affirmations; it merely allows them to guide the way in which the church covenants together, both in personal and church relationships.

Below is a matrix of how the Covenant understands its identity theologically, historically, and relationally.[52]

Theological Commitment	Historical Influence	Relational Sentiment
The authority of Scripture	Protestant Reformation	Where is it written?
New and deeper life in Christ	Pietism	How goes your walk with the Lord?
Evangelism and compassion	Moravian mission	God wants hurting people helped and lost people found.
The Body of Christ	Founding rationale	I am a companion of all who fear Thee.
A conscious dependence on the Holy Spirit	Pentecost	The power to establish unity through all things
Reality of freedom in Christ	Democracy	The decision to retain harmony amid disagreements

Structural

The free vs. state, Swedish vs. American, congregational vs. presbyterian polarities descend into questions of polity. Regarding the free-church and state-church polarity, the Covenant resolved polity in historic Covenant fashion:

50. Erickson, *David Nyvall*, 204-22.

51. The six affirmations can be found in footnote 8 above.

52. Taken and adapted from Kurt Fredrickson, "The Evangelical Covenant Church as Mission Friends: Relational Identities and Missional Practices for a Denominational Future" (Pasadena, CA: Fuller Theological Seminary, 2006), 40. The matrix was initially developed by Gary Walter, executive minister for church growth and evangelism in the Evangelical Covenant Church.

Maybe, we find that the New Testament never opposes these attitudes but unites them as contrasting and yet harmonizing features of one life. . . . Almost every more complete statement as to the nature of the Kingdom of God and the Church of Christ carries with it two views in a harmonious whole.[53]

Here the dialectical view is essential to the Covenant identity. Inherent within the organizing of a fellowship of churches, the Covenant sought to uphold its individual ardor with a communal order.[54] Almost everything in the Covenant has two sides, and this contributes to engaging the challenge facing the church today: how to uphold unity in both ardor and order. Rehearsing the historical, theological, and structural influences on polity highlights the forces that cannot be fully relinquished, but that can be remembered or redeemed in moving forward toward a more missional Ordered Ministry.

History of Ordered Ministry in the Evangelical Covenant Church

The practice of Ordered Ministry is difficult to understand within free-church ecclesiology in general and within Covenant theology in specific.[55] Due to historical influences and biblical hermeneutics, free-congregational churches have always been in tension with the construction of an Ordered Ministry, mainly due to their emphasis on the priesthood of all believers. The history of ordination in the Covenant is often discussed in terms of "ambiguity." The documents written between 1930 and 1977 lack significant theological reflection on the how of ordination, and most of them avoid the difficult questions altogether.[56] The most common rationale for ordination

53. Erickson, *David Nyvall,* 229.
54. Hawkinson and Johnston, *Servant Leadership,* 2.
55. Miroslav Volf, *After Our Likeness: The Church as the Image of the Trinity* (Grand Rapids: Eerdmans, 1998), 152. Volf articulates the primacy of the laity over the confused conception of office for free-church ecclesiology: "The presence of Christ is not attested merely by the institution of office, but rather through the multidimensional confession of the entire assembly."
56. C. V. Bowman, "Something about Ordination" (trans. Sigurd F. Westberg), *Förbundets Veckotidning* (Dec. 15, 1931); C. V. Bowman, "The Pastor's Ordination" (trans. Sigurd F. Westberg), *Förbundets Veckotidning* (Jan. 26, 1932); Earl M. VanDerVeer, ed., "Con-

within the Annual Meeting is for the sake of discipline and pastoral mobility. The conversation about ordination is still rather young in terms of theological understanding, and it is here that the Rules present the greatest obstacles for moving forward.

It is clear that there is a need for pastoral leadership in the church. John Weborg, a Covenant theologian, explains the rise of leadership in speaking of the early church. The need for *office* emerged because of the delayed *parousia;* this delay left the church with a deficit. No longer were the apostles around to give witness to the historic faith, and office filled this void.[57] In this way, the office of the ministry is a continuation of the apostolic historical memory — a connection to Jesus Christ.

The Covenant filled the apostolic deficit by borrowing from two related yet distinct historical narratives. During the days when the Mission Friends of Sweden were welcomed in the Lutheran church as *ecclesiolae in ecclesia,* the narratives of Pietism and mission societies cultivated church leadership from within the laity. *Colporteurs,* or lay preachers, would travel and preach the gospel to immigrant communities.[58] When Mission Friends gathered for worship, lay leaders would administer the sacrament. The society, as noted in Covenant history, was the celebrant, yet this "unforgettable moment" would be short-lived.[59] As functional needs and the pursuit of legitimation increased, the Covenant reverted to former, more clerical-centered narratives.[60] These two narratives have significant tensions between them in defining ordination. On one hand, Pietism was a lay movement engaged in Spirit-filled mission without initial need for clergy; on the other hand, the historic Lutheran narrative developed clergy out of good order, not necessarily apostolic identity.

In the United States the first formal proposal for ministerial credentialing emerged at the organizational meeting in 1885. Two policies were proposed. First, "[t]he Covenant [will] send out experienced pastors

sultation on Ordination" (unpublished, 1970); Sigurd F. Westberg, "Ordination in the Covenant: A Historical Overview" (unpublished, 1977).

57. C. John Weborg, "Ecclesial Service: Permitting the Church to Participate in the Definition of the Self: A Work-Paper for the Study of Licensure and Ordination," in Covenant External Orientation Program, ed., *Reader: The Ordered Ministry of the Evangelical Covenant Church* (Chicago: Covenant Press, 2004), IA4, 5.

58. Weborg, "Ecclesial Service," 139, 225.

59. "Ecclesial Service," 226.

60. Olsson, *By One Spirit,* 325.

as itinerants . . . to encourage, counsel and inspire the churches." Second, ordination was to be left to individual churches unless "assistance from the denomination was requested."[61] In time, the local congregation's ability to ordain was given to the denomination, and after that the practice of ordination became a more presbyterian than free-church form. Currently, clergy are approved by local congregations to enter the ordination process, tested by regional and national committees, and finally approved by the denomination's Annual Meeting for ordination. The denomination holds the credentials of pastors on behalf of local congregations.

Current Affairs in Ordered Ministry of the Evangelical Covenant Church

Amid changing times and a growing denomination, with only one denominational seminary, the Board of Ordered Ministry was commissioned to revise the Rules for Ordered Ministry in 2002. The central tenets guiding this revision were: (1) high view of call to ministry; (2) high view of education; (3) desire to be inclusive; (4) changing needs of the church, including the need to be more flexible.[62]

The board changed the language and clarified a commitment to the Reformation.[63] In the former Rules, the Lutheran notion of Word and Sacrament was absent: "[T]he church sets apart the ordinand to be the servant of the *Word* in the office of holy ministry."[64] Currently, there are two

---

61. *By One Spirit,* 321, 332.

62. Kersten and Lawson, "Looking Ahead with Promise: A New and Improved Version of the Rules for the Ordered Ministry" (Power Point Presentation). The purpose for revising the rules was as follows: "We are called to prepare the church for a new generation of gifted and Godly leaders. These new rules seek to open the door widely to empower them to serve while maintaining the high standards that have always been a part of the Evangelical Covenant Church."

63. Between the older order and the updated order, the threefold responsibility of the Reformed tradition — teach, administer, and bear rule — is emphasized as "authority to preach and teach the gospel, administer the sacraments and rites of the church, and exercise pastoral care and leadership." This threefold responsibility is expected under the rubric of "being set apart . . . to the ministry of word and sacrament." See Rules for Ordered Ministry, available at: http://www.covchurch.org/cov/ministry/rulesforom.pdf (accessed May 22, 2006), or "Rules for Ordered Ministry," IIA3.

64. "Rules of the Board of Ordered Ministry," *The Covenant Yearbook* (1983), 441.

categories of ordination: first, "Ordained to Word and Sacrament" defines one as a resident theologian who has the authority to the three-tiered office of preaching, administering sacraments, and bearing rule;[65] second, "Ordained to Specialized Ministry" calls a person to lead in a specialized ministry of the church, such as justice, administration, children, youth, and so on. Those ordained to Word and Sacrament have the credentials to serve in any office, whether congregational, mobile, regional, or denominational. Those ordained to "Specialized Ministry" serve in accountability to one who is ordained to Word and Sacrament.[66] Those members who are commissioned, licensed, and ordained to Specialized Ministry are technically limited in their vocational locations: they are not allowed to serve in senior pastor roles and many regional and denominational positions without a review of their *academic* record.

The significant difference between the two ordination categories is education. Pietism has always desired educated clergy; this is a cultural value that can and should be maintained. At the same time, the new rules gave educational degrees a castelike character: a master of divinity degree, for example, has more status than other theological master's degrees, including a master of arts in theological studies.[67]

The second distinction worth mentioning is the way accountability

65. The conception of Word and Sacrament as a pastoral vocation emerges out of the Lutheran Reformation as a way to control "good order." The role of the pastor in this system is to control the nature and essence of the church. The church's essence belongs to the ordained, not to the baptized in this historical construction. A look at history, however, suggests that God places the essence of the church in the hands of the baptized. Pastoral leadership is to empower, equip, and encourage the laity to do the work of Word and Sacrament in both the church and world.

66. The rules define one ordained to specialized ministry as follows: "[P]rovides leadership and expertise in an area of specialization, and ministers to the whole congregation of institution of the ECC. Specialized ministry recognizes those persons who are called by God to serve in one of the following designated areas: administration/leadership, adult ministries, camping, children's ministries, health ministries, music ministries, worship ministries, youth ministries, or other professional specialization as determined by the Board. . . . The person ordained to specialized ministry participates in the ministry of sacraments and rites of the church in an accountable relationship with a person ordained to word and sacrament."

67. The Rules, under the heading of "Ordained to Specialized Ministry," declare: "If a person is called to the role of a solo or senior pastor, the standing as ordained to specialized ministry is maintained. The Board may determine that additional education is needed to enhance ministry skills. If a Master of Divinity degree is completed, the candidate may choose to complete the requirements toward ordination to word and sacrament."

functions. Historically, ordination was based on collegiality, much like the Covenant's focus on relationality. In the new rules, accountability between those ordained goes in one direction: Word and Sacrament are tied to the executive position. How is leadership in ministry enacted if an ordained leader is only able to exercise certain functions under the accountability of another peer? The historical desire for minimal structure regarding ordination and church leadership is now experiencing a new level of bureaucratic complexity. The danger is that, within the current rules, the academic degree will increasingly become the distinguishing factor that dictates one's vocational calling, and not necessarily the gifting of the Spirit as discerned by both the local congregation and the denomination.

Engagement with the Rules for Ordered Ministry

The history of the Mission Friends and the Evangelical Covenant Church is rich with lay leadership and nontraditional ideas regarding congregational organization. Early in the life of the Mission Friends — and even in the early work of the Covenant — the priesthood of all believers was active and dominant. At one point, the Covenant even chose T. W. Anderson, a layperson, to be president. The current stratification of Ordered Ministry stands in sharp contrast to the historical and theological roots of the denomination. First, the order was to be simple and was to allow for appointed, ordained leadership centered in collegiality with the denomination and ministerium.[68] Second, placing the stewardship of Word and Sacrament in the hands of just one section of the ordained is contrary to the believer's ecclesiology that is upheld in the Covenant Affirmations. Most leadership literature would favor a rebureaucratizing of the clergy in favor of a clearer, flatter, and more inclusive organization in the church.[69] These are the assumptions that need critique and revision.[70]

---

68. Olsson, *By One Spirit.*

69. Among the most recent publications on ecclesiological leadership, see Eddie Gibbs, *Leadershipnext: Changing Leaders in a Changing Church* (Downers Grove, IL: InterVarsity, 2005); Alan J. Roxburgh, *The Missional Leader: Equipping Your Church to Reach a Changing World* (San Francisco: Jossey-Bass, 2006).

70. On a denominational scale, institutionalization has caused other problems. The office of the president is the *chief executive officer*. Despite the title, the president, based on the current constitution, must be a professional pastor equipped with degrees in theology,

The isolation of Word and Sacrament potentially articulates "no clergy, no church," for without a steward of Word and Sacrament the church cannot continue the ministry of Jesus Christ. However, the ministry of Jesus is located within the life of the church, from which leadership then emerges. The steward of ministry in historic Covenant identity was the believer's church, collectively. The current shift is as much a result of the legitimation and co-optation of the culture within the North American context as it is a theological problem.

Richard Niebuhr articulated the legitimation problem decades ago. As societies (or sects) mature, "an official clergy, theologically educated and schooled in the refinements of ritual, takes the place of lay leadership."[71] The Covenant, as might be expected based on its history, sought legitimation as an immigrant church in the new land. The Covenant has now become a full-blown American denomination, and it elevates role and office. But how might its *radical* historical understanding of the lay ministry, short-lived as that was, be remembered as an impulse for developing a missional polity that reimagines pastoral identity based on its high commitment to perpetual apostolic mission? How might the believer's tradition that focuses on missionary activity approach the formation of leadership with a high Christology that is informed by both missiology and ecclesiology?

Currently, the posture of leadership and service in the church is clouded by the complicated, multiple levels within ordination, commissioning, licensure, and consecration.[72] The *telos* of Ordered Ministry has shifted away from the more missional essence of the denomination. Educated clergy, appointed leadership, apostolic faith, diverse members, and flexibility are goals necessary for church cultures. Now, after several years in action, the present practices should be measured and critiqued against these goals.

---

not executive leadership. Though the person must be ordained to Word and Sacrament, biblical notions of bishop, apostle, or other theologically constructed foundations are absent. This is symptomatic of the confusion between theological leadership and cultural co-optation that is observed in order to satisfy legal status.

71. H. Richard Niebuhr, *The Social Sources of Denominationalism* (New York: Meridian Books, 1957), 20.

72. The schematic for Ordered Ministry can be found at: http://www.covchurch.org/uploads/LQ/s7/LQs7EMRKiTWLoTbwGZQ9Lw/Credentials-schematic.pdf.

Exception Clause

Before moving on to the constructive phase of this argument, I should comment on the Exception Clause within the Rules for the Ordered Ministry.[73] The Covenant is theologically compelled to be open and flexible to diversity in ministry. The Exception Clause has been necessary to cultivate space for such a diverse leadership presence. This will remain necessary as long as the Rules are as tiered, complicated, and focused on educational achievement as they currently are. We can hope that the Exception Clause is but an interim solution, though there have been called and gifted people who cannot accept positions without *exception* because of their failure to meet the specific expectations and qualifications.

Ordaining women and ethnic minorities in the Evangelical Covenant Church is a theological issue that is essential for witnessing to the reign of God (Num. 11:29; Acts 2; Rev. 21). However, in too many cases, the Exception Clause has been used to activate individuals to positions for which they were already gifted and called by God and the church, but who lacked the specific academic or professional qualifications to assume the position "normally." How might the Rules be revised in order to allow a diversity of experiences to serve in a variety of offices without the necessity of an exception clause?

The Exception Clause is a *technical solution* to a larger, cultural, *adaptive* challenge.[74] What began as a desire to have ethnic representation could turn all too quickly into tokenism — and marginalization. According to the current polity, the Covenant asks, "How can we get more women and people of color into Covenant leadership?" The ethnic and gender representation policies and the Exception Clause are the current *technical* solutions.[75]

---

73. Exceptions: "The Board may recommend to the Annual Meeting of the ECC actions that are exceptions to these rules. Such exceptions and the rationale for each shall be clearly stated in presenting the recommendation to the Covenant Ministerium and the Annual Meeting of the ECC." In examining the minutes of the past four Annual Meetings and Covenant Ministeriums, I have found no records of a clear rationale given for execution of the Exception Clause.

74. Ronald A. Heifetz and Martin Linsky, *Leadership on the Line: Staying Alive through the Dangers of Leading* (Boston: Harvard Business School Press, 2002), 33.

75. The ethnic and gender representation policy states that at least two ethnic persons must serve on each board and commission; also, all boards and commissions must have 40 percent female representation.

An *adaptive* question, on the other hand, would be: Which of our values are keeping people of color away from our door, and are we willing to change those values or policies?

The Covenant, in this regard, has started to move forward with women in ministry. In the last several years, the Covenant has produced excellent theological resources on women in leadership.[76] However, though the Covenant is growing in the number of ethnic congregations, there is still more work to be done to ensure their representation at denominational gatherings. Currently, the growth of multiethnic congregations and of diverse leadership situate the Covenant to move forward, but ethnic and female representation is still an adaptive challenge that requires further imagination and innovation.

Toward a Missional Polity: Theology, Ministry, and Organizational Theory

Engaging polity — in this case, the Rules of Ordered Ministry — is a complex matter. Throughout history, polity has emerged in one of three ways. First, churches and denominations have argued, sometimes vehemently, that one's distinct polity is fundamentally biblically based. Borrowing from a small biblical canon, namely the Epistles, Matthew 18, and Acts 15, churches seek to organize themselves by way of an interpretation of these texts.[77] Second, churches organize from their traditions: what has always been, must always be. Whether papal authority (Roman Catholic), Word and Sacrament (Lutheran), or discipline (Calvinist), these polities tend to be static throughout time and space. Third, polities emerge from within a current environment: if this environment becomes the primary influence, less regard is given to biblical-theological foundations or the tradition. A

76. The Covenant began ordaining women in 1979. In 1984, the Covenant presented its first paper on "Women in Ministry." More recently, two volumes have been published that explore the biblical-theological themes of women in ministry: John E. Phelan, *All God's People: An Exploration of the Call of Women to Pastoral Ministry* (Chicago: Covenant Publications, 2004); Sharon Cairns Mann, *Called and Gifted* (Chicago: Covenant Publications, 2006). These represent the kind of theological writing that is necessary for articulating a vision for gender-equality and multiethnic congregations.

77. Steven B. Cowan and Paul Engle, eds., *Who Runs the Church? Four Views on Church Government* (Grand Rapids: Zondervan, 2004).

missional polity does not accept just one of these sources as being normative. Instead, like a missional ecclesiology, it seeks to hold tightly together
theological, historical, contextual, *and* eschatological themes.[78]

Missional polity does not reject the tradition. On the contrary, as the
church is both always forming and reforming, missional polity reflectively
dialogues with the tradition and organizes so that the church gives witness
to the reign of God in new ways. Missional polity has a *telos,* an eschatology: the reign of God. Therefore, conceiving of a missional polity antici-
pates that the church will consider its God-given essence as being primary.
A theological framework is critical for thinking through the essence of the
church. Starting theologically allows for a clearer vision for the ministries
and an organization (polity) that will more fully form and send communities into the world expressing God's reign. "While the church must have
organization, its organizational life must be consistent with the nature of
the church and function in support of its ministry."[79]

Theological Foundations for Missionally Ordered Ministry

Missional ecclesiology, how one defines the essence of the church, begins
with the fact that God, as the creator of the cosmos, is inherently involved
with all of creation. The work of Karl Barth influenced the 1952 IMC Conference in Willingen, and what emerged was a reconceived theology of
mission, the *missio Dei,* which is "God's self-revelation as the One who
loves the world, God's involvement in and with the world, the nature and
activity of God, which embraces both the church and the world, and in
which the church is privileged to participate."[80]

Missional ecclesiology no longer sees mission as a program of the
church for the means of evangelization; rather, mission is embedded in
the very nature of God. Mission is an attribute of God that presupposes
the church.[81] The work of the church becomes a sign, instrument, and
foretaste of the reign of God in Christ. The church is the collective life of

78. Darrell L. Guder et al., *Missional Church: A Vision for the Sending of the Church in
North America* (Grand Rapids: Eerdmans, 1998), 11.

79. Van Gelder, *The Essence of the Church,* 158.

80. David Jacobus Bosch, *Transforming Mission: Paradigm Shifts in Theology of Mission* (Maryknoll, NY: Orbis Books, 1991), 390.

81. Bosch, *Transforming Mission,* 390.

Jesus, whereby the incarnate, visible church is a partner with God, empowered by the Holy Spirit to accomplish the redeeming work of Christ to "the ends of the earth."

Missional ecclesiology understands that its primary identity comes from the God who is revealed in the biblical narrative. The God of Israel raised Jesus Christ from the dead, which serves as the basis for the church's being founded historically — theologically, contextually, and eschatologically. The church is a participant to which God gives authority in this world-concerned movement. The apostle Paul notes it well: "All this is from God, who reconciled us to himself through Christ and gave us the ministry of reconciliation: that God was reconciling the world to himself in Christ. . . . We are therefore Christ's ambassadors" (2 Cor. 5:18-20). The two doctrines of the Incarnation and the Trinity (though others could be used as well) focus the relationship between the congregation and ordained ministry.

Incarnation

Rethinking Ordered Ministry through the Incarnation redirects the role of laity and the role of clergy. Throughout history, especially with respect to Episcopal polities, the Incarnation has taken an iconic approach with the bishop or priest as the "icon of unity."[82] Though the Reformation attempted to subvert this representative reality, it developed its own clericalism based on the same assumptions. The initial intention of the Reformation of a lay-centered ecclesiology and consequent clergy has yet to fully take shape. However, free-church ecclesiology has the resources to proceed in the direction of the Reformation's intent — while continuing to adopt aspects from historical ecclesiologies. The Covenant Church has sought to uphold unity. Therefore, let us borrow from the language of Anglicanism and the historic episcopate in order to reconsider free-church ecclesiology.

In contrast to the episcopate, the congregation became the *icon of Christ;* and, in contrast to the bishop, it became the *icon of unity* in the lit-

82. Volf, *After Our Likeness*, 109-13, 223-28. The historic episcopates understand that one priest or bishop represents unity because "the totality of the congregation cannot be conceived without the unity of office; the *one* must always be a reference to the whole, for only in this way can the unity of the whole be guaranteed and thus the whole exist precisely as a whole" (p. 47).

urgy of Communion.[83] In free-church ecclesiology, the congregation is the constituting factor that serves as both the icon of Christ and the icon of unity. As Karl Olsson notes, before the official structuring of the Covenant Church, the Mission Society became the celebrant.[84] Those congregants who were baptized would be the locus of unity — not one person, such as bishop, a church CEO, or a senior pastor. Instead, the icon of unity would be the plurality of persons gathered in the believers' church (Acts 2:42).[85] The church gathered at the Lord's Supper as both icon of unity and icon of Christ is the mirror into the reconciling reign of God. As icon of Christ while living with the world as the horizon, the congregation — gathered and scattered — becomes the incarnational touchpoint to the world. Incarnation has the world in view through person-to-person encounter:

> If the church is to be in a position to offer all [people] the mystery of salvation and the life brought by God, then it must implant itself

83. I borrow the language and description of "icon of unity" from John D. Zizioulas, an Orthodox theologian. His description of "icon of unity" refers to the theology of the bishop at the Eucharist: the bishop stands at the one altar, in the place of Christ (*alter* Christ), bringing the people to Christ. Zizioulas observes: "[The bishop] was the one in whom the 'many' united would become 'one.' . . . Thus the bishop would become the one through whose hands the whole community would have to pass in its being offered up to God in Christ." John D. Zizioulas, *Being as Communion: Studies in Personhood and the Church* (Crestwood, NY: St. Vladimir's, 1985), 153. This image of unity emerges from Zizioulas's reading of the kefalh (head) tradition. I would like to propose that the concept of icon of unity can be retained, yet relocated in the gathering of the body of Christ. The one behind the table is not responsible to bring the body to the head, but is one participant in this work, where by faith the priesthood presents one another to Christ in the Lord's Supper. So, then, ordination in a free-church ecclesiology does not begin with leadership at the Eucharist as a defining framework; but that does not dismiss the importance of the Eucharist in the gathering of God's people.

84. Olsson, *By One Spirit,* 226. Olsson cites the historical record: "Nevertheless, several of the brethren were still uncertain if it was right to celebrate communion. It was only when they experienced the presence of the Lord on this precious occasion that they, like Thomas, were forced to exclaim, 'My Lord and my God!' It was, in truth, an unforgettable moment." This sacrament was finished not in silence, but in singing.

85. "If one takes the communal confession of faith as the basis of ecclesiality, what, then, is the significance of office . . . for being the church? . . . The presence of Christ does not enter the church through the 'narrow portals' or ordained office, but rather through the dynamic life of the entire church. The presence of Christ is not attested merely by the institution of office, but rather through the multidimensional confession of the entire assembly." Volf, *After Our Likeness,* 152.

among all these groups in the same way that Christ by his incarnation committed himself to the particular and social circumstances of the [people] among whom he lived.[86]

Cruciform Incarnation requires dwelling within the world in its geography, culture, values, lifestyle, and networks.[87] Therefore, dwelling in the midst of internal and external conflict and going through transition is a theological reality for which God leads and guides human action. Incarnation also implies speaking publicly against the injustices and idolatries within a culture. Who, then, is most prepared to dwell in these contexts? The baptized laity — gathered and dispersed. Being both the icon of Christ and icon of unity represents a high calling for an entire congregation to be active in witness.

Taking the approach that the congregation is the primary actor for Word and Sacrament reconceptualizes the identity of the ordained. What, then, does Incarnation offer to ordination? First, the apostolic leader dwells vocationally in the context of the local congregation; second, she or he is acutely aware of God's presence in the forsaken places; third, apostolic leaders are listening to the stories of the people, and hearing of potential locations of God's new work.[88] Through listening, leaders are driven to the edges of the local environment; through sense-making and storytelling, ordained leaders work to discern with the community where God is calling them to participate;[89] with the trust of the community, apostolic leaders then lead congregations into new territory by cultivating environments where the laity can encounter the *other* in the world.

Incarnational ministry needs to guide leadership and impact congregations. Here the polity of the Ordered Ministry emerges out of metaphors and language that transcend the traditional office-bound, dependent concepts of pastor. Metaphors, qualifications, and accountability structures should articulate a clear sense that pastoral leadership equips people for

86. Quoted in *Mission-Shaped Church: Church Planting and Fresh Expressions of Church in a Changing Context, Mission and Public Affairs* (London: Church House, 2004), 87-88. "[A] truly incarnational Church is one that imitates, through the Spirit, both Christ's loving identification with his culture and his costly counter-cultural stance within it."

87. *Mission-Shaped Church*, 12.

88. In this regard, ordained clergy practice the discipline of spiritual direction.

89. Karl E. Weick, *Sensemaking in Organizations: Foundations for Organizational Science* (Thousand Oaks, CA: Sage Publications, 1995).

terrain-crossing ministry. In this respect, Covenant polity could be more explicit in promoting a culture of excellence in leadership. Its polity currently focuses more on discipline and qualifications than the Spirit-filled activity for which ministry is practiced. (I believe that this is too often assumed and hence ignored.) Ordered Ministry that is professionally defined and discipline-centered will continue to erode the possibilities for boundary-crossing and for cruciform-shaped, incarnational ministry.

Doctrine of the Trinity: Sending and Relating

Jesus, as a divine life in the Trinity, is both sent and he sends. As the icon of Christ, the congregation also participates in these activities: the congregation is sent into the world to participate in ministry (John 20:21). In being sent, persons live by baptism into their vocation within their context. This is true for both clergy and laity. Ordained leaders, as called and sent members of the laity, are also gifted differently to serve vocationally: they lead the local church by encouraging, equipping, and celebrating the vocational ministry of the baptized. As the baptized share in the work of Word and Sacrament, the ordained are allowed to emerge as apostles in the world, examining and leading into new frontiers where God is already at work. Appointed as apostles on the basis of the gifts of the Holy Spirit and the affirmation of the church, the ordained lead the laity deeper into the reality of baptism and vocation.[90]

Both the image of Jesus in the Garden and the gathering at Pentecost serve as a background for understanding sentness: Jesus turns to the Father for restoration and vocation — in the cross (Matt. 26:36-39; Mark 14:32-36; Luke 22:39-46); at Pentecost, people gather in celebration and receive the Holy Spirit for the purpose of being witnesses (Acts 1:8). Both situations, though different in tone, are gatherings with God in order that through worship (prayer), they might receive their call. In the case of Jesus, the call was *to* the cross; for those present at Pentecost, the call was to witness *in light of* the cross. The church does not gather for security, but for cross-bearing sentness. Congregations are sent by the power of the Holy Spirit both to bear the cross and to bear witness to God's unity.

90. Jürgen Moltmann, Ellen Charry, and Nicholas Wolterstorff, *A Passion for God's Reign: Theology, Christian Learning, and the Christian Self,* ed. Miroslav Volf (Grand Rapids: Eerdmans, 1998), 229-33.

Therefore, the church as *sent* and as *sending* is participating in God's sending nature. Whether sending missionaries, pastors, stay-at-home parents, lawyers, custodians, or teachers, sentness is not any one individual's reward or call; it is everyone's specialized ministry. All who are baptized are also sent. How, then, is ordination to ministry, especially Specialized Ministry, to be reconceived when sentness is evident through all vocations? Are those currently ordained to Specialized Ministry also gifted and called to be apostolic leaders, albeit with specialized groups?

Providing an answer to these questions lies at the heart of understanding the interrelating power in the Trinity. *Perichoresis* is God's interrelationship or mutual indwelling within Godself and God's creation.[91] God is differentiated, yet symmetrically engaged, as Father, Son, and Holy Spirit in perichoretic relationship (John 10:38). Differentiation allows us to understand that, though we are called to different roles and gifts, no one serves above another.[92] The divine life lives in complementarity, not asymmetrical hierarchy. One example of where this has yet to be activated is that those ordained to Word and Sacrament currently have accountability above those who are ordained to Specialized Ministry. In conceiving an ordained ministry as being rooted in the Trinity, how might a denomination move from a chain of command ordination format to differentiation rooted in perichoretic relationship?

Perichoretically participating in the relationality of the Trinity allows the church to celebrate a reciprocity between pastors and laity who are both *for* and *with* one another. Structurally, then, the church is neither hierarchical nor centralized. Miroslav Volf argues that free-church ecclesiology reflects the Trinity in its decentralized distribution of power and freely affirmed interaction. There are dangers of a mystical communion,

---

91. *Perichoresis* is the analogy that "highlights the *dynamic* and *vital character of each divine person,* as well as the *coinherence* and *immanence* of each divine person in the other two." The perichoretic union is a community of love characterized by mutuality and interdependence. It does not eliminate the monarchy but avoids and reacts against the traditional patriarchy associated with the Trinity; it avoids locating unity in the monism (substance) of the West or in the authoritarianism of the monarchy sometimes associated with the East. *Perichoresis* locates unity in "diversity, in a true communion of persons"; *perichoresis* allows "permeation without confusion." See Catherine Mowry LaCugna, *God for Us: The Trinity and Christian Life* (San Francisco: HarperSanFrancisco, 1991), 270-71.

92. See Jürgen Moltmann, *The Trinity and the Kingdom: The Doctrine of God* (Minneapolis: Fortress, 1993).

yet the intention is that the ordained are given the authority through their indwelling (grounded in the Incarnation) with the congregation, not through position or degree. Authority is animated as the pastor continues to indwell (grounded in Trinitarian relationality) with the people in mutual trust.

Unfortunately, America's fascination with bureaucracy, individualism, and corporate leadership has tended to co-opt a theological pastoral identity. Within the structure of Ordered Ministry, monocentric leadership models have had more influence on the Covenant's polity than the less hierarchical, more team-oriented, decentralized notions of ordained leadership rooted under congregations. In critiquing this, Volf favors a *polycentric polity* that reclaims the priesthood of all believers, albeit one that is differentiated. Volf argues that ordination is not a professionalized, hierarchical claim in the church, but is a gift from God through interaction with the church.[93]

The Ministry of Missional Ordered Ministry

The theology of *missio Dei,* which includes the priesthood of all believers, the Incarnation, and the Trinity, serves as the foundation for the practices and ministry of the church. And the ministry of the church is not a nebulous concept. Ministry flows out of the *missio Dei* in relationship to the reign of God. American pragmatism has tended to bind the church to mere programming without regard to the essence of the church. How the church does ministry conveys to the church why it exists. The church is not a social club, but it is a gathering of people. The church is not entertainment, but it is a dramatic retelling of God's work throughout history. The church is not a political debate, but it does have a public testimony. Ministry in the church must take these tensions seriously as it practices ministry in bold humility.[94]

93. Volf, *After Our Likeness,* 232-33, 236.
94. Craig Van Gelder, in *The Essence of the Church,* has outlined six essential elements that missional ministry (or core missional practices) understands. In moving forward and understanding the core missional practices, each practice invites the practitioners into this reality. The foundations for ministry in the church are: (1) a power encounter between God and the evil one, (2) based on God's disarming the powers through Christ; (3) about unmasking the powers that have been disarmed; (4) to bring God's redemptive reign to all of

The Rules should organize around the practices of the church. This offers a clearer mission and purpose to the *telos* of ordained leadership. The task of the ordained would then be to equip congregations primarily in the core missional practices and not just the daily administration of programs. In this, there is an implicit rejection of programmatic activities that are not articulated within a missional framework.

Stephen Bevans and Robert Schroeder articulate one concept for understanding the ministry of the church as *prophetic dialogue*. Ministry is "prophetic" when the church speaks for the excluded in terms of justice and righteousness, and when the church, amidst pluralism, speaks "unhesitantly, faithfully — and yet respectfully — the name, the vision and the Lordship of Jesus Christ." Ministry is "dialogue" as the church works out of God's perichoretic relationship with the world in "the appreciation of the context of human existence as good, trustworthy and holy."[95] Dialogue believes in the faithfulness of God and the potential of creation, and thus it practices relationship with both friends and enemies. Dialogue expects conversation between laity, clergy, and the world to best know how to prophetically participate as witnesses to God's reign in local communities.

Prophetic dialogue is necessary as the church, in the power of the Holy Spirit, interacts with the world. Prophetic dialogue understands ministry as a complex framework that includes witness and proclamation, liturgy, prayer and contemplation, commitment to justice, peace and integrity of creation, interreligious dialogue, inculturation, and ministry of reconciliation.[96] In an age in which pastors are overly busy with and unclear about organizational practices, a clear conception of ministry allows leadership to implement practices that form the laity in their baptismal commitments.

---

life; (5) to be governed by the word as it is led and taught by the Spirit; and (6) to be grace-based and gift-shaped (p. 156).

95. Bevans and Schroeder, *Constants in Context: A Theology of Mission for Today*. I originally developed these thoughts in my paper "Potential for Prophetic Dialogue: Developing a Contextual Missiology for the Evangelical Covenant Church" (St. Paul: Luther Seminary, 2004; unpublished), 4, 42-66. Bevans and Schroeder have a positivist anthropology that deserves a hearing in the church. However, the reality of sin conceives of the goodness of humanity differently. Miroslav Volf offers a more helpful construction that attains, albeit via a different logic, the same conversational goals of Bevans and Schroeder (in *Exclusion and Embrace: A Theological Exploration of Identity, Otherness, and Reconciliation* [Nashville: Abingdon Press, 1996]).

96. Bevans and Schroeder, *Constants in Context*, 348-95.

Theoretical Foundations for Missional Polity

Missional polity seeks to organize in the best way possible to effectively live out its theological foundations and ministry commitments. Social science and organizational theory have significant insights to offer the organizing aspects of a missional polity. The above theological and ministry framework evidences the fruitful prejudices of the Christian vocation. With regard to theory, the social sciences become helpful to further inform the church's understanding of what God is doing and what God wants to do in local social communities.[97]

If missional leadership believes that God is at work in the world, then God is active across disciplines, including within the prolific literature of leadership and organizational theory. Systems theory, dealing with conflict, and leading in change are areas in which Christian leaders must work. Up to this point, however, much theological research has failed to adequately engage these areas. The church needs to reclaim its form as a human organization.[98] Accordingly, one responsibility for pastoral leadership is *discerning* — based on fruitful prejudices — what aspects of the systems-theory literature are beneficial to the church.

Organizational and leadership literature emerged in the early to mid-twentieth century, and it had largely unnamed assumptions about anthropology. Such unnamed assumptions have also been true for most denominational polities. Beginning with Weber, Fayol, and others, those assumptions have seen humans as being in need of management, accountability, and hierarchy.[99] Predictability and control served as the *modus ope-*

97. Craig Van Gelder, "Hermeneutics of Leading in Mission," *Journal of Religious Leadership* 3, nos. 1 and 2 (Spring and Fall, 2004).

98. James Gustafson, at one time a student at the Covenant's North Park College, argued for a consideration of the church as a human community. See James M. Gustafson, *Treasure in Earthen Vessels: The Church as a Human Community* (Chicago: University of Chicago Press, 1961).

99. What is often misunderstood is that, though Weber develops hierarchy, spans of control, etc., his purpose was not merely command-and-control of the worker, but also the need to understand a worker's rights. Prior to Weber, organizational structures were largely of a charismatic and traditional style of authority, which abused the rights of the worker whether by personality (charismatic) or by arrogant, misappropriated historical precedents (traditional). Weber's construction of the bureaucracy was to protect the workers by removing authority from the person or organizational identity into clear role and responsibility differentiation. His proposal for an ideal type was to deal with issues of abuse of power and

randi, and instead of investing in collaborative models of structure, polity began to evolve with similar bureaucratic constructions. Within these early theories, people were considered incapable of collaboration, accountability, and imagination without structures of hierarchy, division of labor, and command-and-control.

Social science and organizational studies moved beyond these former constraining models toward organizational systems in order to consider the complexities of the human condition. Currently, postmodern organizational theory continues the journey.[100] The theoretical literature has much to offer denominational structures: it can inform current polities and assist in questioning the unnamed assumptions. Missional polities that participate in the *missio Dei* are always open to the unpredictable winds of the Holy Spirit to blow through organizations, disrupting stability without causing catastrophe.[101] But again, we must apply a discerning view rooted in the church's essence to all these resources.

Designing a missional polity is complex and must use both theological frameworks and theoretical insights. We need to start with a missional ecclesiology, which can be stated in simple terms: the church is, the church does what it is, and the church organizes what it does. Together, the theological frames and the theoretical insights expand the horizons for organizing the church based on its *essence*, God's redemptive work in the world, and its *ministry,* practices that announce God's reign. Missional polity is organized around several principles: it is relational not controlling (Trinity), organic not static (pneumatology), contingent not bureaucratic (Incarnation), possible not limiting (creation), and forming and reforming, not standard and biblicist (eschatology and redemption).

---

mistreatment of the worker. He moved from subjective personality-centered leadership to objective role-centered leadership. His proposal was noble, yet his inability to see the people as subjective versus mere objects and his inability to critique the character of the leader within a bureaucracy did not allow him to understand the weaknesses of his model: that is, being chief does not imply virtue.

100. Mary Jo Hatch, *Organization Theory: Modern, Symbolic, and Postmodern Perspectives,* 2nd ed. (New York: Oxford University Press, 2006). Hatch's book is a helpful overview of postmodern organizational theory.

101. Wheatley's new science, based on quantum physics and fractals, acknowledges that what appears as causal may be stale, yet what appears disconnected may be a root cause. This is best noted in the current polity in the multiple layers of credentialing. What was intended to be a system for flexibility turned instead into hierarchical differentiation without symmetrical relationship.

Toward Missional Ordered Ministry for the ECC

For the Covenant, the laypeople in mission are the human instigation for its ecclesiology, as well as its leadership and its organizational structures. The laity have from the beginning ignited the passion to reach people with the gospel, both in matters of personal conversion and social reconciliation. Laity were the backbone of the early Mission Friend days. Without the laity the Covenant would be nonexistent, and the pursuit of a common mission rooted in freedom would be void. The laity are central to the essence of the church.

Ever since the postapostolic episcopate, the Reformation concepts of Word and Sacrament (Luther) and discipline (Reformed), and the emergence of bureaucracy, Ordered Ministry has blindly adopted cultural notions of hierarchy, social status, and professionalization at the expense of theological convictions. However, if the mission-society model taught anything, it was that laity do not need a professional shepherd only to preach weekly and administer the sacrament monthly.

Organizing around the Incarnation and the doctrine of the Trinity changes the ends of Ordered Ministry. No longer is Ordered Ministry for Word and Sacrament alone; baptism and mutual indwelling grant this work to the people. Word and Sacrament are missional concepts, and Lutheran theologians have recently begun to articulate this reality.[102] When Word and Sacrament belong to the entirety of the community, then stewardship of the faith rests with the baptized. The tasks of preaching and administering the sacraments *may* still be incorporated into the work of ordained leadership (though not necessarily); but they are done by the gift of the church, not by right of ordination. When Word and Sacrament are returned to the laity, then the biblical understanding of continuing Christ's ministry is seated in the collective body, not in monocentric leadership structures.[103] Ordered Ministry can now look to the ends of apostolic lead-

---

102. Richard H. Bliese and Craig Van Gelder, eds., *The Evangelizing Church: A Lutheran Contribution* (Minneapolis: Augsburg Fortress, 2005), 61-62.

103. It is important to note that what Jesus did individually, the church does corporately. Arguing from this point of view, I would observe that no task of the church can either be practiced or stewarded by monocentric structures. Christian congregations continue the active ministry of Jesus Christ. Obviously, at times persons will participate in Christ's ministry alone, yet their work is only by the Spirit's power infused and discerned in Christian communities. This has significant implications for Ordered Ministry. First, the task of the

ership. The missional understanding of Word and Sacrament is reconstituted as means toward this end.

Ministerial training, with its current conceptions of Ordered Ministry, is currently organized to train pastors for preaching and worship leadership (and traditional pastoral care). Yet the complexity of today's ecclesial organizations waits for leadership that goes beyond Christendom's tasks of ministry, and which recaptures the dynamic spirit of Ephesians 4:11-13. The two-tiered understanding of ordination confuses the apostolic role of church leadership. Senior (or solo) pastors, as those ordained to Word and Sacrament, are currently considered to be the leaders in the apostolic mission. Those ordained to Specialized Ministry do not have the same apostolic expectation.[104] As Ordered Ministry is divided between Word and Sacrament and Specialized Ministry, the gap between senior pastors and staff grows — without theological basis. Legitimacy for pastors is waning as current pastoral practice is unable to interpret basic understandings of life in congregations.[105]

Historically, denominations have held to mediating, priestly images that envision the pastor as the priest to the people. This image is much like Zizioulas's concept of bishop quoted above. These images have centered on tradition-keeping, stability-sustaining metaphors, such as manager, therapist, and pedagogue. Missional polity requires that ordination be toward different ends, which cannot support such metaphors. Instead, pastoral identity must change: the pastor must not stare primarily into the sanctuary, but she or he must also focus on and animate the same horizon the congregation has in view — outward toward the world. One response in moving forward is to analyze current metaphors for ministry, question their assumptions, and propose changed or new images that are more theologically rooted.

---

ordained emerges from, yet still belongs to, the Christian community; second, the ordained can only participate when the congregation calls them into leadership for their community; third, the work of the ordained is to move the baptized deeper into their identity of Word and Sacrament as sign, instrument, and foretaste of the kingdom of God.

104. "Rules for Ordered Ministry," 46-47. See Sections III.3.1 and IV.4.1. If we compare the descriptions of ordination, there is a sense where apostolic mission belongs to one set of the ordained but not to Specialized Ministry. It is unclear how Specialized Ministry conceives of its ends beyond the task of specialty. Based on the accountability concept, "Ordained to Specialized Ministry" appears as an ordination to assistantship.

105. See section 3 of Alan Roxburgh's essay, chap. 3 above.

New Images for Ordered Ministry

The argument here is that moving toward a missional Ordered Ministry requires new metaphors for the role of pastor and ordained leader. In a church where justifying an ordered ministry was largely based on functionalism, there is a need for continual work in redefining leadership across local, regional, and national lines. There is still work to do in answering how pastors, superintendents, and denominational officers lead the church and connect with local congregations beyond traditional concepts of Word, Sacrament, and Order.[106] This will require a move away from metaphors such as pedagogue, therapist, or CEO. Even the metaphor "resident theologian" limits the ability of all of God's people to participate as theologians within their contexts.

I have used the word "apostolic" elsewhere in this essay. Apostolic has a rich identity, offering both the commitment to God's history and a vision for participation in God's future. It is an action-oriented image rooted and centered in God's larger story. On one hand, apostolic keeps to the inherited faith of the church. On the other hand, apostolic means commitment to the edges. Apostles refuse to leave any stone unturned and are willing to explore new ideas and territory. Apostles yearn to see where God is acting in the world; even more, they invite the people of God to join them in these spaces. Ordination then becomes a living into addressing the leadership deficit that was first perceived in the book of Acts.[107]

The office of the apostle needs to continue today in the leadership of the church. Ordained leadership needs to be recruited and formed with a disposition for apostolic imagination. One may or may not be an apostle per se; yet, by virtue of leadership in the church, one is required to be formed for and capable of living into an apostolic imagination. But it is important to interpret apostolic imagination through the lens of Covenant history. The image connects with our deep commitment to the inherited faith as well as to mission in the world, which is now reconceived of as the *missio Dei*. An apostolic imagination commits leaders to being *storytellers, prophets,* and *missionaries*.[108]

---

106. See Richard Bliese's chapter in Bliese and Van Gelder, *The Evangelizing Church,* 42-44.

107. Weborg, "Ecclesial Service: Permitting the Church to Participate in the Definition of the Self: A Work-Paper for the Study of Licensure and Ordination," IA4.

108. Alan J. Roxburgh, in *The Missionary Congregation, Leadership, and Liminality:*

The *storyteller* "listens to the pain and questioning emerging from the fragmentation and alienation dwelling with modern people — the loneliness of our individualism as experienced by those in our congregations."[109] In turn, the storyteller makes sense of the situation and rehearses it.[110] The storyteller does not create the story anew, but merely rehearses what has been said by both the congregation and the world in order to make a coherent narrative that ignites the imagination of the people in a resounding "yes!" The storyteller receives authority and trust from the congregation through an intimate, yet not romanticized, retelling of the community's story. In practice, the storyteller practices this art in rituals, both formal and informal.

Biblically, the *prophet* engages in bold humility with the people. The prophet knows the story of the people intimately and is able to integrate this story into the work and history of God. The prophet captures the Reformation's historic understanding of Word, and not merely for the passive edification of the church. Indeed, the prophet's is a call to break forth in participation with God in the world. The Word is not a separated activity from the world; rather, it is an invitation to repent, arise, and break forth in missional engagement with the world. The prophet gives ear to the current story and to God's story for interpreting and shaping missional ministry within a certain context.[111] The prophet, in practicing the Word, forms

---

Christian Mission and Modern Culture (Harrisburg, PA: Trinity Press International, 1997), uses three images to express his response to congregational leadership: poet, prophet, and apostle. I borrow from his constructions, but I rename them in order to match the other themes of ministry and sense-making found elsewhere in the essay. *Storytelling* is an ancient art that seeks to connect across race and class. I propose this image instead of poet, because the poem as text has had a narrower audience (unfortunately). I continue to use the image of *prophet* as that which connects deeply to the proposed concept of ministry I have explained earlier. Finally, I propose the image of *missionary* instead of apostle in order to explicitly convey the boundary-crossing movement expected in one angle of apostolicity. It seems that apostolicity is responsible for the threefold identity of storyteller, prophet, and missionary: it is both a reaching back to the inherited faith as well a looking ahead toward new movements of God in the world. One must engage with all three images of congregational leadership in today's ecclesial climate.

109. Roxburgh, *Missionary Congregation*, 58-59.

110. This is Weick's practice of sense-making.

111. The practice of preaching in the black church tradition serves well here. Robert Michael Franklin notes: "Preaching is the ecclesial practice most central to the sacred oral culture of African Americans and most essential for mobilizing and sustaining people for public action. Good black social preaching names and frames crises creatively, analyzes

others in this practice. This is the ancient practice of catechism to which the baptized are still called. Pastors who practice the role of the prophet form congregations that are capable of living by the Word, which is part of their baptismal call. The goal for the prophet, as for Moses, is to say: "Would that all the Lord's people were prophets" (Num. 11:29).

However, storyteller and prophet alone can too often create a congregation aware of but separated from the world. The *missionary* becomes the adaptive call in ordained leadership. The shifting ecclesial situations in our culture of both growth and decline call leadership "to the gospel in lands where old maps no longer work."[112] "Missionary" implies movement, not simply orthodoxy, as the missionary forms missional congregations. "Missionary" also reminds Covenanters of the Mission Friends days, where mission activity meant relationships, embracing the other, and sharing one's faith in the Lord.

Apostolic leadership lives by the Spirit within the culture, yet always toward the reign of God, both as it has come and as it is yet to come. The storyteller embodies the narrative of the community and rehearses it with them weekly; the prophet, in the Pietist tradition, intersects the Word with the world in order to present opportunities for where God is at work; finally, the missionary leader takes the first step into both the known and unknown territories and invites the people of God to join her. The apostolic imagination incarnationally engages the context for the long haul.

"Ordained to Word and Sacrament" can too often imply an institutional, office job for the pastor. Writing sermons and leading worship can too often be void of engagement with the culture. The apostolic pastor has sandals, coat, and parchments (2 Tim. 4:9-15); the apostolic pastor is cultural anthropologist, sense-maker, and catechist; the apostolic pastor is explorer, visionary, and sojourner. If Ordered Ministry understands pastoral identity as storyteller, prophet, and missionary, then ordination has a revised purpose — an apostolic purpose. No longer can structures be articulated in vertical organizational charts, because storytellers, prophets, and missionaries will not stay contained within a vertical structure. Apostolic leadership will topple the vertical chart, and it will move the organization

---

them in biblical perspective, describes solutions using indigenous symbols and images, prescribes specific action plans, and offers hope via celebration." Quoted in James P. Wind and James Welborn Lewis, eds., *American Congregations*, vol. 2 (Chicago: University of Chicago Press, 1994), 281.

112. Roxburgh, *Missionary Congregation*, 61.

forward in mission on earth. The hierarchical chain of command will be overturned by a pneumatological missional engagement. Local congregations will be poised *laterally* in mission.

Pastoral identity is a gift from God through the church for the world. Pastors need to reclaim this call, break forth from any constraining historical expectations, and apostolically lead congregations into new realities of congregational life, realities where the biblical narrative tells the story, and where catechism and historical Christian practices continue to be essential for the apostolic imagination. What is proposed is nothing new, for God's work in the world has always been missional. Yet crucial to this transformational period is the ability to retell the story, hearken to the changing situation, and equip the people of God to embrace a preferred future. This is the structural *telos* of the Ordered Ministry.

Summary

The Evangelical Covenant Church has a rich lay history and tradition. Emerging from the Protestant Reformation, Swedish Pietism, and Mission Societies, the Covenant is grounded in the priesthood of all believers. What it has yet to realize is making this identity distinctly operational within Ordered Ministry. The polity of the Covenant has a unique possibility of reradicalizing the doctrine of the royal priesthood.

As the denomination continues to grow, leadership will need to emerge from within congregations, leaders whom the regional conferences and the denomination will support. Support will come in terms of preparing apostolic leadership as storytellers, prophets, and missionaries, and engaging those as an adaptive challenge is the way forward. Making sense of the situation is essential when the cultural engagement becomes the ministry. God is at work in the world, and ordination is no longer only for Word and Sacrament, for that is the missional task of the baptized. Rather, ordination must be to an apostolic imagination, and that becomes the missional task of the ordained.

CHAPTER 8

Missional Renewal: An Ecclesiology and Polity Proposal for the Baptist General Conference

Todd Hobart

Introduction

The history of the Baptist General Conference (BGC) chronicles a journey of increasing influence and growth. From its humble beginnings among religiously persecuted Swedish immigrants in the 1850s, the BGC has grown to encompass 913 churches, with nearly 145,000 members, and a total income of 240 million dollars.[1] Officially, the BGC is a fellowship of Baptist churches within the United States and Caribbean region, but it has a worldwide presence because of its emphasis on both short- and long-term missionary support. Since the late 1960s, it has continued a strong program of church-planting and evangelism that has nearly doubled its membership from 72,056 in 1960 to 143,200 in 2000.[2] This stands in sharp contrast to the steady decline in membership that many other denominations have experienced during this same period.

These are all positive growth aspects of the BGC, yet there is a further constructive development that this denomination might want to consider, having to do with the BGC's understanding of its own purpose and mission. Such a development would require the use of a missional lens to examine the historical and contextual polity that presently gives shape to the

---

1. The numbers are as of 2003. See: http://www.bgcworld.org/intro/stats.htm (accessed May 25, 2006).

2. http://www.thearda.com/Denoms/D_1066.asp (accessed May 25, 2006).

BGC. Using this lens for this purpose is my intention in this essay. First, I identify some of the historical influences that helped to form the DNA of the BGC; second, I present the foundations that can help shape a missional polity; third, I examine many of the changes in polity that have occurred over the history of the BGC. Finally, I suggest some polity revisions that reflect a missional ecclesiology that is based on theology, organizational theory, and Christian Scripture.

Historical Influences

Many BGC churches today resemble various nondenominational churches, as well as churches of other conservative, evangelical denominations. This is because the BGC was born within a specific context that shaped its initial polity. Specifically, the three factors that have helped the BGC become what it is today are: (1) its Pietist roots; (2) its founding by persecuted and marginalized Swedish Baptist immigrants; and (3) its initial composition, which consisted primarily of poor frontier settlers.

The Importance and Context of Swedish Pietism

Virgil Olson noted the historical importance of Pietism for the BGC in the 1950s, when the Conference[3] was undergoing a "transition into the new forward looking Americanized model." He notes three prior important transitions in the BGC:

1. The free-church Christians in Sweden broke away from the established Lutheran church.
2. The separate group of Swedish Baptists came together as a group to reach other immigrant Swedes with the gospel, which was aided by the creation of a theological seminary and the publication of a religious periodical.
3. The churches made the rapid change from using the Swedish language in their services and meetings to using English.[4]

3. Throughout this paper I will use *Conference* to designate the national level and *conference* to designate the regional level.
4. Virgil A. Olson, "The Baptist General Conference and Its Pietistic Heritage," *Bethel Seminary Quarterly* 4, no. 3 (May 1956): 54-55.

Olson specifies Pietism as the golden thread that ties together the past of the BGC and sets it apart from other Baptist denominations of the time. Pietism was the guiding force that lingered through each of the important changes in the BGC's past, as well as the spiritual perspective that was required to respond to the issue of Americanization. He notes:

> [W]hen we are asked to distinguish our fellowship from some other Baptist group that may be nearly identical in program and objectives, we answer something to this effect: "Our fellowship has a strong dose of pietism in it, and consequently it cannot be identified with ultrafundamentalism, nor hyper-calvinistic Baptists, nor fighting 'come-outer' schismatics."[5]

The other groups mentioned are not as influential within Baptist circles today, but the Pietist heritage of the BGC is still very much alive as an influence on its polity and practices.

In a complex series of ecclesiastical and political events in the 1520s, Sweden exchanged its state-supported Roman Catholic affiliation for a state-governed form of the Lutheran church.[6] Nearly 300 years later, the creative impulses of the Reformation had long since run their course in Sweden, and a morally lax and authoritarian state church had developed. Priests were described as "worldly, sensual, and mercenary," and they preached cold, rationalistic sermons. Likewise, outside of the clergy, the men and women of Sweden consumed more alcohol at the time than in any other European country, which contributed to increased crime and economic depression.[7]

Pietism had already been introduced into Sweden in the eighteenth century, and by the early nineteenth century, conditions were ripe for the Pietists to engage in religious and social reform. The Conventicle Act of 1726 had "placed strict censorship on all pietistic literature and forbade religious meetings in the homes," so the primary staples of Pietism were difficult to come by.[8] The Pietism coming to Sweden then was trans-

---

5. Virgil Olson, "Pietistic Heritage," 55-56.

6. Kenneth Scott Latourette, *A History of Christianity,* rev. ed. (New York: Harper & Row, 1975), 736-39.

7. Adolf Olson, *A Centenary History, as Related to the Baptist General Conference of America, Centenary Series* (Chicago: Baptist Conference of America, 1952), 10-12.

8. V. Olson, "Pietistic Heritage," 59-60.

planted from the Pietist movement that was born in Germany in the late seventeenth century. That movement originated among German Lutherans around 1675, when Philip Jakob Spener (1635-1705) published *Pia Desideria*. Spener proposed six remedies to counter the formalized religion of his day: (1) a return to the Bible; (2) active involvement of the laity; (3) lives of active godliness; (4) charity in doctrinal disagreements; (5) "true Christians" as church leaders; and (6) ministry training that emphasized godliness.[9]

Pietists formed small groups known as "little churches within the church" *(ecclesiolae in ecclesia)*, which emphasized Bible study, common prayer, and accountability.[10] They initiated some of the first modern missionary ventures within Protestantism, while they also encouraged practical good works such as the founding of orphanages and the publication of devotional literature.[11] The influence of the pietistic emphasis on missionary work later played a large role in the development of the polity and self-understanding of the BGC and Swedish Baptist churches in North America.

The later Pietist movement in the 1830s in Sweden was nicknamed the "Readers" *(läsare)* movement. It involved meeting in homes to read devotional books and the Bible. Two outside sources influenced this movement in Sweden: the earlier German Pietism and the free-church influence from England and the United States. The Pietists were not primarily interested in breaking away from the Swedish state church; instead, they wanted reform within Lutheranism. However, where the Readers were particularly numerous in northern Sweden, Baptist views gained ready acceptance and quickly spread.[12]

Pietism did not live on as a movement among Swedish Baptists in the United States. But Virgil Olson notes several characteristics of Pietism that were carried over into the BGC and that have continued to remain influential: (1) the importance of Scripture reading and study; (2) an emphasis on a personal conversion experience; (3) a need for holy living; (4) leadership and participation from among common people; and (5) the regular need

9. Mark A. Noll, *The Rise of Evangelicalism: The Age of Edwards, Whitefield and the Wesleys, A History of Evangelicalism*, vol. 1 (Downers Grove, IL: InterVarsity Press, 2003), 61-62.

10. Douglas A. Sweeney, *The American Evangelical Story: A History of the Movement* (Grand Rapids: Baker Academic, 2005), 34.

11. Noll, *The Rise of Evangelicalism*, 63.

12. V. Olson, "Pietistic Heritage," 60-61.

for revival. Olson further notes in his implications drawn from these trends that the emphasis on conversion and holy living tended to breed a neglect of theology within the denomination. He said that the BGC needed "a careful union of the stress on living faith with a living theology."[13] This is important to note when we address the issue of constructing a missional polity for the BGC.

There is, for example, within the polity of the BGC a relative neglect of biblical or theological rationale related to its organization. The statement of faith is not accompanied by scriptural references, and no attempt is made to explain why particular statements were chosen or how they came into existence. One implicit assumption regarding the structuring of the denomination seems to be that the Bible and theology do not directly relate to decisions regarding organizational forms. Outside of the purpose statement for the denomination, there are no scriptural references in the polity.

One additional connection to note between Pietism and the BGC is the strong emphasis on the importance of mission and evangelism. The early Pietists in Germany in the seventeenth and eighteenth centuries led the way in the development of the modern missionary movement.[14] This emphasis on missionary work became a central, defining tenet of Pietism throughout the movement's growth and eventual decline.

The BGC was first organized in 1879 in the United States as the Scandinavian Baptist General Conference. It centered its life on the task of mission to the unconverted Scandinavians living in the American Northwest at that time.[15] This emphasis on mission has remained constant within the BGC to the present day, and it is reflected in the current purpose statement of the Conference, which is essentially a restatement of the Great Commission (Matt. 28:18-20).[16] This emphasis on mission and evangelism is an important key to constructing a missional polity for the future of the BGC. However, Pietism was not the lone influence on the early American Swedish Baptists. The free-church Swedish immigrants were actually Baptists in the midst of Lutherans.

13. V. Olson, "Pietistic Heritage," 62-65.

14. David Jacobus Bosch, *Transforming Mission: Paradigm Shifts in Theology of Mission,* (Maryknoll, NY: Orbis Books, 1991), 255.

15. The Danish and Norwegian Baptists quickly broke away to form their own conferences in 1882. See J. O. Backlund, *Swedish Baptists in America, A History* (Chicago: Conference Press, 1933), 129.

16. Article IV, section A of the bylaws.

Immigrant Baptist Swedes

Sweden did not tolerate dissident religious groups within the context of its state church system during the mid-1800s. The state had passed an official act of toleration for the free exercise of religion in the constitution of 1809; however, in actual practice, Christian groups who were operating outside the scope of the state-church system were persecuted under the Conventicle Act of 1726. One of the early Baptist pioneer leaders in America, F. O. Nilsson, was banished from Sweden for his free-church beliefs.[17] He served a small Baptist church in Denmark before eventually immigrating to the United States, where he became the founder and pioneer of the Swedish Baptists in Minnesota. Other Baptists in Sweden had their children forcibly taken from them by the police to be baptized by sprinkling according to state law.[18] Mobs often attacked Baptist meeting places and vandalized property. Some Baptists were imprisoned, and many were fined for adhering to their new religious beliefs.[19]

In the midst of this religious persecution, many Swedish Baptists needed little persuasion to make the long and arduous trip to the United States, though economic opportunities in America also convinced many Swedes to emigrate. However, once the Swedish Baptists made the trip across the Atlantic and settled in an area with other Swedes, they often found themselves once again at odds with their Lutheran brethren. Coming from the context of the Lutheran state church, the Swedish Lutherans in the United States considered "all Swedes their parish, and their own church as the authorized Swedish church of America." In addition, "Baptists were regarded as the worst kind of heretics. They undermined the established order of salvation, and denied the blessed sacrament of baptism to little infants." In response, the Baptists had little regard for adhering to denominational boundaries. They recognized that large numbers of Lutherans who had immigrated were quite nominal in their faith, and thus they believed that it was their divine call to proclaim the gospel to them. This set up a natural enmity between the two groups that paradoxically helped both groups thrive for at least their first fifty years in the United States.[20]

17. Arthur Ittermann, "Missionary Administration of the Swedish Baptist General Conference of America" (Th.D. diss., Central Baptist Theological Seminary, 1950), 6.

18. A. Olson, *Centenary History*, 6.

19. Backlund, *Swedish Baptists in America*, 25.

20. A. Olson, *Centenary History*, 18-19, 65-66.

Living on the religious margins, both in Sweden and in the United States, this group forged an identity of the Baptist General Conference in which being a *Baptist* was not an insignificant choice. Therefore, the newly formed fellowship of Baptist churches felt a great need to articulate what made being a Baptist necessary or important. In *My Church: A Manual of Baptist Faith and Action,* first published in 1957 by the BGC, Gordon Johnson outlines eight important principles that he believes distinguish Baptists from other kinds of Christians. This book has been used in courses in Bible schools and seminaries, in educating new church members, and as a leadership training manual. It was revised in 1973, and the title was then shortened to *My Church*; and it was revised again in 1994.[21]

In this book Johnson's first principle is that "the New Testament is the sole and sufficient rule of faith and function." This may not sound all that different from the beliefs of other Christians, but Johnson emphasizes that no creed, confession, or statement of faith is binding on the church. As opposed to the Lutheran confessional context from which they emerged, Swedish Baptists used a simple statement of faith to guide their fellowship of churches. The second principle is: "It is the privilege of each individual to have direct access to God through Jesus Christ." Again, this may not sound particularly different from many Christian traditions; but Johnson is emphasizing the equality that exists between all believers, an equality that removes the distinction between clergy and laity. Again, this set the Swedish Baptist believers apart from their Lutheran counterparts, who held to the priesthood of all believers yet left room for a distinction between clergy and laity.

Likewise, the third principle is relevant to the origins of the Swedish Baptists: "The church and state are to be completely separate in their respective fields." For Johnson, this essentially means that the church and state should stay out of one another's way: "The church is not to interfere with the functions of the state except as it might arouse public opinion about a violation of a biblical or moral issue." But the state should also give liberty for individuals to worship according to the dictates of their consciences. The BGC has included this principle as the tenth point in its official statement of faith.

The fourth principle is a more visible distinguishing characteristic of

21. Gordon Johnson, *My Church: The Baptist Faith and Lifestyle* (Evanston, IL: Harvest Publications, 1979), 5.

Baptists: "The church's government is a simple, democratic form." Johnson unapologetically declares that "[t]he New Testament church was a democracy." Although a pastor is a leader in a local church, he or she is a democratically elected individual who, like any other member, ultimately has only one vote in church decisions. This places an individualistic emphasis within Baptist polity and raises the idea of democracy nearly to that of a biblical principle. Such democratic ideals are played out within all levels of church life.

The fifth principle of belief is reflected in the name "Baptist" itself: "Baptism is for believers only and only by immersion." The Baptist leaders who broke from the Swedish state church were each immersed as adults after being convinced of the importance of Baptist views from their study of Scripture. Johnson's sixth principle is that "church membership is for the regenerate only." This idea was particularly important because Baptists distinguished themselves from the practices of state churches. Baptists require a specific declaration of a person's faith in Christ before that person can become a member of a church, and this allows for specific disciplinary practices within the churches.

"Christ is the supreme Head of the church" is Johnson's seventh principle. Ideally, this would mean that "no group or individual can dominate the wishes of other members within a Baptist church," and that "all are accountable to and under the direction of Christ." However, in practice this is difficult to achieve, given the natural competing interests that can be found in any congregation. After we have said that, though, the principle still applies that Baptist churches are to seek to follow the leading of Christ above all else.

The eighth principle outlined by Johnson is that "the evangelization of the world is our task." He specifically lists the Great Commission as the defining text for Baptists and places on individual believers the responsibility for bearing witness. This principle is in line with the BGC's Pietist beginnings and its historic emphasis on mission. As I have observed above, the Great Commission is the sole biblical text that is used in the purpose statement of the BGC. Though it is not listed among Johnson's eight principles, the independence and autonomy of each local Baptist church is also an important facet of Baptist belief that separates them from several other Christian faith traditions. However, this autonomy must be held in tension with the need for connection with other groups of believers. To Johnson's credit, he notes the interdependence among churches in Acts 15, and he emphasizes the need for churches to cooperate with one another in a larger organization, such as the Conference.[22]

The BGC considers itself a fellowship of Baptist churches and not a denomination as such. Divisive issues are to be resolved by either a showdown vote or through a "live and let live" attitude. Unfortunately, an adequate means has not yet been developed in the BGC for adjudicating differences between powerful local churches in service of a common mission. This is partly due to its Pietist heritage, which seems to value neglecting theological details in favor of valuing a holy life and a commitment to evangelism. It is also due in part to the power that autonomy gives to local churches and to the nearly scriptural level that the idea of democracy has attained.

One would expect that this high view of the Bible would be reflected in the BGC's theological bases for its polity. However, when the District Executive Minister (DEM) for the Minnesota Baptist Conference (MBC) was asked whether the system of boards at the regional and national levels was based more on biblical groups of elders or corporate groups of trustees, he indicated that it was instead founded on a democratic political system.[23] In his book on Baptist principles, Gordon Johnson makes a thoroughly unconvincing argument that the earliest Christian churches used democracy as their preferred means for making decisions.[24] Baptists seem to imply that the only ways to make decisions as a group are either by voting on an issue or having the decision made and handed down by an authority of some sort. This need not necessarily be the case, and there are at

22. Johnson, *My Church*, 26, 28, 37, 42-53.

23. From a personal interview with the District Executive Minister (DEM) of the Minnesota Baptist Conference (MBC), March 30, 2006 (the DEM is the top regional conference representative).

24. Johnson, *My Church*, 108. Johnson asserts, from four New Testament passages, that churches must "preserve the unity of the fellowship," "maintain pure doctrine and practice," "care for the conduct of the ordinances," and "exercise discipline." His primary problem arises when he assumes that Acts 1:23, 26 and Acts 6:3, 5 refer to the democratic election of officers. Each of these passages refer to choosing leaders, but nothing in them implies the means by which they were selected. In fact, Acts 1 involves the casting of lots, which seems like an idea that is directly opposed to a democratic election! Johnson further attempts to back up his assertion with a questionable argument on the basis of a translation of a Greek verb in Acts 14:23. This seems like slim evidence from which to make a broad assertion regarding decision-making in the early church. Though Johnson updated his argument for a later version of his book, his general thrust remained the same.

least two instances in the book of Acts of corporate discernment and problem-solving that would indicate otherwise: Acts 6 and Acts 15.

Poor Frontier People

The early Swedish Baptists were not people of worldly means and power. They existed on the outer margins of society as frontier settlers, and they lived in challenging and sometimes harsh conditions. They were hungry for land, restless, independent, freedom-loving, and they valued democracy. Having been drawn by stories promising great wealth, the poor immigrants often found that this dream was elusive and reckoned instead with a life of courage, sacrifice, and faith. Their homes were simple, usually one-room log cabins or sod houses, and pioneers often found themselves at the mercy of natural forces such as blizzards or plagues of grasshoppers.

This way of life demanded a resilience that could stand against adversity. For the Swedish Baptist settler, this often meant an unswerving devotion to the Bible, one's own interpretation of it, and Baptist distinctives. Revivals were also an important part of the frontier life for Swedish Baptists, both in local churches and in the yearly conference meetings. The early settlers carefully followed another important Baptist practice: they barred unregenerate people from becoming members of their churches. This meant that a candidate for baptism was subjected to all kinds of questions from the members of the church that were meant to ascertain his or her spiritual status.[25] These distinctives of frontier life provided foundational influences for the formation of the BGC as it grew up in nineteenth-century America.

Of course, much has changed in the intervening years since the BGC consisted of poor Swedish immigrant Baptists on the frontier. Today, the BGC is a growing denomination that has several large and influential megachurches among its ranks. It would be fair to say that most of its membership could be considered part of the middle-class socioeconomic group. Yet, within the collective consciousness of the BGC, the memory persists of a time — and to some extent the practices of a time — when the denomination existed on the outskirts of society and represented those without power or influence.

One striking feature about the BGC today is that it apparently does not

25. A. Olson, *Centenary History*, 61-63, 71, 74-76.

understand its own newfound power and influence in the United States. Though the BGC is still relatively small compared to other denominations, it is no longer comprised of poor frontier people who had suffered at the hands of a decadent, foreign state church. It has grown significantly in numbers and wealth since its humble beginnings, yet it seems to have no recognition of the potential of its political, spiritual, or social influence — on local, regional, or national levels. In the St. Paul and Minneapolis area, for example, there are four significant BGC megachurches located in different parts of the metropolitan area, along with many other large and medium-sized churches.[26] This group of churches is capable of having a significant impact on the social, political, and spiritual problems of the region, yet they too often find themselves significantly divided over lesser issues.[27]

Foundations for a Missional Polity

One final point emerging from our consideration of the roots of the BGC is that it must remain true to its historic emphasis on mission. The BGC had its initial start as a missionary group to Swedish Baptist immigrants, and it has kept this missionary heritage strong throughout its growth and development. However, there have been some significant advancements in the broader church regarding what a missiology for North America might look like that could be fruitful for the BGC to consider in a possible revision of its polity. In the mid-twentieth century, the BGC made a successful transition from being a Swedish immigrant church to being a fully Americanized church. A new missionary understanding of the church in Northern America is called for today as well, an understanding that recognizes the implications of living in a time of "posts" in our society:[28] post-Christian, postmodern, and postfunctional Christendom.[29]

26. Though listed as simply Baptist, Bethlehem Baptist Church and Woodland Hills Church are both part of the BGC, along with Wooddale and Eagle Brook churches. http://hirr.hartsem.edu/org/faith_megachurches_database_minnesota.html (accessed May 25, 2006).

27. One example of this is the public disagreement within the BGC several years ago regarding "open theism."

28. Steven Best and Douglas Kellner, *The Postmodern Turn: Critical Perspectives* (New York: Guilford Press, 1997), 3.

29. Darrell L. Guder et al., *Missional Church: A Vision for the Sending of the Church in North America* (Grand Rapids: Eerdmans, 1998), 7, 36-55.

A Missional Ecclesiology: The Missio Dei

An awareness of the changed context for the church in the United States necessitates integrating both missiology and ecclesiology to form a *missional ecclesiology*. This draws attention to the church's intrinsic missionary nature.[30] The authors of *Missional Church* put the issue for churches in North America this way:

> [I]t has taken us decades to realize that mission is not just a program of the church. It defines the church as God's sent people. Either we are defined by mission, or we reduce the scope of the gospel and the mandate of the church. Thus our challenge today is to move from church with mission to missional church.[31]

Given the missionary heritage of the BGC, this idea should be one that easily resonates in the fellowship of churches.

The missional church concept involves a change in the way a church or denomination understands the idea of participating in mission. Mission throughout the nineteenth and much of the twentieth century was understood as an activity primarily initiated by churches, denominations, and parachurch agencies. Today a Trinitarian understanding of mission recasts it so that it is part of the very nature of the triune God. Consequently, an understanding of mission has moved from being *ecclesiocentric* to being *theocentric*. This understanding of mission emphasizes that churches participate in God's mission in the world *(missio Dei)*, not the other way around. Jürgen Moltmann explains:

> It is not the church that has a mission of salvation to fulfill to the world; it is the mission of the Son and the Spirit through the Father that includes the church, creating a church as it goes on its way.[32]

The advantage of emphasizing the *missio Dei* comes by way of shifting the responsibility for mission as the church's work to the church's participation in the work of God in the world. The former relies primarily on

30. Craig Van Gelder, *The Essence of the Church: A Community Created by the Spirit* (Grand Rapids: Baker, 2000), 31.
31. Guder, *Missional Church*, 6.
32. Jürgen Moltmann, *The Church in the Power of the Spirit: A Contribution to Messianic Ecclesiology* (Minneapolis: Fortress, 1993), 64.

a Christological understanding of mission, which consists primarily of obedience to the Great Commission. Historically, this approach has been favored among most Protestants in their understanding of mission. However, perceiving mission in light of the *missio Dei* places it within a Trinitarian understanding. This does not at all exclude a Christological dimension; rather, it places this dimension within an understanding of the mission of the triune God.

A Missional Ecclesiology: The Reign of God

This participation of the church in the *missio Dei* must also include in its focus the New Testament concept of the reign of God (kingdom of God). The *missio Dei* is the means by which God's reign is made evident in this world. Indeed, "*basileia,* the reign of God, is the essence of the *missio Dei.*"[33] This idea of God's kingdom or reign[34] has been relatively neglected by evangelicals today, though it was the central tenet of Jesus' preaching, and its usage can be found throughout the Synoptic Gospels.[35] What are some of the crucial aspects of the message of the reign of God, and how does it relate to the church?

This section focuses on the reign of God as *shalom,* though the idea of the reign of God has many additional aspects that are important for the church.[36] Micah 4:3-7 paints a picture of what the reign of God will look like one day, when the nations travel to Zion to learn the ways of the God of Jacob. This passage pictures the reign of God as a time of peace and prosperity for the nations of the earth. The marginalized and afflicted are given special care under God's providential attention; relationships are restored among opposing groups as they each live under the just rule of YHWH. Jesus clearly showed this healing and restorative aspect of the reign of God in his ministry, for example, in Luke 7:22-23.

---

33. Wilbert R. Shenk, "The Mission Dynamic," in Willem Saayman and Klippies Kritzinger, eds., *Mission in Bold Humility: David Bosch's Work Considered* (Maryknoll, NY: Orbis Books, 1996), 85.

34. I use "kingdom" and "reign" synonymously in this section as translations for *basileia.*

35. Mortimer Arias, *Announcing the Reign of God: Evangelization and the Subversive Memory of Jesus* (Philadelphia: Fortress, 1984), 1-12.

36. Arias, *Announcing the Reign,* chaps. 6-8.

An important reminder regarding the good news that Jesus declared about the reign of God was that it was both *now* and *not yet*. It was an announcement of the inauguration of God's kingdom reign into the present, as well as an announcement of God's future kingdom that would one day be fully consummated. One example of this can be found in the story of the Pharisees' confronting Jesus and accusing him of casting out demons by Beelzebub. In his reply, Jesus told them that his driving out demons by the Spirit of God showed that the kingdom "has come upon you" (Matt. 12:28). This sets up a tension in understanding the kingdom that can only be resolved by understanding it as a future reality that is also breaking into the present. The same present-future tension exists today in how we must understand the reign of God.

The good news of the kingdom was not meant to be left behind by the early churches after Jesus had ascended into heaven. Prior to giving the Great Commission as recorded in Matthew, Jesus said that the end would come only after the Good News of the kingdom was proclaimed throughout the world as a testimony to the nations (Matt. 24:14). The book of Acts makes it clear that the early Christians proclaimed this message of the kingdom (Acts 8:12; 14:22; 19:8; 20:25; 28:23). In fact, just before the end of the Acts narrative, Paul is continuing to explain the Good News of the kingdom to all who will listen to him! (Acts 28:31).

Admittedly, there are fewer references to the kingdom in Paul's Epistles and in the rest of the New Testament than there are in the Synoptic Gospels and the book of Acts. But in the rest of the books of the New Testament the authors often used other terms for "kingdom" or "reign of God." The dynamic ideas of "life" and "eternal life" in the Gospel of John carry with them many of the kingdom connotations.[37] Paul emphasizes phrases and concepts such as "being in Christ," "eternal life," "justification," and the all-encompassing "salvation" in place of "kingdom" as he speaks to gentile audiences who are unfamiliar with Jewish history and theology.[38]

It is important for evangelical churches today to preach not only the gospel *about* Jesus, but also the gospel *of* Jesus. To proclaim Jesus as Messiah is also to announce the reign of God (the kingdom); they cannot be

---

37. *Announcing the Reign,* 62.

38. *Announcing the Reign,* 62-64; Michael Green, *Evangelism in the Early Church,* rev. ed. (Grand Rapids: Eerdmans, 2004), 84.

separated. As John Bright has argued, "To acclaim anyone as Messiah is to announce in him the coming of the Kingdom of God, for it is precisely the business of the Messiah to establish the Kingdom. Messiah cannot be separated from Kingdom."[39] The BGC must recover the language of "kingdom" to incorporate the teaching of Jesus and the full biblical witness into the life of the church. Anything less would deny the high view of Scripture that has been historically important in the BGC.

What, then, is the relationship between the church and the kingdom that Jesus preached? Perhaps the best way to characterize this relationship is that the church represents the reign of God. The holistic way Jesus spoke and lived out his message points to the means by which the church is called to accomplish this representation. Jesus drew around himself a community of followers as he healed and preached; likewise, the church is to represent God's reign as *community, servant,* and *messenger*.[40] The church is called to follow its risen Lord in emulating his threefold earthly ministry of proclaiming the good news, doing works of service, and living in loving community.

Though it may seem very simple, there are three important ideas for helping congregations and denominations in North America today reframe their understanding of their respective roles: (1) recognizing North America as a mission location like any other around the world; (2) understanding that mission originates with the triune God; and (3) seeing that the church participates in God's mission by bearing witness to the reign of God. The suggestions for polity revisions that are discussed below draw on these concepts. But before I develop these points, I need to detail some of the changes in the polity and organization of the BGC that have taken place over its nearly 150-year history.

Historical Polity and Organizational Changes

The roots of the Baptist General Conference, as I have noted above, can be traced back to communities of immigrant Baptist Swedes settling in various communities throughout the Midwest. The first congregation of

39. John Bright, *The Kingdom of God: The Biblical Concept and Its Meaning for the Church* (Nashville: Abingdon-Cokesbury Press, 1953), 215-16.

40. Guder, *Missional Church,* 100, 102.

Swedish Baptists was organized at Rock Island, Illinois, in 1852. Soon after this, larger groupings of local churches (conferences) were organized, largely in accordance with state borders. Because travel was relatively difficult at that time, the idea of a larger national conference that would encompass the state conferences was postponed until a later date.[41] The opportunity for this came in 1879-1880, when the Scandinavian Baptist General Conference was founded as a national organization.[42]

The first constitution of the national conference included emphases on missionary work among Scandinavian immigrants, support for the denominational school and publications, and a desire "to awaken our churches to greater zeal for our faith and for the welfare of our denomination."[43] The constitutional revision of 1892 included these four objectives:

1. To promote missionary work among the Swedes in America;
2. to encourage and support foreign missions;
3. to support the denominational Training School for preachers;
4. to supply and spread denominational literature.[44]

To these objectives was added a fifth paragraph in 1900 about establishing and supporting charitable institutions when the Conference was legally incorporated under the laws of the state of Illinois.[45]

The young denomination experienced slow growth during the first couple of decades of its existence. However, by means of aggressive evangelism efforts and high levels of Swedish immigration, the BGC was composed of 324 churches with 21,769 members at the time of its Fiftieth Jubilee celebration in 1902. It was at this time that the denomination began to realize its increasing strength and began to expand its operations. It established houses for children and the elderly and added a mission secretary along with a corresponding financial secretary.[46]

Two major BGC transitions came about during the first half of the twentieth century, when the denomination began to wean itself from the

41. Backlund, *Swedish Baptists in America*, 39, 129. As I have observed above, the Danes and Norwegians broke away in 1882 to form their own conferences.
42. A. Olson, *Centenary History*, 406-08.
43. Backlund, *Swedish Baptists in America*, 130.
44. A. Olson, *Centenary History*, 415.
45. Backlund, *Swedish Baptists in America*, 131.
46. A. Olson, *Centenary History*, 420, 422, 28-29.

support of the American Baptists. First, it changed from being a predominantly Swedish church to one that used the English language; second, it sought to reach people from other ethnic groups. In 1914, the Swedish Seminary moved to St. Paul, Minnesota, and became independently supported by the Swedish Baptists.[47] Previously, the costs for the seminary had been underwritten by the American Baptists, so this change represented a large financial commitment for this relatively small denomination. The transition away from an ethnically insulated church came about during the two decades following World War I, culminating in 1945, when the word "Swedish" was dropped from the name of the denomination.[48]

Though the organization of the denomination underwent many revisions throughout its history, a few are particularly significant. Between 1914 and 1945, the BGC functioned by way of three main committees of twenty-one members each: missions, literature, and education.[49] These three committees constituted the board of trustees for the denomination, with several subsidiary boards being added over the years. The BGC revised this structure in 1945 and made several changes: it limited the number of those allowed on the boards; it changed the name from "boards" to "committees"; it set term limits for committee members; and it divided the missions board into two separate committees — one for home missions and one for foreign missions.

The BGC added the position of general secretary in 1953 to solidify a strong central position of leadership for the denomination. That position had been preceded, in effect, by the mission secretary position: that person had wielded great influence, though the position was not officially considered the top post in the denomination. A process that took several years culminated in 1987 in another set of sweeping organizational changes for the denomination: an identity statement; a purpose statement; a mission and strategy statement; organizational structure changes; and budgeting and fundraising proposals. This revision also created a board of overseers as the administrative board over the entire denomination: representatives from several other boards and representatives of the districts became members of the new board of overseers. Four other boards were created to

47. A. Olson, *Centenary History,* 415.

48. http://www.temple-baptist.com/history/church_history_inclusive.htm (accessed Feb. 21, 2006).

49. A. Olson, *Centenary History,* 444.

operate under the board of overseers: world missions, home missions, church ministries, and regents. The changes of 1987 also created the office of a president of the denomination to replace the former general secretary position. The president is explicitly referred to as the chief executive officer of the denomination, and the concept of *servant leadership* is specifically referred to regarding this position.[50]

Suggestions for Possible Polity Changes

One of the great strengths of the Baptist General Conference has been its historic commitment to evangelism, church planting, and obedience to the Great Commission. Other denominations may have wavered in their dedication to their evangelistic mandate, but this has not been the case with the BGC. For other denominations, moving toward a missional polity will likely entail a significant renewal in evangelistic practices. In contrast, it would not be out of line to conclude that the BGC considers evangelism and church-planting as constituting the bulk of its mission, with all other matters remaining peripheral concerns. Evangelism and church-planting must continue to play a central role in a missional polity for the BGC. I propose here that the BGC would be well served by reconceiving its mission within the concept of bearing witness to the reign of God. How might this best be achieved for the BGC?

First, adopting a missional polity would entail moving beyond the view that evangelism is simply one of the programs of the church or denomination, no matter how central that program may be. Evangelism must be reconceived as being an integral part of each of the activities of a congregation — or the denomination — whether it be pastoral care, worship, discipleship, or service. While each of these concerns need not have an explicitly evangelistic thrust, each should at least have an evangelistic dimension.[51] As the core part of the mission of any congregation, denomination, or regional judicatory, evangelism should permeate all of its activities, not be simply relegated to a separate program of its own.

50. Donald E. Anderson, ed., *The 1980's in the Ministry of the Baptist General Conference* (Arlington Heights, IL: Board of Overseers Baptist General Conference, 1991), 22. The information in this section on the organizational change of 1987 is from this same source.
51. Darrell L. Guder, *The Continuing Conversion of the Church* (Grand Rapids: Eerdmans, 2000), 149.

A missional polity must also propel the denomination beyond itself to participate in the activity of the triune God in the world. This would necessarily include taking stands on social issues, promoting justice for those who are oppressed, and working to benefit the poor. It could mean promoting prophetic action regarding issues such as war, consumerism, and racism. The list of possibilities here is endless. These simply illustrate some ideas of how a missional polity might call the BGC to expand its view of how it participates in God's mission in the world.

Similar concerns have already been addressed within resolutions adopted by the BGC, but so far these have lacked theological integration into the Conference's polity. In 1966, the BGC adopted a resolution on "social ministries" that claimed that, "[c]onsistent with the example of Christ, the Church fulfills its ministry when it expresses the redemptive love of God for man in his total life situation, both spiritual and social."[52] Later, in the 1979 resolution on "An Affluent Church in a Hungry World," the BGC similarly reaffirmed its historic concern "about the need of the whole man."[53] This present polity proposal seeks to provide a theological foundation within the BGC polity that supports and integrates these previously adopted resolutions and makes their place explicit in the life of the BGC and its constituent congregations. The following specific proposals to amend aspects of BGC polity proceed from the foundations for a missional polity as laid out above, and also from select adopted resolutions of the BGC.

Summaries and Proposed Polity Changes for Consideration

Statement of Faith (Article III of the Bylaws)

The section on the church in article III (see p. 254) is modified by the addition of a sentence regarding the work of the Holy Spirit, since any mention of the Spirit was missing from the original BGC formulation. This adds a Trinitarian dimension to the statement, which recognizes the important constitutive role the Spirit had in the birth of the church as well as in its sustenance (see, e.g., Acts 1:1-8; 2:1-41; 1 Cor. 12). The idea of *mission* was added in the second sentence to emphasize that the church is not simply

52. http://www.bgcworld.org/intro/socmin.htm (accessed Dec. 26, 2006).
53. http://www.bgcworld.org/intro/hungry.htm (accessed Dec. 26, 2006).

ARTICLE III.7 — THE CHURCH

Current polity statement	Proposed changes (in italics)
We believe in the universal church, a living spiritual body of which Christ is the head and all regenerated persons are members. We believe in the local church, consisting of a company of believers in Jesus Christ, baptized on a credible profession of faith, and associated for worship, work and fellowship. We believe that God has laid upon the members of the local church the primary task of giving the gospel of Jesus Christ to a lost world.	We believe in the universal church, a living spiritual body *established and sustained by the Holy Spirit,* of which Christ is the head and all regenerated persons are members. We believe in the local church, consisting of a company of believers in Jesus Christ, baptized on a credible profession of faith, and associated for *mission through* worship, work, and fellowship. *We believe that God has sent the members of the local church into the world for the primary task of participating in His mission, which consists of proclaiming and witnessing to the reign of God and the good news of the gospel of Jesus Christ.*

---

associated for spiritual and functional activities; rather, it exists for mission, which consists of those specific activities that are listed (among others). The last sentence was revised because the original statement said that God makes the church responsible for the task of giving the gospel to a lost world. That emphasis collapses the *missio Dei* into the *missio ecclesiae,* and thus neglects a wider vision about what God is about in the world and how the church might participate in it.

In the section on Christian conduct (see p. 255), the portion advising that Christians should seek for themselves and others the full stature of maturity in Christ was omitted. Then the statement was amended to emphasize the Holy Spirit as the true agent for change, and to show the Christian as simply the one who seeks to cooperate with the Spirit's sanctifying work. This rewording also adds the Holy Spirit to this section — which was completely missing. This perhaps improves on the Pietist leanings from the early years of the BGC that tended to place the responsibility for

---

ARTICLE III.8 — CHRISTIAN CONDUCT

Current polity statement	Proposed changes (in italics)
We believe that Christians should live for the glory of God and the well-being of others; that their conduct should be blameless before the world; that they should be faithful stewards of their possessions; and that they should seek to realize for themselves and others the full stature of maturity in Christ.	We believe that Christians should live for the glory of God and the well-being of others; that their conduct should be blameless before the world; that they should be faithful stewards of their possessions; and that they should seek to *allow the Holy Spirit to realize in themselves* and others the full stature of maturity in Christ.

---

living a holy life and abiding by certain biblical guidelines on the human individual alone.

Identity, Purpose, and Mission Statements (Articles II and IV of the Bylaws)

The identity statement for the BGC (article II of the bylaws — see p. 256) was amended by the addition of the word "inclusive" to signify an attitude of inclusiveness toward those who may be different from those who have traditionally been members of BGC churches. The word "diversity" was also added to the attributes celebrated by the churches to indicate an attitude that values a number of different perspectives. The portion indicating that the purpose of the churches is to fulfill the Great Commission via evangelism, discipleship, and church-planting was omitted in favor of a statement noting that the purpose of the various churches was to participate in the *missio Dei* by bearing witness to the *reign of God*. This adds a more holistic perspective to the mission of the local churches, while it also includes within it the spirit of the Great Commission.

The entirety of Article IV (the purpose and mission statements — see p. 257) was omitted in favor of one singular statement encompassing both aspects of purpose and mission. The two statements are a bit broad, and it is difficult to see how their current form (as stated in Article IV)

ARTICLE II. — IDENTITY STATEMENT

Current polity statement	Proposed changes (in italics)
The Conference is a voluntary fellowship or association of Baptist churches in the United States and Islands of the Caribbean and Bahamas. The Conference is a fellowship of churches whose theology is biblically evangelical; whose character is multiethnic; whose spirit is positive and affirmative; whose purpose is to fulfill the Great Commission through evangelism, discipleship, and church planting; and whose people celebrate openness and freedom in the context of Christ's Lordship.	The Conference is a fellowship or association of Baptist churches in the United States and Islands of the Caribbean and Bahamas. The Conference is a fellowship of churches whose theology is biblically evangelical; whose character is multiethnic *and inclusive;* whose spirit is positive and affirmative; whose purpose is to *participate in the missio Dei;* and whose people celebrate openness, freedom, *and diversity* in the context of Christ's Lordship.

---

could make a practical contribution to the actual organization and practices of the BGC. The sense of mission that is articulated in this proposed polity change includes the biblical terms *kerygma, diakonia,* and *koinonia.* This is a well-supported triad of mission theology of the past fifty years, and it essentially encompasses the overall spirit of the Great Commission in continuing the mission of Jesus here on earth.[54] The triad will also provide a means to reconceptualize the vice-presidential positions, which I will cover in the following section on Articles V-XI.

Summary of Articles V-XI of the Bylaws

One of the most vexing problems for the BGC has seemingly been to find a way to adjudicate differences between powerful pastors of local churches. How can the regional and national structures be changed to better address

54. Guder, *Missional Church,* 102-09; Lesslie Newbigin, *The Gospel in a Pluralist Society* (Grand Rapids: Eerdmans, 1989), 128-40.

ARTICLE IV. — PURPOSE AND MISSION STATEMENT

Current polity statement

Proposed changes (in italics)

SECTION A. — Purpose
The purpose of the Conference is to glorify God by making disciples of all peoples, as stated in Matthew 28:18-20: "All authority in heaven and on earth has been given to Me. Therefore go and make disciples of all nations, baptizing them in the name of the Father and of the Son and of the Holy Spirit, and teaching them to obey everything I have commanded you. And surely I will be with you always, to the very end of the age" (NIV).

The purpose of the Baptist General Conference is to assist and empower its constituent churches to engage in mission through proclamation, service, and fellowship in their local communities and in the world beyond. (Matt. 28:18-20)

SECTION B. — Mission
The mission of the Conference is to glorify God by helping member churches fulfill Christ's mission for His church in all the communities God calls them to serve.

---

this issue? No provisions exist in the polity, as it currently stands, to deal with conflict between churches, though the polity does briefly detail a process for resolving conflict between the regional and national conferences. Perhaps this issue has been downplayed because of the primary principle of the autonomy of each local church. However, for a fellowship of churches whose existence is based on cooperation rather than coercion, this would appear to be an important issue to address.

The primary structure built into the polity on the regional and national levels is that of the singular leader or administrator surrounded by boards, teams, and committees. The board on the regional level consists of men and women from local churches within the region who go through a nomination, caucus, and voting process in order to become part of the board. This allows the district executive minister (DEM) to "hear the voice of the churches" in the region.[55] In the MBC, the board meets four times a year to create and manage the budget and to handle strategy and policy. It also aids in the selection of the DEM.

The board of overseers is the policy-making board of the national conference. It has "the responsibilities and the authority normally granted to the board of directors of like corporations organized under the laws of the State of Illinois" (Article VIII, Section A). This board consists of twenty-five to thirty members, including: the national conference president, the Bethel University president, two DEMs, five or more at-large members, one member for each regional district, and two Cultural Association members.[56] An executive committee exists as a smaller group within the board of overseers that can authorize decisions between board meetings. The board members can serve on one of three standing committees within the board: executive, church planting, or church enrichment. The church-planting and church-enrichment committees can include two additional members who are not board members.

There are two other important committees in the conference: the Conference Leadership Team and the District Executive Ministers' Council. The Conference Leadership Team is composed of some of the same members of the board of overseers (with some additions), but its role seems to be largely ambiguous. It seeks to "coordinate and strengthen the unified efforts of the ministry partners and to increase the mutual accountability of these ministry partners" (Article VI, Section B). The District Executive Ministers' Council is composed of all the various DEMs, and it serves as a liaison between the regional districts and the national conference.

The various officers of the national conference include a president, executive vice president, vice president of church-planting, vice president of church enrichment, treasurer, secretary, and other possibilities as well. The president, vice president of church-planting, and vice president of church enrichment are all elected positions: they are filled by a nomination from the board of overseers to the annual assembly of the national conference.

---

55. From a personal interview with the District Executive Minister (DEM) of the Minnesota Baptist Conference (MBC) (Mar. 30, 2006).

56. The Cultural Associations are groups of at least ten churches within the BGC that represent a different cultural or linguistic group from the majority of the churches.

The annual assembly is a key part of understanding how the denomination works on a national level. Each church is entitled to at least two delegates to the national assembly, and several ex officio delegates are also provided for from the board of overseers, Bethel University, and other sources. With a recommendation from the board of overseers, a church can be held accountable at the national assembly for "failure to cooperate in the objects and purposes of the Conference, or for departure from the life and historic teachings of Baptist churches . . ." (Article VII, Section B). The polity actually lists very few other uses for the annual assembly.

Proposed Polity Changes for Articles V-XI of the Bylaws

There are numerous boards and committees on the national level in the BGC that may not all be necessary, particularly the Conference Leadership Team. The president likely spends a great deal of time attending to redundancies arising from the business and meetings of these various bodies. The need for a smaller group within the board of overseers seems reasonable, but that also speaks to some possible flaws in the current organization of the conference. Perhaps those two groups could be collapsed into one.

Given a change in the mission/purpose statement, as proposed above, the two vice-presidential positions could be recast as three vice-presidential positions, with each corresponding to a facet of the BGC's new understanding of mission. The vice president of church planting could become a vice president of communal witness; the position of vice president of church enrichment could be changed to a vice president of church community; a new vice president position could be created that would focus on issues of justice and acts of service by the denomination and its constituent churches in local communities and in the broader world. These organizational changes would correspond to the purpose and mission of the denomination and would represent its natural outgrowth.

The Process of Polity Change

Article XV of the bylaws states that official revisions to BGC polity can only be made by a two-thirds majority vote of the delegates who are present at an annual assembly. This procedure requires that a copy of the proposed amendment has been presented to the board of overseers three months beforehand and that member churches have received written notice of the proposed change at least one month prior to the annual assembly. The only exception to this rule is Article III, the statement of faith. A change to this article can only be accomplished by a proposed amendment that has been ratified by a simple majority at one annual meeting and passed by a two-thirds majority at the next annual meeting.

A constructive change in the polity of the BGC to reflect a missiological ecclesiology would constitute a significant challenge. Officially, it would need to begin at the congregational level, the level that sends the greatest number of representatives to the national assembly and the level that must be in favor of any changes to the polity. Any polity revisions that include alternative visions to problem-solving would first need to travel through the existing system, and would require coalition-building to achieve a two-thirds majority vote. However, the process of embracing a missional ecclesiology would necessarily mean much more than a polity change for the BGC; it would need to begin at a deeper level. Just as some authors have proposed that Lutherans need to embrace an evangelizing church culture, the BGC would also need to embrace a culture that is receptive to a missional ecclesiology.[57] The process of change for the churches, conferences, and systems within the BGC that do not currently value a missional ecclesiology would necessarily involve addressing the narratives, traditions, values, and beliefs that have helped to shape their culture(s). The elaborate issues surrounding a change process such as this have been noted elsewhere in this volume.[58]

Conclusion

The Baptist General Conference has much to celebrate in its nearly 150 years of existence. It successfully weathered the challenges of frontier life, carving out an existence among difficult financial and environmental conditions and competing religious groups. It successfully made the transition

57. Richard H. Bliese and Craig Van Gelder, eds., *The Evangelizing Church: A Lutheran Contribution* (Minneapolis: Augsburg Fortress, 2005).
58. See, esp., Alan Roxburgh's essay, chap. 3 above.

from a Swedish Baptist immigrant group to a fully Americanized Christian fellowship of evangelical churches. It persevered through years of slow growth and stagnation to ultimately take off in the late twentieth century. But the BGC still has room to grow. I hope that this proposal will be seen as a helpful suggestion for the denomination as it begins the process of becoming a fellowship of missional Baptist churches that are guided by a polity reflecting that reality.

THE STORY OF ONE DENOMINATION SEEKING TO BECOME MISSIONAL

Sometimes it is helpful to be able to tell and hear a story in order to begin imagining what something might look like. Stories are illustrations and they bring to life insights into how something actually works. The Reformed Church in America (RCA) has been on a journey now for over a decade trying to bring a missional imagination into both its ecclesiology and its polity. This work has been led by the general secretary of the denomination, Wesley Granberg-Michaelson. We invited Wes to speak at a special banquet held during the 2006 Missional Church Consultation so that he could share with the participants the lessons the RCA had learned about developing a missional identity from this journey of more than ten years.

The style and tone of this chapter are somewhat different from the other chapters in this volume: what follows is an edited transcript of the story that Wes told at that banquet. Readers will be both inspired and challenged as they read this story, for it is an honest telling of a real journey that has seen both successes and failures. Our thanks to Wes for allowing us to join him and the RCA on their journey.

CHAPTER 9

Insights into Becoming a Missional Denomination: The Reformed Church in America

Wesley Granberg-Michaelson

Introduction

The Reformed Church in America (RCA) began as a mission outpost. Our first pastor, Dominie Jonas Michaelius, was sent by the Classis of Amsterdam in 1628 to lead a congregation on an island in the new world. His ministry has often been characterized simply as a chaplaincy to the commercial interests of the Dutch West Indies Company, but to so characterize it is dismissive of the missional DNA that is embedded in the core of that work — and of our historic denomination.

The founding of the RCA, and its journey to become rooted in this foreign American soil, reflected an impulse to plant the gospel in new cultural contexts. But inevitably mission outposts became settled churches. As the RCA grew over the next centuries, and its congregations sank roots into American society, this denomination — its churches and its members — became part of the social establishment in a culture presumed to be Christian. We did what we did well: preaching the Word, performing the sacraments, providing catechetical instruction to our youth. In time, whether in Hull, Iowa, or Hackensack, New Jersey, or South Blendon, Michigan, or Bellflower, California, we felt like comfortable colonies in the land of Zion.

But how can we be comfortable with the place of the church in today's culture? The challenges confronting us include such things as soccer leagues for our kids on Sunday mornings; personal values and behavior shaped more by the media than family or church; spiritual curiosity that is detached from institutional religious expression; and the alienation of younger generations from the organized life of the church. On any given Sunday, fewer than half of American adults attend a house of worship, and in many communities that figure is in the single digits.[1] People ready to talk about God are alienated by the way faith is practiced. The average age of many congregations, and certainly the RCA as a whole, continues to rise significantly above the median age of the population. One study has shown that there is not a single county in the United States where the percentage of those who regularly attend religious worship services is higher than that of a decade ago.[2]

Something profound has happened to the place of the Christian faith in North America. The church needs to enter into a new missional age. There is no other clear way to put this. The relationship between the church and the culture in North America has fundamentally changed, and we can't go back to the way it used to be. RCA congregations should no longer expect to have a comfortable, cozy relationship with the emerging culture. Indeed, if our only comfort is that we belong — body and soul, in life and in death — to our faithful savior, Jesus Christ, then we need to be ready to embrace a fresh missional engagement within contemporary society.

Pat Kiefert, in his recent book *We Are Here Now,* describes these sweeping changes in church and culture as being like a tsunami that has washed ashore, upsetting and tossing in every direction the multiple boats that previously moved comfortably together in fleets.[3] Now all of them are desperately trying to navigate their way forward, often individually, in the midst of the massive sea change. That's a picture that works for the RCA, where we often describe the churches in a classis (our regional judicatory), from the term's derivation, as a "fleet of ships."

Therefore, in my view, which is based on my service as the general secretary of the RCA, I offer the following challenge: The most critical challenge facing the Reformed Church in America today is making the transition from being a "settled" denomination to becoming a "missional"

1. Forty-seven percent of American adults attend church in a typical weekend, not including a special event such as a wedding or a funeral (The Barna Group, 2005: www.barna.org).

2. Information available from http://www.thearda.com/ (accessed Dec. 17, 2007).

3. Patrick Keifert, *We Are Here Now: A New Missional Era* (Eagle, ID: Allelon Publishing, 2006).

church. This challenge compels us to rediscover a courageous missional identity that can and should be at the core of our Reformed identity. This transition is essential to fulfilling the shared commitment of "Our Call," the path we have embraced as God's calling for our future.[4]

What Do We Mean by "Missional"?

What do we mean when we speak of becoming a "missional church"? Here's the definition I would offer: A missional church places its commitment to participate in God's mission in the world at the center of its life and identity. "Mission" places the focus on what God is doing in the world, recognizing that God's mission is always ahead of us, already active through the Spirit in the world. It is our task to join, and in the words of our 1997 Statement of Mission and Vision, "to follow Christ in mission, in a lost and broken world so loved by God."[5] As Christ's body, the church, we are called, gathered, formed, and sent, a cycle of growth that repeats itself continually through our lives and ministries.

For the missional church, mission is not an activity or a program; rather, it lies at the center of the church's identity. Moreover, it is linked to participating in the life of the Trinity. God sent Jesus. "For God so loved the world that he sent his only son. . . ." And Jesus sent the Spirit. In the book of John, before his death Jesus explains to his disciples: "I am now going to him who sent me . . . if I do not go, the Advocate will not come to you, but if I go, I will send him to you. . . ." And so Jesus tells the disciples, "As the Father has sent me, so send I you."

The early church lived out of this missional identity. In an alien culture, its very life was a testimony to what God's power could do. People were transformed through the power demonstrated in the life, death, and resurrection of Jesus Christ, and they were called into a community that

4. "Our Call" in the Reformed Church in America is to build on the foundations of discipleship, leadership, and mission and to renew existing congregations and start new churches. See http://www.rca.org/NETCOMMUNITY/Page.aspx?pid=1457&srcid=220.

5. The full statement reads: "The Reformed Church in America is a fellowship of congregations called by God and empowered by the Holy Spirit to be the very presence of Jesus Christ in the world. Our shared task is to equip congregations for ministry — a thousand churches in a million ways doing one thing — following Christ in mission, in a lost and broken world so loved by God."

lived as his body. They were sent out — to Antioch, to Ephesus, to Rome, and to the ends of the earth. Mission defined the church's identity, and these believers were caught up in the movement of God's Spirit. As a result, the ancient world was transformed. Listen to how sociologist of religion Rodney Stark describes the early church's growth:

> The movement began with perhaps no more than a thousand converts; three centuries later more than half the population of the empire (perhaps as many as 33 million people) had become Christians. The result can be attributed to the work of missionaries only if we recognize a universal mission on the part of all believers.[6]

This is what we mean by a missional church. Our focus is on God's work, transforming lives through the power of the gospel of Jesus Christ, transforming communities through the justice and love that break into the world through God's kingdom, and seeking the transformation of the world, so that God's will might be done on earth. Again, as our Statement of Mission and Vision said a decade ago, we are "called by God and empowered by the Holy Spirit to be the very presence of Jesus Christ in the world." Our focus is placed not solely on how well we attract people into the church, but also on how well people are empowered to be sent into the world.

The Journey of the Reformed Church in America

The first thing I need to say is that I am convinced that either denominations will figure out how congregations are empowered for missional engagement, or denominations will atrophy and will become increasingly irrelevant. The church is called, gathered, centered, and sent. We follow Jesus to join in God's work in the world. Mission, I think, means crossing boundaries in word and deed to share God's transforming love in Jesus Christ in the church at every level. Every assembly in our church must recover this missional identity in order to anchor its life and to find its own sense of self and to seek its future. You could say it this way: the way we structure our consistories in the Reformed Church; the way we train people for pastoral service; the way we invite people into the Christian faith;

6. Rodney Stark, *One True God: Historical Consequences of Monotheism* (Princeton, NJ: Princeton University Press, 2001), 60.

the way we form them into Christian faith and discipleship; the way we offer ourselves in worship; the way we use our governing assemblies; the way we prioritize our budgets; the way we form expectations for pastors — all this and more will be dramatically reshaped by a radical commitment to join in God's ongoing mission in the world.

You could also say that whenever the church becomes settled, established, comfortable, and preoccupied with preserving its power in privileged position, its faith begins to wither. Its ministry loses vitality, its theology becomes dry, its worship becomes static, and its life becomes boring. I think that this is really the challenge before us.

Personal Preparation for the Journey

I want to say a quick word about my personal narrative and where I learned missional theology. I was recently asked, "So where did you first learn missional theology?" It was before the phrase "missional church" became popular. It was when I was in Washington, D.C., at the beginning of my work there at Church of the Savior. This remarkable church, as I think back on it now, was the embodiment of a congregation whose polity and structure were shaped by a missional ecclesiology. As a member of that church, you were also a member of a small group in which you were held accountable both for your inward spiritual journey and for your outward engagement in the world. Each group was called a mission group because each group had a particular mission to which it was called. Hence, *koinonia* did not exist for its own sake, but it was centered on mission. You became part of such a group because you discerned God's call to a particular mission. Whether that might be Jubilee Housing or working in the Potter's House or serving in Wellspring or whatever it was, your group's outward call to mission shaped you into a fellowship in which you were held spiritually accountable for your life with Christ. It was a journey described as being both a journey inward and a journey outward. That is really where I learned what we are now calling the journey of the missional church.

When I became general secretary of the Reformed Church in America, my assumption was that what a denomination should do is figure out how to empower congregations for outreach and mission with a holistic gospel. This is a gospel that both believes in the transformation of people's lives through the grace and love of God in Christ and in the transformation of the communities and societies in which those congregations are placed. What I did not realize was how much our life as a denomination reflected a settled church, and how deep the need for change would be. It would require a change not simply in structure and style but a change in *organizational culture* and *ethos*.

First Moves toward Change

Our journey toward trying to become a missional denomination began to take shape particularly as we led up to the year 1997. When I first became general secretary, I remember being told about the governing structures that we had. We had not only the General Synod that met every year, but also the General Synod Council, a group of sixty-seven people that met three times a year. Each time they met, they had a book that was very thick, and the former general secretary said to me, "Well, when we finish one General Synod Council, then staff begins working on preparing the workbook for the next one." It was a classic case of how you disempower boards by giving them too much information. We were simply duplicating the levels of governance rooted in a culture that pretends to be organizationally efficient. But at its root there is really a sense of mistrust and a need for a constant overlay of bureaucratic governance. I made the suggestion that we go to a retreat center in Phoenix for one of these meetings: we would go on retreat, have no notebook, read the book of Acts, and reflect together during that time on where we might be called as a denomination. That began a process that took another two years and that eventually led to our embracing of a statement of mission and vision.

I think that the most important thing we discovered during those early days is that we needed to carve out some open space within our complex structure, space where people could really reflect and be together and pray and ask, "What are the directions to which God is calling us?" rather than simply gathering in governing structures in order to do the administrative and managerial work that was put before that particular group. Eventually, the two-year process led to a formulation of mission and vision, and this formulation became a document that has lasted. It was the first time that we in the Reformed Church in America even tried to adopt something called a statement of mission and vision. Before we did so, people said "We have the book on church order and we have confessions that say who we are. So why would we even need to do this?" But it was clear to me that we needed to try to articulate what it meant to be a church at this particular time. We put it this way:

> The Reformed Church in America is a fellowship of congregations called by God and empowered by the Holy Spirit to be the very presence of Jesus Christ in the world.

It was important, when we reflected on this theologically, that we first talked not about what the church *did* but what the church *is* — that it is the presence of Christ that is situated in the world. We then said what our shared task was:

> To equip congregations for ministry — a thousand churches in a million ways doing one thing — following Christ in mission in a lost and broken world so loved by God.

What is interesting is that now, almost ten years later, I hear these same phrases at classis meetings, I hear them in congregations, and I see them in bulletins. In some way that I think can only be attributed to the mystery of God's Spirit, they have woven their way into the words of the church because they reflected a hunger that existed within the denomination.

The outcome of the journey at that time was not simply a mission and ministry statement. We tried to imagine laity and pastors unleashed and hungry for ministry. We tried to imagine congregations that were mission-minded and authentic and healing, that were growing and multiplying, and that were alert to the opportunities around them. This was not how anyone would have described most RCA congregations in 1997, but it was what we were trying to imagine. We were also trying to imagine a different classis. (In our own polity, classis is the assembly that is closest to the congregation; it's the first level up from congregation.) We began to imagine classes and synods as communities of nurture and vision that would be accountable, responsible, sustained in prayer, alive to the Spirit. That is not the way the majority of RCA members experience the functioning of most assemblies. There were other imaginings, but I just want to mention one that provoked the most animated response. At that time we said:

> To live out this vision by consistories, classes, synods and staff, our decision-making will be transformed by a pervasive climate of wor-

ship, discernment and biblical reflection. We will no longer do business as usual, nor our usual business.

It was that last sentence that got quoted most often, both by those who loved it and those who hated it. It was the most remembered.

Building on Earlier Gains

Since the time we first said those words, we began to ask, "What does it mean to live them out?" Any denomination can get an assembly to pass some words; denominations do that constantly. But we were trying to ask: "What would it mean to really say we want to claim a missional identity as a denomination?" These are words we not only want to say, but to also live by. The first thing I ran into was that it took a year to convince my staff that something was going to be different. I had left them out of the process because I didn't want anyone to think this was staff-driven. It was one of the biggest mistakes I made, and I literally had to spend the next year saying, "No, this isn't just something we passed, this is something we're actually going to do, and we should pay attention to it." Eventually, they did become convinced.

We then conducted a missional audit of our structures. As I look back, I think that we implemented what was recommended to us; we did some very wise structural things. But it was a mistake — and a predictable mistake — to so quickly go from mission to structure.

We also decided to look at how we do General Synod. In the year 2000, we gathered together in what we called Mission 2000. We took what was normally a legislative assembly of the church, transformed it into a gathering of representatives from the whole church in New York City, and then immersed everyone into what mission meant within our context in this time. Because our gathering was over Pentecost, we engaged in a discernment process by dividing the large group of over a thousand people into small groups and then having everyone work through the same process. I still think the results were miraculous in that we came up with something we called a "Pentecost Letter." It became a letter that went from that assembly to all our congregations, and it emphasized the missional call, declaring that we had entered into a new century and a new millennium.

Early on, we began to work on questions of ministerial formation. We had two summits of all the major stakeholders, recognizing that the patterns of ministerial formation were ones that tended to be too constricted and were blocking potential avenues for leadership. In that process we established what we call "commission pastors," which is something akin to what many polities now have. It is a way for persons to pastor in a given place for a given time with pastoral authority, but they are different from what we call ordained ministers of Word and Sacrament. We also approved an alternate route, a way in which one could get to be ordained without getting an M.Div. These were small but important steps to try to open up our ministerial formation process.

Early in the process, we also conducted two events that we called "Spring Sabbath." This was important because we recognized that whenever those in the church gather — its pastors, its leaders — they usually gather for legislative purposes. These legislative purposes too often tend to be divisive and are not altogether happy experiences. What we lacked was how to nurture pastors in their relational ability together. Spring Sabbath invited pastors to simply come and spend a weekend with one another, with very little input, and not a word or pamphlet or any kind of denominational promotion. Pastors would come simply to be there for one another. The response of the pastors was strong and grateful. It proved to be a model program, and the Presbyterians are now doing something quite similar. Again, it was an attempt to carve out space within a denominational system where pastors could relate to one another concerning questions of nurture and fellowship rather than merely questions about governance.

But we also had to work with the question of how we make decisions. That work is not yet done, and it's very difficult work; but I am convinced that a transition to a missional ecclesiology reflected in our polity will never be possible if we remain locked in patterns of political decision-making that are principally informed by our American political culture. I think that this is one of the biggest hurdles we face. We have experimented with developing a discernment-process approach: some feedback has been positive, and some has been negative.

We have also looked at what is going on around the world. This past summer, several of our senior staff were in Australia to look at how the Uniting Church of Australia does its work. This denomination is, I believe, one of the most advanced in making decisions by consensus. The World Council of Churches also has changed its whole decision-making process to a consensus approach. A whole lot of exploration is going on, and it's still in an experimental phase: there's a good deal of confusion, with questions about what we mean by consensus and what we mean by discernment. But beneath it is a search for a different way for practicing decision-making within our governing bodies.

Further Issues to Address

Within our legislative sessions, there is a clear need for the transformation of the style of the General Synod itself. We need to move from a gathering that is primarily defined as being legislative to a gathering that does legislative work in a context that is shaped by worship, vision-casting, and by inspiration cultivated through the building of a shared fellowship. This entails a pretty fundamental transformation of how the General Synod functions, but we have been making progress in implementing it over the past ten years.

In 2004, we also began a significant transformation of our executive committee of the General Synod, a practice of Carver Policy governance. This is a step toward saying, "A board of the church should really focus itself up and out instead of down and in, should look at major policy questions rather than micromanaging, and should redirect the way in which it functions."[7] It is too soon to know the lasting effect that this will have on the governing structures in our church.

After being clear about moving toward a missional engagement, we then asked, "What will this concretely look like and what specific goals will that commit us to?" In response, the Synod adopted what we term "Our Call" in 2003. This has now become a commitment in which we have crystallized what our missional engagement means. It is focused primarily on congregational revitalization and church multiplication. These are all phrases that anyone in any denomination might adopt and say are a good thing. But this is what we are trying to say: "Revitalizing congregations has to come particularly through strategies and new ways of relating together that we think have some promise of working."

We have adopted two such means. One is the development of sup-

---

7. John Carver, *Boards That Make a Difference: A New Design for Leadership in Non-profit and Public Organizations* (San Francisco: Jossey-Bass, 2006).

portive pastoral networks with the help of grant money from the Lilly Endowment, Inc. We have found that pastors who fail are pastors who are alone: what pastors most need are contexts of collegiality, transformational learning, accountability, and support. We now have sixty-two such groups established for our pastors, with deep accountability and clear commitments. Their groups are equipping them to reflect on what missional engagement with their congregations really means and what it means for their own personal journey in ministry. The second means is our use of "natural church development," which we are finding to be an extremely useful tool as an assessment for congregations as they reflect on where God is calling them.[8] The use of that tool is now probably out to about one-third or more of our congregations. In some areas we have all the churches in a classis using it more than once and sharing their results. Those are simply a couple of means that we find are working.

In church multiplication, what we have committed ourselves to is a very different approach, but again, an approach that is not new or revolutionary. This is actually going back to the future. Today, denominational bureaucracies and program agents will not start new churches; it is congregations that will start new churches, and we are seeing a major movement in church multiplication beginning to emerge in fresh ways. In the past twenty years we have basically started as many churches as we have closed, which is a typical pattern for mainline denominations. What we are saying now is that a movement involving church multiplication by congregations will be at a rate that will increase church multiplication threefold. For the RCA, this means establishing about 400 new churches by the year 2013. At least one-third of those will be of a racial and ethnic composition that will be different from the majority of RCA churches. The best way to describe this is that it no longer feels like a denominational program — because it isn't. The pastors of our new churches and the pastors of churches that are parenting those new churches have made it clear that this thing is now out of control. That is exactly what we had been praying for: it is now beginning to build on its own momentum.

All this is undergirded by a commitment to discipleship and leadership in mission. When we think about congregations that are called, gathered, centered, and sent, it is the part about "being centered" that I think

---

8. Christian A. Schwarz, *Natural Church Development: A Guide to Eight Essential Qualities of Healthy Churches* (St. Charles, IL: ChurchSmart Resources, 1996).

becomes so crucial for us. It is also so difficult to do because most of the traditional models of education have been profoundly informed by the Christendom motif and paradigm of the church. How we do discipleship within a missional framework is one of the really big challenges for us to try to figure out.

Having said all that, if I really reflect carefully on where we are, I must also acknowledge some of the key secular authors who have studied change in secular/business organizations. One of the most helpful here is Jim Collins, and many of the ideas in his book *Good to Great*, I believe, also apply to the church.[9] We have found that his analogy of the flywheel best describes how our staff members now feel. It has taken a long time, but we feel that we are at the place where the flywheel is just now beginning to move, and we pray that that perception is correct.

Eight Challenges

Let me reflect briefly on eight challenges that I think we in the RCA have in front of us. See if these have any relevance for your own situation.

1. *The Definitional Challenge.* We still have a definitional challenge. We don't have an agreement about what "mission" is. For some people it means evangelistic outreach; for some it means social-justice ministry. Some are afraid that "mission" is simply a rehash of church growth and thus all about numbers. For others, you say "mission," and they say, "Well, maybe I can figure out how I want to do the agenda I have always done for social justice but now I just put a new label on it." What needs to happen is a really biblical and theological reflection about what mission means that breaks through that dichotomy that still divides far too much of the church today. I like to think of mission as simply being the work of the Spirit to turn our congregations inside out to the world. The fundamental movement is how a congregation in its own life gets turned inside out so that it is oriented first to the world and to what God is doing in the world, gets redirected to where they're being called in the world.

9. Jim Collins, *Good to Great: Why Some Companies Make the Leap . . . and Others Don't* (New York: Harper Business, 2001).

2. *The Confessional Challenge.* This comes in a couple of ways. First, it concerns what it means to be both missional and confessional. For us the question is: What does it mean to be missional and Reformed? We, in fact, have looked at our congregations and have developed a little four-part grid for thinking about how we describe them: (1) least missional and least Reformed; (2) least missional and most Reformed; (3) least Reformed and more missional; and (4) most Reformed and most missional. Within your own polity, I suggest that you go through that kind of exercise. There is another, more foundational way that this affects us. We're a confessional church that has three confessions: the Belgic Confession, the Heidelberg Catechism, and the Canons of Dort. Those confessions don't have any missional words in them; they barely contain a missional comma. They were written at a time when the criteria we have before us today were simply not what they spoke to. As valuable as they are, they are not confessions that help us learn what it means to be missional.

So we have been asking this question: If we are a confessional church, what would it mean to adopt another confession? Our church has obviously not done so since the 1600s. In the ebb and flow of the past ten years, the confession that we have been dealing with is the Belhar Confession, a confession that is rooted in justice and reconciliation and unity. At the General Synod of 2007, we adopted the Belhar Confession as a provisional confession for the next two years; we will vote on it again in 2009. I believe that this is an important discussion, because a denomination like ours needs to root missional engagement in our confessional identity.

3. *The Ecclesiological Challenge.* People need to understand that mission is the identity of the church — how we understand the church's being. That is clear. For us there is even a more practical ecclesiological question and challenge: How do you define a church? When do you call a church a church? As an example, we have about a hundred places, with about ten to twelve thousand people who are worshiping and experiencing the life and grace of God in Christ, that are not considered churches because they are not yet organized and do not yet meet the criteria of what our order calls a church. The more we become missional and the more we start new churches, which begin now in a whole variety of ways, the more this issue will become a pressing one for us. It is a question of how we understand and define

what a church is: when we are committed to missional engagement, that changes the discussion.

4. *The Sacramental Challenge.* How do we understand the practices of baptism and communion within a missional context? The typical story we get from pastors of new churches goes something like this: a person who was baptized as an infant — let's say as a Roman Catholic — left any semblance of the Christian faith by the age of twelve. Now, at the age of thirty-five, he has experienced what he would call a dramatic conversion. He has discovered the grace of God in his life, and the life of his family has been totally transformed. He comes to the pastor and says, "Pastor, baptize me!" But most RCA pastors will hesitate and probably say no because the church does not believe in rebaptism and they want to be true to what they believe. We must find ways — liturgically, confessionally, and practically — to celebrate what has happened in this person's life that acknowledges the work of God. This is one example of how we need to transform the way we have typically thought about the sacraments. There is even a greater question and challenge we need to face regarding a missional understanding of the church: Are leaders called to be ministers of Word and Sacrament, or are leaders called to lead congregations in mission? There needs to be a whole discussion about how we understand the gifts of our sacraments, and that discussion becomes more intense the more missionally engaged we become.

5. *The Multiracial Challenge.* A colleague of mine recently asked, "What do you think is the biggest challenge out there?" I answered: "I think it has to do with what it means for us to become a denomination that truly embraces a multiracial future as God's intended future for us." In a way, this again involves how to think in missional terms. Every mainline denomination has passed statements saying, "We need to increase our racial diversity." The situation is so stark that we even set goals for these resolutions and initiatives, but virtually none of them has been met. I believe it's because we frame the issue principally as a political challenge. I think this is a missiological challenge. When we frame it in terms of mission, we will finally be able to really make breakthroughs toward the kind of future that we all really do believe God intends for us.

Our denomination, like many others as they moved through the 1960s and 1970s, came to institutionalize expressions of solidarity with civil rights that were very important for that time. But the question we now face is: How do we move in order to embrace a multiracial future that we know is God's intention for the future? This raises deep structural as well as theological issues. I admire the leaders of the Evangelical Covenant Church because, in their own life, they have passed what sociologists will call the "20 percent threshold." You can't talk about anything being genuinely multiracial until 20 percent of the body is of a race different from the dominant majority. Very few mainline denominations can claim that, but the Covenant has been able to do it by means of a very concerted and intentional effort. They take leaders, black and white, put them on buses, and travel through the South visiting civil rights sites, as they talk and share views and experiences toward the building of racial understanding. We must embrace efforts like these if we really believe that a multiracial future is the future that God desires. I am convinced that this is the only missional future that makes any sense at all within American society.

6. *The Formational Challenge.* I have already touched on it above, but there is a real challenge regarding how we continue to understand the task of ministerial formation and the formation of other leadership. This is related — deeply, I believe — to the multiracial challenge. When one looks at the patterns of growth in mainline denominations, the most interesting century — in the history of the Reformed Church in America at least — was the nineteenth century. From 1800 to 1900, the RCA increased to 923 churches, a growth of 764 percent. There were two reasons for that. Up to that time, all who would be pastors in the RCA were still being sent back to Amsterdam to be educated and ordained. The U.S. church made the courageous decision to establish its own seminary to educate and ordain ministers of Word and Sacrament within the United States — under its control. The RCA made a commitment to leadership, which in this case led them to found New Brunswick Theological Seminary, to contextualize theological education, and to raise up leadership. This led to the century of astonishing growth, only one-quarter of which was due to immigration. Three-quarters of that growth came from starting new churches. I am convinced that we face exactly the same challenge today. It has just gotten much more complex. What does it mean within a multiracial society to contextualize ministerial forma-

tion in more and more ways and to make an enduring commitment to raise up leaders? The challenge of ministerial formation remains ahead of us.

7. *The Procedural Challenge.* This is the challenge of figuring out patterns of governance. How do we transform decision-making styles? How do we transform our understandings of the ways governing structures function? Particularly in the Reformed tradition, our governing structures are built so much around the principle of mistrust. We have to balance two things: an awareness of sin and power with what the New Testament clearly says about the giftedness and embracing of gifts for leadership in the church. The heritage of the present polities, at least within the broad Reformed tradition, relies heavily on the first and very little on the second. I have already referred to decision-making styles and the way boards should properly function, how boards should be empowered to do what governing bodies can do best, and how staff can then be freed to do what staff do best in proper accountability on such boards. These become crucial for a missional engagement. There are different models; we have gone toward the Carver model, and we are now in the process of figuring out how to adapt it. Some are also working on what it might mean to adapt Carver governance to congregational settings. In my mind, this is an extremely provocative and important discussion for us to have.

8. *The Structural Challenge.* I place this as the last challenge because it is not the place to start. One of my first mistakes when I became general secretary was my attempt to begin with a structural change. That is not the place to start. You have to start by being clear about how to identify the vision that you believe God has given to you, and then you have to persistently clarify your mission. When you've moved clearly ahead with a sense of mission and vision that is informed by those values, the dysfunctionality of your structures will be revealed. Only then will you have the capacity to make the structural changes that are really sensible to make, and only then will you have the political capital to actually do it. You will no longer have to fight about structure, which is a fight the church does not really want.

Conclusion

The various writers of the essays in this book have said that the authority structures within most of our present denominations focus their attention on the internal life of the congregation or of the assembly. When that happens — for example, with a classis — the majority of the pastors and elders encounter the wider denomination at that level. They encounter an assembly that is devoted almost exclusively to administrative management; they encounter an assembly that is dealing with the often divisive and mundane issues of such management. What pastors are yearning for is a place for collegiality and support that nurtures their ministry and their missional journey. We need to find ways for those governing structures that are closest to those who are doing ministry to reinforce their deepest yearnings. We need to develop an approach in which the governing and regulatory functions that are necessary in our denominational assemblies don't overwhelm the nature of those assemblies.

What we have experienced in the RCA is that creating space and being clear about mission reveal how present structures are not functioning in the best way possible. This begins to open up space and opportunity for change. But it doesn't automatically lead to change — especially when it comes to structure. A proposal before the 2007 General Synod to carve out open space for experimenting in different ways regarding how we do our governing structures was defeated. However, that does not change the underlying reality. We need to examine and rework our polity, because it is clear that the way we are presently functioning is not empowering the missional engagement of our congregations.

What, then, have we learned in the end? What does it take to move from a settled denomination to becoming a missional denomination? First, it is essential to be honest. It is very important to look at the brutal facts, and denominations do not typically want to do that. It has been hard for us in the RCA, but it has been crucial. Second, it is essential to have a compelling vision of God's preferred future, to be consistent in the focus on mission, and then to do the realignment necessarily implied by that vision and focus. Third, it is essential to take time. This has taken much longer than I think any of us imagined it would. But one thing we've learned is that, if you are engaged in deep change, if you are making changes that go to the level of culture and ethos and style, those changes will take much longer. In order for a congregation or an assembly to be truly missional, however, those are by far the most important changes to make.

Fourth, it is essential to have continuity in leadership. The issue of turnover in leadership is one of the major problems we have in Reformed polity. It affects all of our assemblies. Is that because we don't trust anyone? We constantly change the leadership of our assemblies, and that constantly makes maintaining a consistent direction very difficult. It requires what I would call a "community of change agents" to become what some have called a "guiding coalition." Some stable group needs to carry the vision of change forward over time. In the RCA case, we've been able to get our regional synod executives and senior staff to come together and say, "We will be the guiding coalition for missional change." You have to develop such an ongoing vision in some way.

Fifth, it is essential to establish and maintain the biblical roots in all this, to ground this work in the story of God's people, and to have such a biblically integrated process that anyone who examines it can say, "This is spiritually driven, not managerially driven."

When I think about what lies ahead of us, I think of the narrative in Luke 10, where, early on, the disciples are called out by Jesus into the missional journey: he tells them that they are not allowed to bring along a staff or bag or bread or money, or even an extra tunic. They are being asked to have this sense of a radical dependence on God. Such dependence means that we don't have the props that ensure us against risks. We become vulnerable to and dependent on the hospitality of those to whom we minister and to whom we proclaim the Good News. I think these are probably the deepest challenges that lie ahead of us. But then, in that same passage, we have the picture of the disciples returning and Jesus gathering them together. They share such awesome joy and wonder! There we have a glimpse of the church that is not gathering in order to be sent, but the church that is gathered because it has been sent. I believe that that is where we all must go.